Grandparents' Rights

Your Legal Guide to Protecting Your Relationship with Your Grandchildren

Fourth Edition

Traci Truly

Attorney at Law

SPHINX® PUBLISHING
AN IMPRINT OF SOURCEBOOKS, INC.®
NAPERVILLE, ILLINOIS
www.SphinxLegal.com

Fourth Edition: 2005

Published by: **Sphinx® Publishing, An Imprint of Sourcebooks, Inc.®**

Naperville Office
P.O. Box 4410
Naperville, Illinois 60567-4410
630-961-3900
Fax: 630-961-2168
www.sourcebooks.com
www.SphinxLegal.com

This publication is designed to provide accurate and authoritative information in regard to the subject matter covered. It is sold with the understanding that the publisher is not engaged in rendering legal, accounting, or other professional service. If legal advice or other expert assistance is required, the services of a competent professional person should be sought.

From a Declaration of Principles Jointly Adopted by a Committee of the American Bar Association and a Committee of Publishers and Associations

This product is not a substitute for legal advice.

Disclaimer required by Texas statutes.

Library of Congress Cataloging-in-Publication Data
Truly, Traci.
  Grandparents' rights / by Traci Truly.-- 4th ed.
    p. cm.
  Includes index.
  ISBN-13: 978-1-57248-526-6 (pbk. : alk. paper)
  ISBN-10: 1-57248-526-4 (pbk. : alk. paper)
  1. Custody of children--United States--Popular works. 2. Visitation rights (Domestic relations)--United States--Popular works. 3. Grandparents--Legal status, laws, etc.--United States--Popular works. I. Title.

KF547.Z9T78 2005
346.7301'73--dc22
                                                            2005025780

Printed and bound in the United States of America.
BG — 10 9 8 7 6 5 4 3 2 1

Contents

Using Self-Help Law Books vii

Introduction xi

Frequently Asked Questions xiii

Chapter 1: Overview of Grandparents' Rights 1
    Kinds of Rights Available
    Legal Research
    Summary of Custody Laws
    Summary of Visitation Laws

Chapter 2: Should You File for Visitation? 9
    Troxel v. Granville
    Reasons to File
    Reasons Not to File
    Additional Considerations

Chapter 3: Filing for Visitation 21

Preparing Your Petition

Complaint/Petition for Grandparent Visitation (form 1)

Petition for Grandparent Visitation (form 2)

Complaint for Grandparent Visitation (form 3)

Original Petition for Grandparent Access (form 4)

Petition of Grandparent(s) for Intervention in Suit Affecting the
    Parent-Child Relationship (form 5)

Request for Mediation

Court Procedures

Notifying the Other Parties

After the Court Order

When Grandparents Divorce

Modification of Visitation

Chapter 4: Should You File for Custody? 37

Qualifying to File for Custody

Reasons to Consider Filing for Custody

Obstacles to Getting Custody

Grounds

Uniform Child Custody Jurisdiction and Enforcement Act

More on Child Abuse

Chapter 5: Filing for Custody 49

Preparing Your Petition

Complaint/Petition for Custody (form 15)

Original Petition in Suit Affecting the Parent-Child
    Relationship (form 16)

Petition of Grandparent(s) for Intervention in Suit Affecting
    the Parent-Child Relationship (form 17)

Financial Affidavit (form 26)

Court Procedures

Notifying the Other Parties

Chapter 6: Role of the Lawyer 57

Tips for Selecting a Lawyer

Tips for Working with Your Lawyer

Chapter 7: Court Procedures 63
Filing Your Petition
Notifying Others
When You Cannot Locate the Parent
Default Judgments
Uncontested Cases vs. Contested Cases
Agreed Orders
Motions
Courtroom Manners
Evidentiary Rules
Trial Procedures
Final Order
Appeals

Chapter 8: Evidence You Will Need 89
Visitation
Custody

Chapter 9: Specific Case Examples 93
Visitation
Custody
Conclusion

Glossary 99

Appendix A: State Laws 101

Appendix B: Resources 133

Appendix C: Sample, Completed Forms 143

Appendix D: Blank Forms 165

Index 229

About the Author 235

Using Self-Help Law Books

Before using a self-help law book, you should realize the advantages and disadvantages of doing your own legal work and understand the challenges and diligence that this requires.

The Growing Trend

Rest assured that you will not be the first or only person handling your own legal matter. For example, in some states, more than 75% of the people in divorces and other cases represent themselves. Because of the high cost of legal services, this is a major trend, and many courts are struggling to make it easier for people to represent themselves. However, some courts are not happy with people who do not use attorneys and refuse to help them in any way. For some, the attitude is, "Go to the law library and figure it out for yourself."

We write and publish self-help law books to give people an alternative to the often complicated and confusing legal books found in most law libraries. We have made the explanations of the law as simple and easy to understand as possible. Of course, unlike an attorney advising an individual client, we cannot cover every conceivable possibility.

Cost/Value Analysis

Whenever you shop for a product or service, you are faced with various levels of quality and price. In deciding what product or service to buy, you make a cost/value analysis on the basis of your willingness to pay and the quality you desire.

When buying a car, you decide whether you want transportation, comfort, status, or sex appeal. Accordingly, you decide among choices such as a Neon, a Lincoln, a Rolls Royce, or a Porsche. Before making a decision, you usually weigh the merits of each option against the cost.

When you get a headache, you can take a pain reliever (such as aspirin) or visit a medical specialist for a neurological examination. Given this choice, most people, of course, take a pain reliever, since it costs only pennies; whereas a medical examination costs hundreds of dollars and takes a lot of time. This is usually a logical choice because it is rare to need anything more than a pain reliever for a headache. But in some cases, a headache may indicate a brain tumor, and failing to see a specialist right away can result in complications. Should everyone with a headache go to a specialist? Of course not, but people treating their own illnesses must realize that they are betting on the basis of their cost/value analysis of the situation. They are taking the most logical option.

The same cost/value analysis must be made when deciding to do one's own legal work. Many legal situations are very straightforward, requiring a simple form and no complicated analysis. Anyone with a little intelligence and a book of instructions can handle the matter without outside help.

But there is always the chance that complications are involved that only an attorney would notice. To simplify the law into a book like this, several legal cases often must be condensed into a single sentence or paragraph. Otherwise, the book would be several hundred pages long and too complicated for most people. However, this simplification necessarily leaves out many details and nuances that would apply to special or unusual situations. Also, there are many ways to interpret most legal questions. Your case may come before a judge who disagrees with the analysis of our authors.

Therefore, in deciding to use a self-help law book and to do your own legal work, you must realize that you are making a cost/value analysis. You have decided that the money you will save in doing it yourself outweighs the chance that your case will not turn out to your satisfaction. Most people handling their own simple legal matters never have a problem, but occasionally people find that it ended up costing them more to have an attorney straighten out the situation than it would have if they had hired an attorney in the beginning. Keep this in mind while handling your case, and be sure to consult an attorney if you feel you might need further guidance.

Local Rules   The next thing to remember is that a book which covers the law for the entire nation, or even for an entire state, cannot possibly include every procedural difference of every jurisdiction. Whenever possible, we provide the exact form needed; however, in some areas, each county, or even each judge, may require unique forms and procedures. In our state books, our forms usually cover the majority of counties in the state or provide examples of the type of form that will be required. In our national books, our forms are sometimes even more general in nature but are designed to give a good idea of the type of form that will be needed in most locations. Nonetheless, keep in mind that your state, county, or judge may have a requirement, or use a form, that is not included in this book.

You should not necessarily expect to be able to get all of the information and resources you need solely from within the pages of this book. This book will serve as your guide, giving you specific information whenever possible and helping you to find out what else you will need to know. This is just like if you decided to build your own backyard deck. You might purchase a book on how to build decks. However, such a book would not include the building codes and permit requirements of every city, town, county, and township in the nation; nor would it include the lumber, nails, saws, hammers, and other materials and tools you would need to actually build the deck. You would use the book as your guide, and then do some work and research involving such matters as whether you need a permit of some kind, what type and grade of wood is available in your area, whether to use hand tools or power tools, and how to use those tools.

Before using the forms in a book like this, you should check with your court clerk to see if there are any local rules of which you should be aware or local forms you will need to use. Often, such forms will require the same information as the forms in the book but are merely laid out differently or use slightly different language. They will sometimes require additional information.

Changes in the Law

Besides being subject to local rules and practices, the law is subject to change at any time. The courts and the legislatures of all fifty states are constantly revising the laws. It is possible that while you are reading this book, some aspect of the law is being changed.

In most cases, the change will be of minimal significance. A form will be redesigned, additional information will be required, or a waiting period will be extended. As a result, you might need to revise a form, file an extra form, or wait out a longer time period. These types of changes will not usually affect the outcome of your case. On the other hand, sometimes a major part of the law is changed, the entire law in a particular area is rewritten, or a case that was the basis of a central legal point is overruled. In such instances, your entire ability to pursue your case may be impaired.

Introduction

The purpose of this book is to help you secure visitation with, or obtain custody of, your grandchildren without hiring a lawyer. If you decide to hire a lawyer, this book will help you to work with your lawyer more efficiently and effectively.

This is not a law school course, but a practical guide to get you through *the system* as comfortably as possible. Legal jargon has been nearly eliminated. The emphasis is on practical information in plain English. For ease of understanding, certain terms and language will be used in order to avoid confusion when talking about the grandparents, the parents, and the grandchildren. This book is written in language that assumes you (the reader) are a grandparent. Therefore, the words "you" and "grandparent" will be used interchangeably. The word "parent" refers to the parent of your grandchild. The word "grandchild" will be used instead of the word "child" as much as possible, so there is no confusion about whether it is your grandchild or your son or daughter who is being discussed. However, there will be times, especially when talking about statutes, that the word "child" will be used to mean your grandchild. Many statutes use this terminology, so it is necessary at times to use it as well. Occasionally, it will be necessary to refer to "your son or daughter" to distinguish between the parent to whom you are related and the other parent. Finally, the words "parent" and "parents" are used interchangeably, as are "grand-child" and "grandchildren."

One difficulty in writing a book of this type is that court procedures and laws are different in every state, and sometimes in various courts in the same state. While general forms are provided in Appendix D of this book, you will need to do some research to determine exactly what forms are required for your state and county. More information about this is discussed later in this book.

Be sure to read the entire book before you begin preparing any of the forms in this book. You may want to make several copies of the forms and save the originals, so you can make more copies if you need them.

Frequently Asked Questions

If you are reading this book, you are probably facing some problems in regard to your grandchildren and the amount of time you get to spend with them. Maybe it is simply a question of not getting to see them enough. Perhaps you are considering trying to get legal custody of them either because they are already living with you or because their parents have encountered problems. In either case, you probably have some questions about the legalities of your relationship with your grandchildren. Answering some of your basic questions is a good way to get started.

Q: I hear a lot about *grandparents' rights*. What does that really mean?

A: Usually, people are talking about the grandparents getting court orders to have visitation with their grandchildren.

Q: What are my rights as a grandparent?

A: Your rights as a grandparent depend on the laws in the state where your grandchild lives. Parents have a fundamental, constitutionally protected right to make decisions for their children, but grandparents do not have any fundamental rights to their grandchildren. The only rights grandparents have in regard to their grandchildren are those granted by the state legislature and set out in the laws of the grandchildren's home state.

Q: Do all states have grandparent visitation laws?

A: Yes, all states have passed some form of a grandparent visitation statute. However, the laws are not all the same. Also, just because your state has a statute on the books does not mean it is still valid. Courts review statutes all the time, and there are some statutes that still show up in the books but have been ruled invalid by the courts.

Q: What does it mean to me if my grandchild lives in a state where this has happened?

A: It means that, as a practical matter, there is not a grandparent visitation statute available to you. You will need to keep up with what is happening in the state legislature and watch to see if a new law is passed to fix the problems the court found in the other version.

Q: I have read or heard about a U.S. Supreme Court case that deals with grandparent visitation. What is it?

A: That case, *Troxel v. Granville*, is discussed in this book. It is a very important case, because it has affected the grandparent visitation statutes in most states. You will need to read the section covering this case carefully and understand as much as you can about how it affects the laws in your state.

Q: Will this book tell me for sure whether or not the visitation law in my state is still valid?

A: Sometimes, but not always. Every effort has been made to give you the most current information, but the law is always subject to change. Where possible, a citation to a grandparent visitation case has been given, so you have a starting point for researching the law in your state. If it is a case that held the law in your state to be unconstitutional, that information is given.

Q: What does it mean if my state does not have a case cited?

A: It may mean that there simply have not been any cases on grandparent visitation appealed in your state, even if the version of your state's law has been around for a long time. However, many states have recently changed their laws to comply with the *Troxel* case, and it may be that your state law is too new to have any reported cases that talk about it.

Q: If I am not being allowed to see my grandchildren, is that enough to get me court-ordered visitation?

A: No. Every state has a set of requirements you must meet before the court can give you visitation.

Q: If I meet the basic requirements, will I automatically get visitation?

A: No. The judge still has the last word, and will make a decision as to whether or not giving you visitation is in your grandchild's best interest.

Q: If the judge gives me visitation, how much time will I get?

A: It varies depending on the state law, the views of the particular judge who hears your case, and the facts of your case. However, as a general rule, you will not get as much visitation as a noncustodial parent would.

Q: What if the parents object to me getting visitation?

A: Obviously, this makes it much harder for you to win. In some states, it may make it virtually impossible.

Q: Can I get visitation if my grandchild's parents are still married to each other and living together?

A: This is the hardest situation of all in which to get court-ordered visits. If you are in this situation, you will need to research the laws of your state to learn if you are even eligible for visitation in this setting. If you are, you will need to know as much as you can about what you have to prove in order to get visitation and have very strong evidence to back up your request. In many states, you may not even qualify to file under the visitation law.

Q: I am seeing my grandchild some, but not as much as I would prefer. Can I still file for visitation?

A: You may be eligible to file for visitation, but this is a situation in which you should carefully evaluate what you can gain in court versus the risk that you will lose what you have now. Courts and laws are more sympathetic to grandparents whose access has been cut off completely. If you are getting some visitation and you go to court, the parents may become so upset that they restrict the time you have with your grandchild even more. If you lose in court, you take the chance that they will end the visits entirely.

Q: I have gotten visitation in court. Can it ever be taken away from me?

A: Yes, it can. Many states have specified criteria in their laws about when visitation can be modified. Even if it is not specifically set out in the grandparent visitation statute itself, there are probably other laws in place that allow visitation schedules to be changed if the circumstances change.

Q: What if I am the grandparent of an adopted grandchild? Are the rules different?

A: If you are an adoptive grandparent, the rules are the same for you as they are for a biological grandparent. On the other hand, if you are a biological grandparent and your grandchild gets adopted, you will need to check the laws of your state. You may not have *any* visitation rights.

Q: Do I need a lawyer?

A: One of the purposes of this book is to help you make that decision. Every case is different, and no one answer is right for everyone. Please review the chapter on working with an attorney for more information.

Q: How much will it cost to use an attorney?

A: It depends. Different lawyers charge different rates, and rates vary depending on your geographical location. Also, every case is different. The more complicated your case, the more the total cost will be.

Q: How long will my case take?

A: This depends on how complex the case is. It could be anywhere from a month or two to several years if the case gets appealed.

Q: What if both sets of grandparents want visitation? What happens then?

A: The court will decide whether either set gets visitation. The fact that one set gets visitation does not mean the other set will.

Q: What if my spouse and I have grandparent visitation, and we get a divorce?

A: You will have to divide the time you have between the two of you. It is not likely that the court will grant more total grandparent time just because of a divorce between the grandparents.

Q: What if I think I need more than visitation? Can I get full custody of my grandchild?

A: Yes, under some circumstances you can. Most states have a presumption that the parents should have custody, but there are situations in which that presumption can be overcome. Please review the section on custody for more information.

Q: Will I need a lawyer for a custody case?

A: You do not absolutely have to have one, but it is easier to have one because custody cases are difficult.

Q: How much will a custody case cost?

A: Once again, it depends on the case. A very complex custody case can end up costing thousands of dollars.

Q: If I decide to represent myself, what do I do when I get to court?

A: You will have to know the rules, just as if you were a lawyer. You should carefully read the chapters in this book on court procedure and evidence.

Overview of Grandparents' Rights

The relationship between grandparents and their grandchildren has become increasingly complex and less traditional over the past ten to twenty years. More and more, grandparents find themselves looking to the courts to set the parameters of their time with their grandchildren. The rising divorce rate, soaring single parenthood, increased drug use among the adult population, and a troubled economy have all played a part in these changes, as they have altered the entire American family structure.

For various reasons, a significant number of grandparents have assumed full-time responsibility for rearing their grandchildren. An even greater number have sought the assistance of the courts to get regular visitation with their grandchildren. As a result, the various state legislatures have been forced to set standards for grandparent visitation and for custody to nonparents.

The purpose of this book is to examine the laws of the various states regarding grandparent visitation and custody. Additionally, a review is made of different family situations that can affect your decision to file for custody or visitation. You will also learn about court proceedings involved in custody and visitation cases.

If you decide to go to court to seek custody of or visitation with your grandchildren, one of the decisions you will have to make is whether or not to hire an attorney. Chapter 6 addresses the various factors involved in that decision, as well as the pluses and minuses of representing yourself in court. There is an overview of the types of evidence you will need in order to prepare a custody or visitation case.

Obviously, the laws relating to grandparent visitation and custody vary from state to state. In the back of this book, Appendix A contains a summary of the laws of each state. Before you move forward with a case, you will need to study the law of your state to be sure you meet the qualifications to file and to be sure you know how to file.

KINDS OF RIGHTS AVAILABLE

There are two basic types of rights available to grandparents in relation to their grandchildren—custody and visitation. *Custody* refers to the legal rights and obligations that go along with assuming the role of full-time parent to your grandchildren. Deciding to file for custody of your grandchildren involves making a big commitment, especially if the children's parents fight your attempt to obtain custody. In that event, you should review your situation very carefully before you file.

The second right is that of *visitation*. This involves the court setting a schedule for you to spend time with your grandchildren. Once again, the laws vary from state to state, and you will need to study Appendix A before you file. The fact that you are not getting to see your grandchildren will not, by itself, be enough to qualify you for court-ordered visitation.

LEGAL RESEARCH

Once you have reviewed this book and carefully studied your state's listing in Appendix A, you will need to consult your nearest law library or public library with a legal section. If your public library does not have a legal section, or if it does not contain the information you need, you may be able to find a law library in or near your county courthouse. If you live near a law school, you will also find a library there. The librarian will be able to direct you to the proper books, but cannot tell you what forms to use or how to fill them out, because they are not allowed to give legal advice.

In the legal section, you will find several types of books. A discussion of the various types follows.

Statutes or Codes

One set of books that you will need to use is the set of statutes or codes for your state. These are the books in which the laws passed by the state legislature are found. References to these books are contained in the state law section in Appendix A.

You will notice that many of the state statutes have the words *revised* or *annotated* in the title. (For example, *Vernon's Texas Codes Annotated* and the *Hawaii Revised Statutes*.) *Annotated* just means that the statutes also contain a listing of some court cases that have been decided under a particular section of the statute, and a summary of the court decision immediately following the text of the statute section itself. *Revised* means the books have been updated with changes in the laws. The *Vernon's* in the Texas statute example refers to the publisher. Many state statutes contain the name of the publisher in the book title.

Every time your state legislature meets, it is possible that some change to the law that governs your case will be made. It is important that you use the most current version of the law. Therefore, when you look in these books, be sure to check for the most current *supplements*. These may be found attached to the main volume or in a softcover book kept near the main volume.

Practice Manuals

You will also find practice manuals that contain forms and practical pointers for handling different kinds of cases. If there is a conflict between the forms contained in this book and the forms you find in a practice manual for your state, you should use the form from the practice manual that is tailored specifically for your state.

Court Rules

The procedural rules for your state are usually kept in a book called *court rules*. The court rules may not be in their own book, and may be made part of another book containing laws and procedures, so you may need to ask the librarian. The rules about how to notify people of court filings and hearing dates are found in the court rules.

Reporters   Another set of books that will be helpful to you is the *reporter*. These books contain the written opinions of courts, usually appellate courts, as to how and why each case was decided the way it was. The cases for your state will be found in the reporter for your region. The following is a list of reporters and the states they cover.

Abbreviation	Full Name of Reporter	States Covered
A. and A.2d	Atlantic Reporter	Connecticut, Delaware, District of Columbia, Maine, Maryland, New Hampshire, New Jersey, Pennsylvania, Rhode Island, Vermont
Cal. Rptr., Cal. Rptr.2d, and Cal. Rptr.3d	California Reporter	California
N.E. and N.E.2d	North Eastern Reporter	Illinois, Indiana, Massachusetts, New York, Ohio; also, New York Court of Appeals
N.Y.S.	New York Supplement	New York
N.W. and N.W.2d	North Western Reporter	Iowa, Michigan, Minnesota, Nebraska, North Dakota, South Dakota, Wisconsin
P., P.2d, and P.3d	Pacific Reporter	Alaska, Arizona, California Supreme Court since 1960, Colorado, Hawaii, Idaho, Kansas, Montana, Nevada, New Mexico, Oklahoma, Oregon, Utah, Washington, Wyoming
S.E. and S.E.2d	South Eastern Reporter	Georgia, North Carolina, South Carolina, Virginia, West Virginia
So. and So.2d	Southern Reporter	Alabama, Florida, Louisiana, Mississippi
S.W., S.W.2d, and S.W.3d	South Western Reporter	Arkansas, Kentucky, Missouri, Tennessee, Texas

Cases are referenced (cited) in a certain way as follows:

Jones v. Jones, 165 S.W.3d 859 (Tex. 2005)

You would find this case by looking in volume 165 of the *South Western Reporter 3d Series* and turning to page 859. The "(Tex. 2005)" means that the Texas Supreme Court decided the case in 2005. Sometimes you will see a fairly recent case cited similar to the following:

Smith v. Smith, No. 2920-39 (Cal. 2006)

This is a case that is too recent to have made its way to the reporter. The citation refers to the case number used by the particular appellate court.

Digests One way to locate particular cases that apply to your situation is by looking at the annotations following the statute itself. Another source is the *digest*. A digest contains brief summaries of cases and tells you where to find the full text of the opinion. The cases are grouped together according to subject matter. Digests contain indexes to help you find the right subject heading.

Legal Encyclopedias A *legal encyclopedia* can also be a good source of information. *American Jurisprudence* and *Corpus Juris Secundum* are two legal encyclopedias that are national in scope, but your state may have its own. (*Texas Jurisprudence* is an example of a state legal encyclopedia.) Once again, the material is grouped by subject matter. In a legal encyclopedia, you will find a summary of the laws on a particular subject and a few cases listed.

Law Librarian You should check with the law librarian to see what is available for your state. He or she can also help make sure that you have the most current information. The law is constantly changing, and you need to check to see if the courts have changed the interpretation of the statute as it is written or if the state legislature has amended the statute itself. Once you have done these things, you will be better prepared to confront the legal system, either on your own or with the assistance of a lawyer.

SUMMARY OF CUSTODY LAWS

All fifty states have passed some form of grandparent visitation (the District of Columbia has not), and of course, all have laws governing child custody. In terms of custody, all states have adopted a form of a law called the *Uniform Child Custody Jurisdiction and Enforcement Act* (UCCJEA). This law is basically designed to provide a method for resolving disputes between courts when more than one state is involved. In today's mobile society, it is not unusual for parents to have been married in one state, lived in several others, separated, and moved to two different states. The UCCJEA sets out the guidelines for determining which state should have the primary right to rule on child custody issues in a particular case. If you are in a situation in which more than one state is involved, you will need to study this law and comply with its provisions. There are, however, additional laws in each state that govern child custody.

In each case, you will need to review the laws of the state in which the court that will decide the custody case is located. A number of states have fairly specific statutes setting out the factors to be considered in deciding custody, and you will need to tailor your evidence to these factors. Other states will give you very little guidance in the statute. For example, it may only say that the *best interest of the child* is the controlling factor. If your custody case is filed in one of these states, you will need to read some of the court decisions that have interpreted the custody statute, so you know what will and will not be helpful to you in the way of evidence. Even if your state has a fairly specific statute, you would be well-advised to read some of the cases involving the law.

SUMMARY OF VISITATION LAWS

Grandparent visitation is governed by statute and by case law interpreting that statute. Each state has its own version of a grandparent visitation statute. You will find that many states have recently amended their laws to comply with the United States Supreme Court case on grandparent visitation. This case, *Troxel v. Granville*, is discussed in more detail in the next chapter.

In some states in which the legislature has not changed the law to comply with *Troxel*, the courts have added rules about grandparent visitation that come from *Troxel*, but may not be written out in the statute. You will need to follow the rules created by these cases, just like you would if they were actually written in the statute. In other states, there is still a version of a grandparent visitation statute on the books, but the court system in that state has declared it unconstitutional. If you are in one of these states, the fact that a grandparent visitation statute is still in your state law means nothing. In effect, until your state passes a new law, there is no grandparent visitation statute available for you to use.

Before you file a grandparent visitation case, you need to check the laws of your state for the most current status. The information given here is current as of the time of the writing of the book, but by the time you read it, things may have changed. The various aspects of visitation laws are discussed in the next chapter.

Should You File for Visitation?

chapter 2

If you are contemplating seeking the court's assistance in getting visitation, it is probably because you are having difficulty with one or more of the parents, and are not seeing your grandchildren regularly. Perhaps there are problems in your grandchildren's home environment. You most likely tried to reach some kind of agreement with the parents but were not successful; otherwise, you would probably not be reading this book. The assumption is that the parents are unwilling to allow you visitation.

This book is written based primarily on the grandparent laws that are *on the books* in the various states. You need to be aware that these laws are always subject to change, either by the state legislature or by court decision.

TROXEL V. GRANVILLE

Before you make a decision about filing for visitation, you must be familiar with the United States Supreme Court decision *Troxel v. Granville,* 120 S. Ct. 2054 (2000). Although this case was decided on the basis of and applies to a previous version of the Washington grandparent visitation statute, you need to pay careful attention to the analysis and reasoning of this case, as it may have serious implications for the constitutionality of the statutes in your state. It also means that your state legislature may be making changes to the statute in your state as a result of this case. Because of the complexities involved, you may wish to invest in at least a consultation with an attorney to help you determine the status of grandparent visitation in your particular state.

The *Troxel* case is based on an early version of a Washington law that permitted any person to ask for visitation at any time. The only thing they had to prove was that the visitation was in the best interest of the child. The Troxels are the grandparents of two girls; the father of the children is the Troxels' son, Brad, who is deceased. Tommie Granville is the mother. The Troxels were getting frequent visitation with the children after the death of their son, but the mother at some point decided to limit their visits to one per month. In response, the Troxels filed for visitation.

The trial court granted more visitation than what was offered by the mother, so she appealed. Ultimately, the Washington Supreme Court ruled that, as written, the visitation statute was unconstitutional, and that the Troxels were not entitled to visitation. The Troxels appealed to the U.S. Supreme Court.

The Supreme Court cited a number of cases under the Fourteenth Amendment to the U.S. Constitution that set out the fundamental liberty interest parents have in regard to the care, custody, and control of their children. The Court ruled that Washington's statute unconstitutionally infringed on that fundamental right. The Court's concern was that the statute basically subjected any decision by a fit parent to court review without giving any consideration or weight to the decision of the parent, and the Washington Supreme Court had declined to give the statute a narrow interpretation. The majority opinion held that there is a presumption that a fit parent will act in the best interest of the child, and that some sort of special weight must be given to the parent's decision before the Court can intervene.

However, the Court specifically limited its ruling to the *sweeping breadth* of the statute and the way the Washington Supreme Court applied that unlimited power. They passed up the opportunity to define the scope of the parental due process right, and they did not rule that harm to the child was necessary before a court could intervene and order visitation.

The Impact of Troxel

This meant that the only statute specifically invalidated by the ruling was this version of the Washington law. Obviously, if you are in a state with a similar statute and interpretation, it is likely that your statute will be held to be unconstitutional. The Supreme Court seemed to approve of the wording of statutes in California, Maine, Minnesota, Nebraska, Rhode Island, and Utah, but these statues were not specifically reviewed and ruled upon by the Court. You will need to check the wording of the statute in your state to see where it fits.

You will need to know whether or not your state courts have ruled on the constitutionality of your state statute. Look especially for cases that were decided after the *Troxel* decision was announced in 2000. You need to be particularly aware of this situation in Florida, Iowa, and Washington.

Florida has a long history of struggle with the constitutionality of its grandparent visitation statute. Even before *Troxel*, Florida's Supreme Court had repeatedly declared parts of its visitation statute unconstitutional. What often happens is that the legislature passes a new version of the statute, and the process gets repeated. The present status of the law in Florida is that the courts have once again declared the statute that is *on the books* to be unconstitutional. In *Sullivan v. Sapp*, 866 So.2d 28 (Fla. 2004), the court invalidated the present law. In the written opinion on that case, the judges sent a message to the Florida legislature telling them to stop passing grandparent visitation statutes based solely on the best interest of the child. The court said that any law that does not require a showing of harm to the child from the denial of visitation will not pass constitutional muster.

Iowa is one of the states in which its state supreme court has ruled the existing visitation statute unconstitutional. The statute was first held unconstitutional in *Santi v. Santi*, 633 N.W.2d 312 (2001). You will find a more detailed discussion of the facts of this case in Chapter 9.

The state of Washington has had similar struggles with grandparent visitation. The *Troxel* case originated in Washington and resulted in the invalidation of one version of the grandparent visitation statutes. The Washington legislature had already passed another version of a grandparent visitation law by the time the *Troxel* ruling was announced. Since that time, the Washington Supreme Court has ruled on the new version. In *Appel v. Appel*, 109 P.3d 405 (Wash. 2005), the present grandparent visitation law was determined to be unconstitutional.

If your case will have to be filed in South Carolina, there is case law that you should carefully weigh before you file. The South Carolina Supreme Court, although it has not invalidated the grandparent visitation statute, has let grandparents know that it will not always be easy in South Carolina to get grandparent visitation. There is language in a case that says that it is seldom in the child's best interest for grandparents to have visitation when the grandparent's child, who is the parent of the grandchild, has access to the child.

In other states, the courts have not ruled that the statute itself is unconstitutional but have ruled that it was unconstitutionally applied in a particular case. If you are in a state in which there is case law with this kind of language, you need to be sure that your evidence meets the *Troxel* standard, even if it is not required by the language of the written law. Maryland residents need to pay particular attention to this area because your state has some cases that said the statute was constitutionally applied and some said it was not.

There are numerous states that have attempted to keep their grandparent visitations statutes constitutional by adding the *Troxel* standards by way of court interpretation. If you are in one of these states, you need to read some of the cases so you know what the courts will require you to prove. You cannot rely on the wording of the grandparent visitation law itself. Appendix A contains entries for states where this is already an issue and includes a citation to at least one case to get you started in your research. These states include California, Colorado, Connecticut, Kansas, Kentucky, Louisiana, Massachusetts, Vermont, and Wisconsin.

By contrast, Arizona's grandparent visitation statute is in much better condition, as the Arizona Supreme Court upheld the validity of the statute. This case, *Jackson v. Tangreen*, 18 P.3d 100 (AZ 2000), was appealed to the United States Supreme Court, which refused to take the case. However, by case law in Arizona, the *Troxel* rules still apply. As long as you keep in mind that the cases impose a presumption that a fit parent acts in the child's best interest and his or her decision about visitation gets special weight, you should be able to have a greater degree of confidence that the Arizona law will remain constitutional.

In October 2005, the Ohio Supreme Court issued a ruling in *Harrold v. Collier*, 2005 Ohio LEXIS 2241, holding that their grandparent's visitation statute is constitutional. The court ruled that, because the Ohio statute contained a requirement for the trial court to consider the parent's wishes before ordering visitation, the statute complied with the *Troxel* requirements. Because this decision was so new at press time, check the subsequent history of this case to be sure of the final outcome.

As you review the rules for your state, always keep the *Troxel* guidelines in mind. Assume the court will presume that the parent's decision is in the best interest of the child, and be prepared to show some sort of physical or emotional harm to the child if visitation is denied. Look to the case law of your state to learn what factors the courts will consider most important for you to prove.

REASONS TO FILE

A variety of situations may exist that will indicate whether an action for grandparent visitation may be appropriate. For example, if the parents are engaged in a bitter divorce and custody battle, and you have always been close to your grandchildren, court-ordered visitation may help give the grandchildren some continuity and stability. This particularly may be the case when you, as grandparents, are the parents of the noncustodial parent. In those instances, the custodial parent may be unwilling to permit the soon-to-be former in-laws to visit the grandchildren. As the parents of the noncustodial parent, you may not want to infringe on your son's or daughter's limited time with his or her children. It may be necessary, therefore, to seek the court's assistance in carving some additional time from the custodial parent's time. Other situations that are good candidates for court-ordered visitation are when your child is the noncustodial parent and lives a great distance from you, or when you do not have a good relationship with your child and do not see your grandchildren when they are with your child.

Keep in mind, however, that the situations just described may not be good reasons in your particular state to seek visitation. There are states that will not let a set of grandparents get visitation time taken from the parent to whom they are not biologically related. In other cases, the fact that you have a poor relationship with your own child may be used against you to keep you from having visitation—some states, by statute, look at the grandparent's ability to foster a good relationship between the child and the parents. If you do not get along with your child, he or she may use that to say you will undermine the parent-child relationship, and that is why he or she is not granting you visitation.

Death of a Parent

If one or both of the parents have died, you may consider filing in order to continue a regular relationship with the grandchild. This is especially true if your child is the parent who is deceased. The remaining parent may not emphasize keeping up family contact with the deceased parent's relatives. Here, court-ordered visitation is generally available.

One word of warning—any time your grandchild is adopted by someone, you may lose all rights in relation to that child. This is because the rights of the biological parents are terminated in an adoption proceeding. A parent whose rights have been terminated is legally a stranger to the child, and so are the grandparents. Legally, the child is no longer your grandchild. Nonetheless, the majority of states have an exception to the termination of grandparent visitation rights if the adoption is by a stepparent or other relative. Conversely, if your son or daughter adopts a child, you will qualify for grandparent rights to that grandchild if you meet the requirements in your state.

Failure to Exercise Visitation

Another reason you might consider filing for visitation is if the non-custodial parent does not or cannot exercise visitation periods. If you qualify under the statute, the court is likely to find that the visits are in your grandchild's best interest because they serve to strengthen your grandchild's sense of family.

Stability for the Grandchild

If the parents are unstable, either emotionally or financially, and you otherwise qualify for visitation in your state, visitation may be important. This is not only for your grandchild's security, but also allows you an informal way of monitoring your grandchild's situation to see if more serious action needs to be taken.

Conflict with Parents

If you are seeing your grandchildren but there is frequent conflict over scheduling, having the court set ground rules may remove a source of conflict. Of course, while the reduction of conflict is desirable, the courts are now reluctant to use that as the basis for awarding visitation. In fact, if you are getting visitation but are perceived as wanting too much time (thus interfering with the child's schedule and the parent-child relationship), you run a chance that you will lose in court. In the process, you will have angered the parents, and you may end up losing the visitation that you were getting by agreement. While it is true that the unreasonable restriction of contact between the grandchild and grandparent is a factor that can be used to rebut the fit parent presumption, you should approach this area with caution. Be realistic about how much time you are already getting and how much time you could get in court. If there is not a significant difference, then consider this a factor that pushes you more toward not filing than filing.

If your relationship with both parents is bad, court intervention may be your only hope of maintaining a relationship with your grandchildren. Although the fact that you have a poor relationship with the parents may be used by the parents in an attempt to block the visitation you have requested, courts generally realize that the grandparent statutes were passed to accommodate families with fractured relationships. Most judges will expect some difficulties in the relationship between the parents and grandparents, and will not be unduly alarmed if the parents oppose you.

REASONS NOT TO FILE

One of the pitfalls of seeking court-ordered visitation is that you may do permanent damage to your relationship with your son or daughter. Any unresolved emotional issues between you and your child will likely flare up if you file a lawsuit against your son or daughter demanding visitation with your grandchildren. If you are in this sort of situation, you must weigh the possible problems caused with your own son or daughter against the need for court intervention in order for you to see your grandchildren.

If the relationship between the parents and grandparents is poor, it is important for all parties to remember that the grandchild loves all of you, benefits from a close relationship with all of you, and does not belong in the middle of a bitter court battle between his or her parents and grandparents. None of you should disparage the other to your grandchild.

It is vital for the grandparents to determine whether the benefit to the grandchild of court-ordered visitation outweighs any problems this will cause at home for your grandchild with parents who resent your intervention. Just keep in mind that, while the court will expect opposition from the parents (or you would not be in court at all), the judge is obligated by law to give extra consideration to the decision the parent made. The burden is on the grandparents in these cases to overcome the fit parent presumption—not on the parents.

There are also cost factors, both in terms of time and money, even if you elect to represent yourself. If you are getting some access now, you may not be able to improve your situation enough to offset the financial and emotional costs of going to court. You must also give consideration to the age of your grandchildren. Courts may be reluctant to send infants off for visitation periods (in order to avoid trauma to the child). Courts are also hesitant to order unwilling, uninterested teens to go for visitation with a grandparent, and will likely encourage the teen, the parents, and the grandparents to resolve the issues themselves without the help of the court.

If there are allegations substantiated by evidence that you have been abusive—either physically, emotionally, or sexually—to any child, the court can certainly find that visitation with you is not in the best interest of your grandchildren and deny your request. In some states, a conviction for child abuse automatically excludes you from obtaining visitation. Even in states where such a conviction is not a statutory exclusion, you should recognize the difficulty of convincing the court that visitation with you is in your grandchild's best interest.

ADDITIONAL CONSIDERATIONS

Some courts are more generous than others in the amount of access they typically give to grandparents. You may get as little as a few hours every two or three months, or as much as a weekend every month. You should not realistically expect to approach the level of the every-other-weekend schedule normally available to the noncustodial parent. Of course, the circumstances of your particular case may warrant an exception to any general rules or policies. The amount of grandparent access is left strictly to the discretion of the judge. You may want to make inquiries or consult an attorney to get an idea of what policies the judge who will hear your case has for grandparent visitation.

Parents Presently Married

The requirements and qualifications for visitation are dependent in many states on the status of the parents' relationship. In the majority of states, you will not be entitled to visitation if your grandchild's parents are still married to each other and living together. Only Connecticut, Delaware, Idaho, Kentucky, Maine, Montana, New York, North Dakota, Oklahoma, Tennessee, and Wisconsin have statutes providing for visitation while the parents are still together. All states add some requirements, such as:

- the grandparent has established a substantial relationship with their grandchild (Idaho and Maine);

- some special condition exists that necessitates consideration of grandparent visitation (New York);

- the visitation does not interfere with the parent-child relationship (North Dakota); or

- a relationship exists between the grandparent and grandchild that is similar to the parent-child relationship (Wisconsin).

In some states, grandparents may be entitled to visitation while the parents are still married if certain other conditions are present. In three states (Arkansas, Colorado, and Iowa), grandparents may petition for visitation if the grandchild is in the custody of someone other than the parents, regardless of the status of the parents' relationship. If one of the parents is absent, Arizona, California, and Florida statutes provide for grandparent visitation. If the grandparents have been denied visitation for a specified period of time, several states provide for visitation even if the parents remain together. These states are Missouri, New Mexico, Pennsylvania, Rhode Island, West Virginia, and Wyoming. Minnesota allows for visitation if the grandchild has previously resided with the grandparents. Illinois allows visitation if one of the parents joins the grandparents in the request. In South Carolina, the grandparent must show exceptional circumstances to get visitation. Texas also has provisions for grandparent visitation under certain conditions while the parents remain married; for example, if one parent is in jail. Many states listed allow for visitation under more than one of the type of situation described. For a complete list of situations giving rise to visitation, refer to the listing for your state in Appendix A and to the statutes for your particular state.

Divorce   In most states, the filing of a petition for divorce, dissolution of marriage, or for legal separation triggers eligibility to file for grandparent visitation. In some states, it is sufficient that some sort of proceeding for custody or separate maintenance be filed to authorize a request for grandparent visitation, even if there is not a request to dissolve the marriage before the court. In Illinois, Massachusetts, Mississippi, and New Jersey, physical separation (as opposed to legal separation) is a ground for grandparent visitation.

Arizona requires that the parents' marriage is dissolved for at least three months before grandparent visitation is permitted. Florida, Indiana, and Maryland provide for visitation after dissolution of the marriage.

Deceased Parent   All states that have specific requirements relating to the condition of the parents' marriage in order to qualify for grandparent visitation treat the death of a parent as a condition giving rise to visitation. The laws vary as to which grandparents qualify to apply for visitation when a parent dies. Some states permit visitation for either set of grandparents in the case of the death of a parent. Other states limit the visitation to the parents of the deceased parent of the child. As always, you will need to check the statute for your state to see which version applies to you and to determine whether or not there are any additional requirements that apply in this situation. For example, Wyoming allows visitation in this situation only if the grandparents' child has died and the person who has custody of the grandchild has refused visitation.

Children Born Out of Wedlock

Another condition that may enable grandparents to seek visitation is when the child has been born out of wedlock. Many states have specific provisions for this situation. As a general rule, mothers of children born out of wedlock have full parental rights to that child. The father, however, has no parental rights to the child until some action is taken under the paternity or parentage laws to declare him the legal father. Since most states require that the father be declared the child's legal father (using the procedures set out in the paternity or parentage laws). For grandparent visitation to be awarded, paternal grandparents will need to determine the status of their son's legal relationship to the child in order to know whether they are eligible for grandparent visitation.

Native American Children

If your grandchild is a Native American, you will need to review a specific federal law—the *Indian Child Welfare Act*. This law may govern some or all of your case, and may even override the law of your particular state.

Filing for Visitation

Now that you have made the decision to file in court for visitation, the next step is to prepare your paperwork for filing. How and what to file depends on the status of any legal proceedings between the parents, the contents of the specific state statute for grandparent visitation, and the provisions of the state procedural rules. In addition to the information contained in this book, you will need to refer to the procedural rules for your state.

Generally, the petition should contain:

- the names of the grandparents seeking visitation;

- the names, addresses, and dates of birth of the grandchildren with whom visitation is sought;

- the names and addresses of the parents and any other individuals or entities with court-ordered relationships with the children;

- the grounds from the statute that authorizes your visitation (see Appendix A); and,

- a request that the court order the visitation.

(There is additional information about how to complete the forms and file them in Chapter 7.)

Massachusetts provides a standard complaint form in the grandparent visitation statute. For illustration purposes, refer to a copy of this form in Appendix C (see form B, p.147), which has been filled in using the following facts.

> John Doe and his wife, Jane, are the parents of Robert Doe, who was married to Wanda Smith in 1990. Robert and Wanda have two children, Sam Doe and Sara Doe. Sam is 8 and Sara is 4. In 2002, Robert and Wanda were divorced in Massachusetts. Wanda got custody of the children and Robert was awarded visitation. In their Judgment of Divorce, no mention was made of the grandparents. John and Jane have decided to go to court and file for visitation.

The document they would file with the court in order to begin the proceedings is found in Appendix D. (see form 3, p.173.) With some modifications, this form should be sufficient in most states.

Some states, however, have additional requirements. Massachusetts also requires that a *care and custody affidavit* be included. Some type of affidavit is also required in Colorado, Florida, Maine, and Michigan. New York specifically requires that the action be brought by a *special proceeding* or by *writ of habeas corpus*. (These are names of legal proceedings and documents. You will need to refer to additional sources for New York to determine the requirements for these proceedings.)

Missouri

Missouri has created an additional procedure for resolution of grandparent disputes that does not require the filing of a formal complaint. Section 452.403 of *Vernon's Annotated Missouri Statutes* permits a grandparent who has been denied visitation to make a written request for mediation. In that event, the court can order all parties with custody and visitation rights to attend a session with a neutral mediator appointed by the court. This mediator will attempt to help the parties reach an agreement about visitation rights for the grandparents. The mediator does not have the power to order the parents to permit visitation; he or she can only facilitate a voluntary agreement. One warning—the statute requires that the grandparents bear all of the costs of the mediation. Form 11 in Appendix D is the Missouri form to request mediation. (see form 11, p.189.) Many other states have provisions that allow for mediation between the parties at some point during the litigation. Information regarding mediation may be found in the grandparent visitation statutes in some states, in the general domestic relations code in other states, in the state procedural rules, or in the statutes relating to *alternative dispute resolution*.

Pending Case
If you are seeking grandparent visitation as a part of a divorce or other legal proceeding between the parents, your request should be in the form of an intervention in the parent's case. A sample Texas intervention using the Doe family from the Massachusetts complaint (but changing the facts so that the grandparents are making their request for visitation as a part of the parent's divorce) is included in Appendix C. (see form C, p.148.) A sample Texas order for grandparent visitation based on the post-divorce complaint, as opposed to the intervention in the pending divorce, is also included in Appendix C. (see form H, p.155.)

Adoption
Timing can be very important, particularly when adoption is involved. If your son or daughter is giving up his or her parental rights, you may lose your grandparent rights if you do not file your petition before your child's parental rights are terminated. This may be true even if the law in your state says that adoption does not automatically terminate your rights as grandparents.

Great-Grandparents
If you are great-grandparents, you will need to check the laws of your state carefully. Some states specifically include great-grandparents in their visitation laws, while other states exclude great-grandparents. There are also states whose statutes do not address this issue at all.

PREPARING YOUR PETITION

In all cases, you begin legal proceedings by filing some sort of initial paper. These documents vary depending on the type of case and type of proceeding. Everything you file with the court should be typed and double-spaced. Some states require that documents be filed on legal-sized paper, some states require letter size. You can find out what the requirements for your state are by asking the court clerk.

All documents have a heading, called the *case style*. Case styles vary from state to state. To find out what form is appropriate for your state, ask the clerk to let you see a pending case file or look in a form book in your law library. Generally, the style will contain the name of the state and county, and the court designation (for example, *13ᵗʰ District Court*), as well as the names of the parties.

There will also be a docket number assigned to your case. If you are intervening in a pending divorce case, the docket number for your pleadings will be the docket number assigned to the divorce case. If you are filing a new lawsuit, leave this line blank on your first pleading. The clerk will assign you a case number when you file the pleading. Use that number for all future filings in that case.

Just before the body of your pleading should be the title of the document. Refer to the forms included in Appendix D. They have titles like *Petition in Intervention* and *Complaint for Grandparent Visitation*. All your documents should have titles like this, and the title will vary depending on what you are filing. Visit your law library or look at a case at the court clerk's office to find out what title to use.

Some states use the word "complaint," whereas others use the word "petition" to describe the document you will file. Similarly, some states use the words "plaintiff" and "defendant" while others use "petitioner" and "respondent." Some may even use "petitioner" and "defendant."

A typical case style might appear as follows.

IN THE FAMILY COURT OF THE STATE OF WASHINGTON,
IN AND FOR THE COUNTY OF KING

JOHN DOE and JANE DOE,
        Plaintiffs,

VS.   CASE NO. _06-2394-A_

ROBERT DOE and WANDA DOE,
        Defendants.

COMPLAINT FOR GRANDPARENT VISITATION

The same basic information will be included in the case style for all states, although different states will vary the order or location on the page of the information. If you look at forms 2, 3, and 4 in Appendix D, you will see examples of the variations for Florida, Massachusetts, and Texas. Except for the forms for these three states, you will find an area at the top of each form marked "case style" that covers approximately the top one-third of the page. This should give you enough room to type in the proper case style for your state and county.

At the end of your pleadings, you should close with a paragraph telling the judge what it is you want him or her to do. For example, look at paragraph 4 of the **COMPLAINT FOR GRANDPARENT VISITATION**. (see form A, p.145.) Additionally, you should always sign your documents and then type in your name, address, and phone number. Some states have fill-in-the-blank forms or check-off forms. Before you begin preparing this paperwork, check with the court clerk to see if they have forms available. If they do, use the forms from the clerk.

The forms contained in Appendices C and D of this book are either generic or geared to a specific state. This is because the forms vary from state to state. You may use the forms in this book as a guide, but you should be sure you have adapted the form to fit your particular state.

COMPLAINT/PETITION FOR GRANDPARENT VISITATION (FORM 1)

COMPLAINT/PETITION FOR GRANDPARENT VISITATION is a general complaint or petition form for use in seeking visitation in all states except Florida, Massachusetts, and Texas. (see form 1, p.167.) (These states have their own forms, which are discussed in the following subsections of this chapter.) However, after researching the requirements for your state, you may find you need to modify this form.

– Warning –

If you live in Florida, Iowa, or Washington, be sure to read the section on *Troxel v. Granville* on pages 9–13 before preparing this form or taking any other action to seek a court order for visitation.

Complete the **COMPLAINT/PETITION FOR GRANDPARENT VISITATION** as follows.

⬥ Complete the case style portion of the form according to the information in the previous section of this chapter. Follow the language and format commonly used in your state and county.

⬥ In the first unnumbered paragraph, fill in the names of the grandparents seeking visitation on the first line. The second line (after the phrase, "hereinafter called the…") is for your designation as a party (your state will likely use either "Plaintiff," "Petitioner," or "Movant"). In the third line, type in the word "Complaint," "Petition," or whatever word or phrase you used as a title. In the line after the word "against," type in the name or names of the parents (the same person or persons listed as defendants or respondents in the case style). The last line is for the parents' designation, which will be either "Defendant" or "Respondent."

⬥ Paragraph #1 is to identify the relationship of all of the parties. On the first line, type in your designation as a party ("Plaintiff," "Petitioner," or "Movant"). On the second line, type in either "maternal grandparents" or "paternal grandparents," whichever applies to you. Type your address on the third line. The next two lines are for the parents' designation as parties ("Defendants" or "Respondents") and their address. If they are living apart, list both addresses. (see form A, p.145.) In the last two lines, type in the names of the children (your state may also require their ages or birth dates to be listed; if you are not sure, you may want to include them just to be safe), and their current address.

⬥ Paragraph #2 is for you to state the legal *grounds* for why you are entitled to visitation. The first blank in the grounds section should contain either your name or your party designation ("Plaintiff," "Petitioner," or "Movant"). The second blank is where you enter the items from your state statute under which you qualify for visitation. Be sure to read the listing for your state in Appendix A and consult your state's statutes before filling in this space. It is a good idea to use the language of your state's grandparent visitation statute as closely as possible. For example, the listing for Alabama in Appendix A gives five grounds for a grandparent filing for visitation:

1. if one or both parents are deceased;

2. the marriage of the parents has been dissolved;

3. when a parent has abandoned the child;

4. the child was born out of wedlock; and,

5. when the child is living with both parents who are still married to each other, and parental authority has been used to prohibit a relationship between the child and the grandparents.

If you fall into the last category, you might say something like, "The Plaintiffs have attempted to have a relationship with the grandchild. The parents, who are married to each other, have used their parental authority to prohibit Plaintiffs from having a relationship with the child."

◈ Paragraph #3 is for you to tell the court if there is any other case pending that relates to visitation or custody. In the blank, type in your designation as "Plaintiff," "Petitioner," or "Movant." If there are no other cases, type the word "none" in the space after this paragraph. If there is another case, type in the case style from that other case (name of the court, parties' names, and case number).

◈ Paragraph #4 is for you to tell the judge what you are asking him or her to do. The first blank in the relief section is for your designation as "Plaintiff," "Petitioner," or "Movant." In the second blank, state the specific visitation schedule you want. (see form A, p.145.)

◈ Fill in the date, sign your name, and fill in the name, address, and telephone number on the appropriate lines.

PETITION FOR GRANDPARENT VISITATION (FORM 2)

PETITION FOR GRANDPARENT VISITATION is designed for use in filing for grandparent visitation in Florida. (see form 2, p.169.)

– Warning –

Before preparing this form, and before doing anything about seeking a visitation order in Florida, be sure to read about the Florida Supreme Court decisions on page 11.

Complete the **PETITION FOR GRANDPARENT VISITATION** as follows.

◈ Type in the number of the judicial circuit and the county where the court is located in the first two lines of the case style. This should be the court for the county where your grandchild lives.

◈ Fill in your name (and your spouse's, if you are both filing) on the lines above the word "Grandparent(s)," and the names of your grandchild's parents on the lines above the word "Respondent(s)."

◈ Type in your name (and your spouse's, if you are both filing) on the line in the first unnumbered paragraph.

◈ In paragraph 3, fill in the name, birth date, age, and sex of each grandchild with whom you seek visitation.

◈ In paragraph 4, check the appropriate boxes to fit your situation.

◈ In paragraph 5, check the lines before any items that apply to your case. If you check "a" or "c," you will need to check the appropriate box for "mother" or "father." The items in paragraph 5 are the statutory grounds for a grandparent obtaining visitation in Florida. If none of these situations apply, your petition will be dismissed.

◈ In paragraph 6, describe the visitation you would like. For example:

Unsupervised visitation, in our home, on the third Saturday of each month, from 9:00 a.m. to 6:00 p.m.

◈ In paragraph 7, type in a brief explanation of why you believe the visitation will be in the best interest of your grandchild. For example:

The grandchild has developed an emotional attachment and relationship with the grandparents, and such visitations will be the only opportunity for the child to maintain this relationship and to see his aunts, uncles, and cousins.

◈ You (and your spouse, if filing together) need to sign before a notary public on the appropriate signature line, and type in your name, address, and phone information on the lines below the signature line. One of you will need to do this on the second page of the form, and the other on the third page.

◈ Complete form 6, the **UNIFORM CHILD CUSTODY JURISDICTION AND ENFORCEMENT ACT AFFIDAVIT**, and file both forms with the circuit court clerk. These will need to be served on the parents by the sheriff or other approved process server.

COMPLAINT FOR GRANDPARENT VISITATION (FORM 3)

COMPLAINT FOR GRANDPARENT VISITATION is the form you will use if you are filing in Massachusetts. (see form 3, p.173.) Complete the form as follows.

◈ The first two blanks you see (for the "Division" and "Docket No.") should be left blank. If a division needs to be filled in, you can get this information from the clerk and fill in the blank. The docket number should be left blank. The clerk will assign your case a number when you file the complaint.

◈ The blank above the word "Plaintiffs" is where you put in the names of the grandparents seeking visitation.

◈ The blank line above the word "Defendants" is for the names of the parents.

◈ In #1 on the form, you should put the full names and dates of birth of each of the grandchildren. The address of the grandchildren goes in the second blank.

◈ The first blank in #2 on the form is to identify which grandparents, paternal or maternal, are seeking visitation. Your address goes in the second blank.

◈ #3 contains blanks for the names and addresses of the parents.

◈ #4 is the section in which you identify for the court the grounds under which you are eligible for visitation. Item A should be self-explanatory—just fill in the date of the parents' divorce if you are using the parents' divorce to qualify. Items B and C refer to children born out of wedlock. Use B if there was a contested court proceeding that determined the child's father. Item C is for use when the parents have followed the procedure whereby they both acknowledged paternity. Item D should be checked if you are relying on the separation of the parents as your visitation ground. Note that the parents must have been to court to obtain temporary orders before you can get visitation. Check E if one of the parents is dead, and F if both parents have died.

◈ When you have completed the form, sign and date it, and fill in the name, address, and telephone number information on the appropriate lines.

ORIGINAL PETITION FOR GRANDPARENT ACCESS (FORM 4)

ORIGINAL PETITION FOR GRANDPARENT ACCESS is for use in Texas if there is no divorce or other lawsuit pending involving custody or visitation. (see form 4, p.175.) This form is self-explanatory as to what information needs to be filled in on each line. (Form D on page 150 is a completed example.)

Complete the **ORIGINAL PETITION FOR GRANDPARENT ACCESS** as follows.

◈ In the case style section, leave the case number line blank—the clerk will assign the number. The grandchildren's names go in the space just below the words "In the interest of."

◈ Your name goes in section #1, along with your age and address. After the words "who are the," type in either "maternal" or "paternal," whichever describes you.

◈ In section #3, fill in the information for your grandchildren.

◈ In sections #4 and #5, type in the parents' names and addresses.

◈ In the last paragraph in section #8, your names go on the first line after the word "Grandparents," and the specific visitation schedule you want goes on the line after the word "from."

◈ This form then needs to be signed by you (and your spouse, if he or she is joining in the petition) on the lines after the word "by."

PETITION OF GRANDPARENT(S) FOR INTERVENTION IN SUIT AFFECTING THE PARENT-CHILD RELATIONSHIP (FORM 5)

PETITION OF GRANDPARENT(S) FOR INTERVENTION IN SUIT AFFECTING THE PARENT-CHILD RELATIONSHIP is for use in Texas if there is already a divorce or other lawsuit involving custody or visitation. (see form 5, p.177.) A sample can be found in Appendix C. (see form C, p.148.)

Complete the **PETITION OF GRANDPARENT(S) FOR INTERVENTION IN SUIT AFFECTING THE PARENT-CHILD RELATIONSHIP** as follows.

◈ Since you are intervening in an ongoing lawsuit, use the heading from that lawsuit.

◈ The first line in the first unnumbered paragraph is for your name (and your spouse's name, if you are both filing).

◈ In section #1, the first four blanks are for the names and ages of you and your spouse. The fifth blank should be completed by filling in either "paternal" or "maternal," as appropriate. The final blank in this section is for your address.

◈ In section #3, fill in the blanks for each grandchild with whom you seek visitation.

◈ In sections #4 and #5, type in the parents' names and addresses.

◈ In section #6, the form assumes that no other persons have any court-ordered relationships with your grandchildren. However, if some third party or agency has been awarded legal rights to the child (temporary legal custody, for example), you will need to change this section to reflect those relationships.

◈ In the last paragraph in section #8, your name goes on the line after the word "Grandparents," and the specific visitation schedule you want goes on the line after the word "from."

◈ This form then needs to be signed by you (and your spouse, if he or she is joining in the petition) on the lines after the word "by."

◈ In the "Certificate of Service" section, fill in the names of the other parties and the date you sent them copies of your petition. This should be the same day you filed the petition. If you are modifying this form for use outside of Texas, you will need to check the laws of your state to see if you need to do something more than send the parties copies by certified mail. (For more information about formal notification to other parties, see Chapter 7.)

REQUEST FOR MEDIATION

The **REQUEST FOR MEDIATION** is the form used in Missouri, but it may also be used to request mediation in other states that have provisions for mediation after a lawsuit has been filed. (see form 11, p.189.) Complete the **REQUEST FOR MEDIATION** as follows.

◈ Complete the case style portion of the form according to the information in the previous section of this chapter.

◈ In the first paragraph, type in your name on the first line. On all of the other lines in the three main paragraphs, type in the word "Plaintiff," "Petitioner," or "Movant," whichever term is used in your state.

◈ Sign your name on the "signature" line and type in your name, address, and telephone number on the lines indicated. File this with the court clerk. The judge will fill in the order portion of the form.

COURT PROCEDURES

After you complete your complaint or petition, you will need to file it with the court, notify the other parties, prepare for and attend a court hearing, and prepare an order for the judge to sign after he or she makes a decision. See Chapter 7 for information about the procedures to follow once your complaint or petition is completed.

NOTIFYING THE OTHER PARTIES

After you have completed your complaint or petition, you will need to notify the other parties involved (usually the parents) that you are filing court papers for visitation. See the section in Chapter 7 titled "Notifying Others" for more information about notification.

AFTER THE COURT ORDER

After you have been to court and have been successful in convincing the judge to grant you visitation, you are all set to begin enjoying regular time with your grandchildren. Ideally, this turns out to be a very stable situation for the grandchild with minimum conflict between the parents and grandparents. This enables the grandchild to have the many and varied benefits of a close relationship with his or her grandparents. In this situation, the parents get to be parents and the grandparents get to enjoy being grandparents. Sometimes, though, the family situation does not work out this way, and you, as grandparents, may find yourselves facing the decision to seek custody of your grandchildren. (see Chapters 4 and 5.)

WHEN GRANDPARENTS DIVORCE

If you are grandparents covered by an existing court order for visitation and you get a divorce, the divorce will have some effect on your visitation schedule. Unless the two of you intend to see the grandchild together, you will need to reach an agreement on how the visitation time you have with the grandchild will be allocated. If you cannot agree, you may find yourselves back in court trying to modify the visitation schedule. If at all possible, the grandparents should reach an agreement on this point. If you end up back in court, you may be giving the parent an opening to try to reduce your court-ordered visitation time.

Obviously, if you are already divorced when the visitation action takes place, this same issue is not a problem for you. It may be that the other grandparent also files for visitation, and you will have to accept the fact that you will get less time with the child if that happens. The court is not going to give each individual grandparent a weekend a month or even a weekend every couple of months in most cases, because it will cut into the parents' time with the child too much.

MODIFICATION OF VISITATION

Once you have been granted visitation, you cannot assume that your order is set in stone and will never be changed. Many states have specific provisions governing how often and under what circumstances visitation can be modified. Generally, what is required is some sort of *change in the circumstances* of the parties or some sort of *good cause* shown by the parent to reduce or terminate the visitation. Even if your state does not have specific statutory guidelines for visitation modification, the order can probably be changed. The requirements are likely similar to the ones found in states with specific laws.

If you are a grandparent who is facing a lawsuit to reduce or eliminate your visitation, or a parent who is thinking of filing to reduce visitation under a court order, you should review the laws of your state and try to find some cases to learn what the rules are for your situation.

Should You File for Custody?

chapter 4

Over the past twenty-five years, the number of grandparents rearing their grandchildren has risen dramatically. Over four million children live with their grandparents, with nearly one million of those living away from their parents. Most commonly, those parents are absent as a result of drug or alcohol abuse, making them either unable or unwilling to parent their own children. Other factors influencing the rising rate of grandparents rearing their grandchildren include the divorce rate and the economy. Many parents, especially single parents, are unable to afford to care for their children. Sometimes, abuse by a parent or stepparent is a factor that prompts grandparents to seek custody of their grandchildren.

QUALIFYING TO FILE FOR CUSTODY

Just as grandparent visitation statutes establish prerequisites for visitation, the states have requirements that grandparents must meet in order to obtain legal custody. In order to have standing to seek custody in most states, you will have to establish that you had significant past contacts with your grandchild. Assuming that the parents appear in court and contest your attempt to get custody, the greatest hurdle you will have to overcome is the parental preference.

In the overwhelming majority of states, the court starts out presuming that the parents should have custody. The burden is on the grandparents to overcome that presumption. Various states use different words and phrases to describe what it takes to overcome that burden, but generally you must prove that the parents are unfit in order to take custody from them. In states that do not have the parental preference, the *best interest of the child* is the determining factor. Regardless of the standard used by your state, there may be a number of reasons or situations that will cause you to consider filing a lawsuit to get custody of your grandchildren.

REASONS TO CONSIDER FILING FOR CUSTODY

Before you make the decision to file for custody, you will need to weigh the factors that might help you win a custody case and the factors that might cause you to lose. Although each case is different and there may be factors unique to your case that you should also consider even though they are not covered in this book, there are some frequently occurring situations that you should know about.

Abusive or Neglectful Parents

In today's society, there are more reported cases of abuse and neglect than ever before. Sometimes, this is a reflection of drug or alcohol addiction. There are many causes of abuse.

Addicted parents may leave their children with the grandparents, forcing them to seek custody. In other cases, the grandparents may become the primary caregivers for their grandchildren as a result of action by a child welfare agency. Often, grandparents may become aware of instances of abuse or neglect on their own and decide to seek custody in order to protect their grandchildren.

Regardless of how the grandparents become involved in custody litigation relating to abuse or neglect, a contested custody suit of this nature is likely to be very messy. Most parents who invest the time and money to contest a custody case will vigorously deny that they have abused or neglected their children, especially if the possibility of criminal charges stemming from the abuse or neglect exists. Physical abuse can be difficult to prove, unless there are injuries that could only be the result of abuse that have been documented by third persons. For example, a scar or bruise in the shape of a coiled extension cord is difficult to explain as anything other than abuse—a black eye is subject to many explanations. Sexual abuse is even more difficult to prove. There is rarely any physical evidence of sexual abuse of children. In fact, the only evidence may be the testimony of the child.

Very young children are not legally competent to testify. Older children, although allowed to testify, are easily confused about dates, times, and sequences of events. Children are also easily suggestible, as they tend to be eager to please, and their allegations of sexual abuse are often countered by the *coaching defense*. The coaching defense involves claims by the alleged abuser that some adult, usually the person bringing forward the allegation, has coached or manipulated the child into saying he or she has been sexually abused.

Undertaking a case of this nature is a very serious endeavor. It requires a major investment of time and money (even if you represent yourself) and is difficult to handle without a lawyer. There is also the very real possibility that if you are unable to convince a judge or jury that the abuse has occurred, you will be totally excluded from the lives of your grandchildren. In spite of those odds, it is also difficult to stand by and do nothing if you have reason to believe that your grandchildren are being abused.

Neglect is also difficult to prove, as there may not be much evidence other than the testimony of family members, many of whom will not want to take sides in a custody fight. The testimony of family members is also more easily attacked than that of disinterested third parties, especially when there is little or no physical evidence to back the claim. In some cases, however, third party evidence will be available. For instance, if the police or child welfare investigators are called in because the children have been left alone somewhere, you will have the testimony of the police officers or investigators to help your case.

If you are able to establish the existence of abuse or neglect, this will be sufficient in most instances to show that the parents are unfit.

This alone, however, will not entitle you to custody. You will also have to convince the judge or jury of your fitness as custodian, and show that awarding custody to you is in the best interest of your grandchildren. There may be problems in proving these matters to the satisfaction of the court. (Some of the obstacles are discussed later.)

Unstable Parents

Another situation that may give rise to a custody fight is when the parents are unstable. Instability can refer to a number of situations within the family. A family may be financially unstable or emotionally unstable. When taken in conjunction with the laws of the particular state, the nature and severity of the financial instability determine whether or not a grandparent can get custody. For example, if the financial instability involves frequent job and residence changes, that alone will not be enough for a nonparent to get custody in most states. However, if the financial instability means that the child is living in substandard housing without the basic necessities, the grandparents stand a much better chance of having enough evidence to win. The same may be said of emotional stability. Particularly in states where the parents have a statutory preference for custody of their children, it will take a significant amount of instability to defeat the presumption. The presence of significant instability is a factor that triggers an evaluation of whether or not a grandparent should seek custody of the grandchildren.

Absent Parents

Parents may be absent from their children's lives for a number of reasons. The most obvious reason for a parent to be absent is death. Another reason is due to drug and alcohol abuse. An addicted parent may leave his or her child with the grandparents and vanish from the scene. No matter what the reason for the absentee parents, this situation will likely force a grandparent into court to seek custody. In that instance, the grandparents will need custody for legal reasons, such as to consent to medical care and to enroll the child in school. The basic problems involved in a contested custody case do not apply in this situation, as the absent parents are not likely to be in court contesting the change of custody to the grandparents.

OBSTACLES TO GETTING CUSTODY

When the parent does contest the custody case, there are some significant obstacles facing the grandparents.

Age
One difficulty a grandparent may encounter is age. One of the factors a court considers in making a custody determination is long-term stability of the child's situation. All other things being equal, a younger grandparent will have an advantage over an older one. Whether accurate or not, an older grandparent is at a disadvantage. Especially when the custody of younger children is involved, the court will question the remaining life span of older grandparents. Health problems, either existing or potential, are also a factor the courts use in the custody equation. The judge will wonder whether the older grandparent will be physically able to care for the child until the child reaches adulthood. This is the reason the younger, healthier grandparent has an edge over a grandparent who is older or who has health problems.

Your Track Record as a Parent
A second factor in the custody equation is the grandparents' track record as parents. If you are competing against your son or daughter for custody of your grandchild, you should expect your son or daughter to bring up every mistake you ever made as a parent. If the discipline methods you employed as a parent would be considered abusive by today's standards, you will have a disadvantage to overcome, regardless of the methods you use to discipline the grandchild. If you were a largely absent parent who left your own children mostly with other relatives or sitters, this fact will count against you in the eyes of the judge or jury. On the other hand, if there is not any negative evidence, or only minor negative evidence, this can be an advantage for you.

Your Relationship with Your Children
A third potential disadvantage to grandparents seeking custody is the current state of their relationships with their own children. A grandparent who has a poor or nonexistent relationship with some or all of his or her children will be at a significant disadvantage when compared to a grandparent with good relationships with all of his or her children. Another issue contained within the overall parent-child relationship is the grandparent's motivation for seeking custody of a grandchild. Are you filing because you still feel the need to control your son's or daughter's life? Are you filing to fulfill some maternal or

paternal need of your own? Are you filing because you wish you were your grandchild's parent? A "yes" answer to any of these questions indicates that you should reevaluate the need to file in light of your motivation for filing. Filing to punish your son or daughter for some affront or misdeed is also not well-considered.

Your Financial Situation

Your financial situation may also become an obstacle in a contested custody case. Another of the many factors that goes into a determination of what is in the child's best interest is the ability to meet the financial needs of the child. Everyone recognizes that rearing a child is an expensive proposition. Many grandparents will find themselves in the position of being on a fixed income. With costs rising every year, your income may not be sufficient to take on the expenses of caring for your grandchild. While this issue may not be the one that solely determines the outcome of your case, it is something that may make a difference in a close case.

Parental Preference

Another factor involved in custody disputes is one that has been previously mentioned. That factor is the law of parental preference. This obstacle is one that should not be taken lightly. Even if you are fairly young, healthy, and financially secure, with a wonderful record as a parent or grandparent, and could easily prevail in a state where the only test is the best interest of the child, you may not be able to get custody in a state with a parental preference. This law, by itself, may be enough to keep you from getting custody of your grandchild. The parental preference is stronger in some states than in others, and you will need to determine the strength as well as the existence of this policy. Before you file a lawsuit for custody, you need to evaluate the evidence you will be able to use in court in light of the presumption favoring the parents in custody cases. To determine whether or not the parental preference applies in your state, check the listing for your state in Appendix A of this book.

GROUNDS

As a general rule, the qualifications for obtaining custody are not as specific as those for visitation. However, that does not necessarily mean that your state does not have any requirements. These requirements are often referred to as *having standing to sue* or just *standing*.

For example, Texas has specific Family Code provisions that govern standing to sue (§102.003 and §102.004). These laws say that a suit affecting the parent-child relationship (Texas terminology for a custody suit) can be filed by the following:

- ✪ a parent;

- ✪ the child through a court-authorized representative;

- ✪ a custodian or person having the right of visitation with or access to the child appointed by an order from another state or country;

- ✪ a legally appointed guardian of the child;

- ✪ a governmental entity;

- ✪ a licensed child-placing entity;

- ✪ a man claiming to be the biological father of the child; or,

- ✪ a person with whom the child has resided or who has had actual care, control, or possession of the child for at least six months, ending not more than ninety days prior to the filing of the suit.

A grandparent is given additional specific standing if the court order requested is necessary, because the child's present circumstances would significantly impair the child's physical health or emotional development, or if both parents, the surviving parent, or the managing conservator or custodian consented to the suit.

Once you have reviewed your status in light of the parental preference and have decided to seek custody, the next standard you will run into is the *best interest of the child*. Some states simply define this general concept, while other states have specific statutory guidelines for determining the best interest. Typical of these guidelines is §25.24.150 of the Alaska Statutes, which includes the following:

> *...the physical, emotional, religious, and social needs of the child; the capability and desire of each parent to meet these*

needs; the child's preference if the child is sufficient age and capacity to form a preference; the love and affection existing between the child and each parent; the length of time the child has lived in a stable, satisfactory environment and the desirability of maintaining continuity; the desire and ability of each parent to allow an open and loving frequent relationship between the child and the other parent; any evidence of domestic violence, child abuse, or child neglect in the proposed custodial household or a history of violence between the parents; evidence that substance abuse by either parent or other member of the household directly affects the emotional or physical well-being of the child; and other factors that the court considers pertinent.

Even if your state does not have specific guidelines included in its statutes, the Alaskan guidelines will be similar to what courts in your state will consider as part of the best interest standard. As a reminder, if the parties reside in different states, the provisions of the *Uniform Child Custody Jurisdiction and Enforcement Act* will also apply.

UNIFORM CHILD CUSTODY JURISDICTION AND ENFORCEMENT ACT

As noted before, the *Uniform Child Custody Jurisdiction and Enforcement Act* (UCCJEA) is a law designed to avoid conflicts between courts of different states in child custody situations. All fifty states and the District of Columbia have enacted some version of this law, and most provisions will be the same in every state. However, before you file anything in a case in which the UCCJEA is involved, be sure to check the laws for your state, as it is possible for state legislatures to make modifications to the provisions.

Generally, the courts in a particular state can hear a child custody case in any of the following situations.

- ✪ If that state is the home state of the child on the date the legal proceeding began.

- ✪ If that state has been the child's home state within six months of the date the legal proceeding began.

✪   If the child has been removed from that state by someone and a parent continues to live in the state.

✪   If the child and at least one parent have a significant connection with that state, other than mere physical presence in the state.

✪   If the child is physically present in the state and has either been abandoned or is in danger of being abused or neglected.

✪   If another state has deferred to your state.

If you otherwise qualify for a court in your state to hear a custody case, the court can still refuse to hear your case. One reason for this refusal might be that another proceeding concerning custody of the child was already on file in another state. Another reason might be that your state's court decides that it is an inconvenient forum. In making this determination, the court will consider the best interest of the child, the connections the child and his or her family have to other states, and the availability of substantial evidence in the other state. If you have wrongfully taken the child from another state or engaged in similar reprehensible conduct, a state can also decline to exercise jurisdiction.

Uniform Child Custody Jurisdiction and Enforcement Act Affidavit (form 6)

Assuming your state can hear your custody case, there are some specific provisions in the UCCJEA with which you must comply. The most important of these relates to information that must be provided to the court in or with the first document you file. This information must be provided in the form of an affidavit. Form 6 in Appendix D is a UNIFORM CHILD CUSTODY JURISDICTION AND ENFORCEMENT ACT (UCCJEA) AFFIDAVIT, which can be used if you cannot find a specific form for your state. (see form 6, p.179.) Some states require a form like this to be filed in all domestic relations cases involving children, if for no other reason than to assure the judge that the UCCJEA does not apply. Some states may allow the same information to be included in the petition. The court clerk may be able to tell you if you need to file such an affidavit.

The UCCJEA AFFIDAVIT requires very specific information. Complete it as follows.

◈ Complete the case style portion exactly the same as in your complaint or petition.

◈ Fill in the child's name and present address (#1).

◈ Write the places where the child has lived within the last five years (#2).

◈ Write the names and present addresses of the persons with whom the child has lived during that period (#3).

◈ Detail whether the party has participated (as a party, witness, or in any other capacity) in any other litigation concerning the child (#4).

◈ Indicate whether the party has any information of any other pending proceedings relating to the child (#5).

◈ Explain whether the party knows of any other person not already a party to the lawsuit who has physical custody of the child, or claims to have custody or visitation rights with respect to the child (#6).

It is important to remember that if any of this information changes or you become aware of new information, you must provide that information to the court.

There are also provisions applicable to the recognition of court orders from other states, as well as the enforcement and modification of those orders. If you are trying to change an order from another state or enforce such an order, you will need to familiarize yourself with these provisions. For example, you must first register the out-of-state order in your new state before it can be enforced or modified. You will need a certified copy of this order to get it properly registered in the new state.

MORE ON CHILD ABUSE

Earlier in this chapter, the legal aspects of child abuse as it relates to a custody case were discussed. Of course, there is more to child abuse than just how it impacts the evidence in a lawsuit. First, grandparents (and parents also, in many instances) face the hurdle of determining whether or not a child has even been abused. Generally, there are three categories of abuse—physical, sexual, and emotional. Often, physical abuse is the easiest to verify for a concerned grandparent, because there may be visible bruises or scars that are suspicious. Combined with a report from the child, the grandparent may have reliable information on which to base a claim of child abuse.

Sometimes, grandparents may witness physical or emotional abuse, and can provide testimony about the behavior. This testimony can be used not only in custody cases, but also in visitation cases, to overcome the presumption about fit parents acting in the best interest of the child. In this instance, your evidence would be focused not on the validity of the decision itself but on the fitness of the parent. Sexual abuse is much more challenging to identify because of the lack of witnesses discussed earlier.

So what is a grandparent to do if he or she believes that a grandchild is being abused? If the child is being abused, by whom? If the child discloses abuse to you, as a grandparent, and the perpetrator is someone outside the family, then the obvious choice is to relay the information to the parents. In that scenario, there is no need for the grandparents to take any further action unless the parents fail to act to protect the child.

The situation is more complicated when the abuser is a member of the child's family. In an intact family in which the child accuses one or both parents, the grandparent has no choice but to go outside the family for help.

Every state has laws requiring people who believe that a child is being abused to file a report with the authorities. In fact, you may be subject to criminal liability if you know that a child is being abused and fail to report it. However, particularly in the situation in which a family member is accused and the family is no longer intact, you may face allegations that you are manufacturing the abuse allegation to help your child gain an advantage in a divorce or custody suit, or are acting vindictively against the other parent because of your personal feelings for that person. The same thing can be true if it is your own child that you believe is abusing the grandchild.

There is a fine line that you must walk, balancing all of the competing interests. If you honestly believe that child abuse has occurred, you are obligated to act to protect the child, at least by filing a report with the authorities. However, if you are wrong or the allegations cannot be proven, then you have damaged your relationship with one or both of the parents of the child, and may end up losing contact with your grandchild. There is no one answer that fits for every case. You have to evaluate what you think is really happening with the child and make the best decision you can based on those facts. It is a hard truth of the legal system that not every allegation of child abuse is true, and there are people who make these claims in order to gain an advantage, especially in a divorce situation. Not every valid claim of child abuse can be proven to the satisfaction of the courts, either. Finally, if you make a claim of child abuse, and you cannot prove your allegation and it is not substantiated by an official investigation, then you may end up worse off than you were before you filed the report. It is a challenging problem, and sometimes things do not work out as you think they should.

Filing for Custody

In order to obtain custody of your grandchildren, you will have to file pleadings in court. (*Pleadings* are simply documents filed with the court.) The exact documents you will file depend on the status of any legal proceedings between the parents. If there have been previous proceedings between the parents and a court has entered an order for custody of the children, you will need to file a lawsuit to modify the custody order. If the parents are in the process of divorcing or obtaining a legal separation, you will be filing an intervention in the proceedings between the parents. If there have been no custody orders entered by the court, you will file an original lawsuit.

PREPARING YOUR PETITION

In all cases, you initiate the legal proceedings by filing some sort of initial pleading. It will usually be called a *complaint* or a *petition*. These documents vary depending on the type of case and type of proceeding. Everything that you file with the court should be typed and double-spaced. Some states require that documents be filed on legal-sized paper, some states require letter size. You can find out what the requirements for your state are by asking the court clerk.

All documents have a heading called the *case style*. Case styles vary from state to state. To find out what form is appropriate for your state, ask the clerk to let you see a pending case file or look in a form book in your law library. Generally, the style will contain the name of the state, county, and the court designation (for example, *13ᵗʰ District Court*), as well as the names of the parties.

There will also be a *docket* or *case number* assigned to your case. If you are intervening in a pending divorce case, the docket number for your pleadings will be the docket number assigned to the divorce case. If you are filing a new lawsuit, leave a blank space for the number on your first pleading. The clerk will assign you a number when you file the pleading. Use that number for all future filings in that case.

Just before the body of your petition should be the title of the document. Refer to the forms included in Appendix D. They have titles like *Petition in Intervention* and *Complaint for Custody*. All your documents should have titles like this, but the title will vary depending on what you are filing. Visit your law library or look at a case at the court clerk's office to find out what title to use. Some states use the word "complaint," whereas others use the word "petition." Similarly, some states use the words "plaintiff" and "defendant," whereas others use "petitioner" and "respondent." Some may even use "petitioner" and "defendant."

A typical case style might be as follows.

STATE OF MICHIGAN
SIXTEENTH JUDICIAL CIRCUIT, MACOMB COUNTY

JOHN DOE and JANE DOE,
     Plaintiffs,

VS.   CASE NO._____

ROBERT DOE and WANDA DOE,
     Defendants.

COMPLAINT FOR CHILD CUSTODY

At the end of your pleadings, you should close with a paragraph telling the judge what it is you want him or her to do. For example, see paragraph 4 of the **PETITION FOR CHILD CUSTODY** in Appendix C, form I. Additionally, you should always sign your documents and then type in your name, address, and phone number. Some states have fill-in-the-blank forms or check-off forms. Before you begin preparing this paperwork, check with the court clerk to see if they have forms available. If they do, use the forms from the clerk.

COMPLAINT/PETITION FOR CUSTODY (FORM 15)

COMPLAINT/PETITION FOR CUSTODY is for use in all states except Texas. (see form 15, p.197.) Before using this form, look at specific forms tailored to meet the requirements of your state. Then, modify this form as necessary. A filled-in example of this form is included in Appendix C. (see form I, p.157.) Complete the **COMPLAINT/PETITION FOR CUSTODY** as follows.

◈ Complete the case style portion of the form according to the information in the previous section of this chapter. Follow the language and format commonly used in your state and county.

◈ In the first unnumbered paragraph, fill in the names of the grandparents seeking custody on the first line. The second line (after the phrase, "hereinafter called the…") is for your designation as a party. Your state will likely use either "Plaintiff," "Petitioner," or "Movant." In the third line, type in the word "Complaint," "Petition," or whatever word or phrase you used as a title. In the fourth line, type in the name or names of the parents (the same person or persons listed as defendants or respondents in the case style). The fifth line is for the parents' party designation, which will be either "Defendants" or "Respondents."

◈ Paragraph #1 is to identify the relationship of all of the parties. On the first line, type in your designation as a party ("Plaintiff," "Petitioner," or "Movant"). On the second line, type in either "maternal grandparents" or "paternal grandparents," whichever applies to you. Type your address on the third line. The next two lines are for the parents' designation as parties ("Defendants" or "Respondents") and their address. If they are living apart, list both addresses. In the last two lines, type in the names of the children (your state may also require their ages or birth dates to be listed—if you are not sure, you may want to include them just to be safe) and their current address.

◈ Paragraph #2 is for you to state the legal *grounds* for why you are entitled to custody. The first blank in the grounds section should contain either your name or your party designation ("Plaintiff," "Petitioner," or "Movant"). The second blank is where you describe the facts (using the factors from your state statute) that you believe justify your request for custody. Be sure to read the listing for your state in Appendix A and consult your state's custody statutes before filling in this space. It is a good idea to use the language of your state's custody statute as closely as possible, and include a summary of the facts that indicate that custody should be changed. For example, the listing for Indiana in Appendix A indicates that the custody statute may be found in section 31-1-11 of the Annotated Indiana Code (this is the notation "A.I.C. §31-1-11 et seq."). If you look up section 31-1-11.5-21, you would find that custody is to be determined by what is in the child's best interest, considering the following factors:

✪ the age and sex of the child;

✪ the wishes of the parents and the child;

✪ the interaction and interrelationship between the child and the parents, siblings, and other significant persons;

✪ the child's adjustment to home, school, and community; and,

✪ any special educational or medical needs of the child.

You would want to relate your grandchild's situation to as many of these factors as possible to show why he or she would be better off with you. For example:

*The child has expressed a desire to live with the peti-
tioners, has substantial past interaction with the
petitioners, and has not adjusted well to his new school
since his parents' divorce, and could return to his original school if in the petitioners' custody.*

In most states, to overcome the presumption that a child is
best off in the custody of his or her parent, you would have to
show that your grandchild is suffering, or is likely to suffer,
harm if he or she remains with his or her parents. This usually
would require additional statements claiming some kind of
abuse, neglect, or some type of improper home environment.

❖ Paragraph #3 tells the court whether there are any other cases
pending that relate to visitation. If there are no such cases,
type in the word "none" in the space after this paragraph. If
there is another case, type in the case style from that other
case (name of the court, names of parties, and case number).

❖ Paragraph #4 is for you to tell the judge what you are asking
him or her to do. The first line in the relief section is for your
name or party designation ("Plaintiff," "Petitioner," or
"Movant"). On the second line, fill in exactly what you want
the judge to order with regard to custody. An example of how
this form can be completed is included in Appendix C. (see
form I, p.157.)

❖ Fill in the date, sign your name, and fill in the name, address,
and telephone number information on the appropriate lines.

ORIGINAL PETITION IN SUIT AFFECTING THE PARENT-CHILD RELATIONSHIP (FORM 16)

ORIGINAL PETITION IN SUIT AFFECTING THE PARENT-CHILD RELATIONSHIP is for
use in Texas when there is no divorce or other lawsuit pending that
involves custody or visitation. (see form 16, p.199.) This form is fairly
self-explanatory as to what information needs to be filled in on each
line. An example of this completed form is included in Appendix C.
(see form J, p.159.)

This form may be adapted to other states, but you will need to change the legal term for custody. In Texas, primary custody is called *managing conservatorship*, but in other states, this will be referred to by some other term or phrase, such as *physical custody*, *legal custody*, or perhaps just *custody*. You can review form 16 for additional guidance, but you will also need to look at specific forms tailored to meet the requirements of your state. Complete the ORIGINAL PETITION IN SUIT AFFECTING THE PARENT-CHILD RELATIONSHIP as follows.

⬦ In the case style section, type in the number of the court district and the name of the county. Leave the case number line blank—the clerk will assign the number. Your grandchildren's names go in the space just below the words "in the interest of" and in section #3. The rest of the blanks in #3 apply to the grandchildren as well.

⬦ Your name goes in section #1, along with your address.

⬦ In section #4, type in the parents' names and addresses.

⬦ In section #7, type in the names of the parent or parents you believe should pay child support.

⬦ This form needs to be signed by you (and your spouse, if he or she is joining in the petition) on the lines after the word "by."

PETITION OF GRANDPARENT(S) FOR INTERVENTION IN SUIT AFFECTING THE PARENT-CHILD RELATIONSHIP (FORM 17)

PETITION OF GRANDPARENT(S) FOR INTERVENTION IN SUIT AFFECTING THE PARENT-CHILD RELATIONSHIP is for use in Texas when there is already a divorce or other lawsuit involving custody or visitation. (see form 17, p.201.) Form 17 will be completed the same as form 16, except that the case style will be exactly the same as the case in which you are intervening. Also, in the CERTIFICATE OF SERVICE (form 7), fill in the names of the other parties and the date you sent them copies of your petition. This should be the same day you file the petition. If you are modifying this form for use outside of Texas, you will need to check the laws of your state to see if you need to do something more than send the parties copies by certified mail. (For more information about formal notification to other parties, see Chapter 7.)

FINANCIAL AFFIDAVIT (FORM 26)

Some states may require you to file a **FINANCIAL AFFIDAVIT**. (see form 26, p.219.) The two main purposes for this would be to show that you have the financial ability to care for your grandchild and for the court to determine the amount of child support the parents should pay to you. If your state or court requires a **FINANCIAL AFFIDAVIT**, you may need to use an official form provided by the court clerk or some other state agency. If a **FINANCIAL AFFIDAVIT** is required, but there is no official form, you can use form 26 in Appendix D. Just fill in the required information on each line.

COURT PROCEDURES

After you complete your complaint or petition, you will need to file your papers with the court; notify the other parties; prepare for and attend a court hearing; and, prepare an order for the judge to sign after he or she makes a decision. See Chapter 7 for information about the procedures to follow once your complaint or petition is completed.

NOTIFYING THE OTHER PARTIES

After you have completed your complaint or petition, you will need to notify the other parties involved (usually the parents) that you are filing court papers for visitation. See the section entitled "Notifying Others" in Chapter 7 for more information about notification.

Once you have your pleadings filed, you will have to begin preparing your evidence. A more thorough discussion of what you will need in the way of evidence is found in Chapter 8. However, you may find the idea of representing yourself in court intimidating. You may even be considering hiring a lawyer. The following chapter evaluates the pros and cons of hiring a lawyer, and contains some tips for selecting an attorney.

Role of the Lawyer

As with anything, there are advantages and disadvantages to hiring a lawyer to represent you in court. The advantages are fairly obvious. An attorney knows the law and the procedural rules, things you will be responsible for knowing if you choose to represent yourself. The lawyer also has experience in trying custody and visitation cases. He or she will know what evidence will play favorably in front of the judge or jury, and what evidence will hurt your chances of victory.

Another advantage is that a lawyer has objectivity. You are a party to the case, and as such, have a big emotional investment in the outcome. There are also likely to be emotions involving the other parties at play. No matter what emotional strategies are employed by the other parties, your lawyer will be able to help you maintain perspective and make decisions regarding your case with a clearer head and distance from the emotional issues.

With a lawyer, you may be taken more seriously by the court and the other parties, including your children. You also do not have to be responsible for all of the administrative details that go along with a lawsuit if you use an attorney.

Of course, this freedom from details comes at a price. Cost is usually the most serious disadvantage to using a lawyer. Most lawyers will charge you an hourly rate and probably require you to make a deposit in advance to handle a custody or visitation case. The hourly rate will vary depending on your geographical location and the experience of the lawyer. You should always receive an itemized bill from your lawyer so you know how your money is being spent.

The next biggest disadvantage is losing the ability to personally keep your case moving through the system. Most attorneys handle a heavy caseload, and sometimes work on your case will come behind the more pressing demands of other cases.

TIPS FOR SELECTING A LAWYER

If you decide the disadvantages of representing yourself outweigh the advantages, you will face the decision of which lawyer to hire. It is important that you hire an attorney who is knowledgeable about domestic relations cases. It is also important that you feel comfortable with that lawyer. If you do not already know a good family law attorney, there are several sources of referrals. One of the best ways to find a lawyer is through someone you know. Ask acquaintances for names of lawyers they have dealt with and liked. You can also call the local bar association. Most bar associations, especially in larger towns and cities, maintain referral services. Of course, you can also check the telephone book.

Feel free to schedule consultations with more than one attorney. Some will give you a free initial consultation, others will charge you. You should be able to find out what the charge will be for the consultation when you schedule the appointment. When you meet with the attorney, do not hesitate to ask the lawyer about his or her educational background and experience.

You should also come away from your initial consultation knowing how the lawyer intends to handle your case and what you can expect during the course of your lawsuit. You should feel comfortable with that person and have confidence in him or her. Remember—if at any time you become dissatisfied with your lawyer, you can always discharge that lawyer and hire another.

TIPS FOR WORKING WITH YOUR LAWYER

Once you have made the decision to hire an attorney, there are several things you can do to make the experience better. One of the keys to a good relationship with your attorney is to understand what is going on with your case and the law that applies to the case. If you do not understand something, keep asking questions until you do understand. The law can be complicated, and you should not be embarrassed if you do not understand something the first time. Your lawyer should be willing to take whatever time is necessary to answer your questions.

It is also important that you tell your lawyer everything that might apply to your case. It is much better to let your lawyer decide what is important, as things that may not seem important to you may be very important. If you withhold information because it is damaging, your lawyer will not have an opportunity to minimize the damage to you if he or she hears that information for the first time in court. Remember, anything you tell your lawyer is confidential and cannot be revealed without your consent.

Another key to being satisfied with the way your case is handled is to be realistic. In many more instances than you may realize going in, the system is not going to work the way you think it should, and the law may not seem fair to you. These are things over which your lawyer has no control. Being angry with your attorney because of these problems accomplishes nothing, except to damage the working relationship between the two of you. When you find yourself in that situation, do not vent your frustration on your lawyer. Instead, accept the situation and do your best to work with your attorney within the system to get the best outcome you can.

You will also need to be patient. Our legal system will often move at a frustratingly slow pace. In many places, the courts are very busy, and it may take a long time before your case can be heard. There is nothing your lawyer can do about these scheduling problems, and your relationship with your attorney will be much better if you refrain from demanding that he or she schedule things according to your schedule instead of the court's.

You will also need to be patient with your attorney. You are not the only client your lawyer has. It is unrealistic to expect your lawyer to always be available for you. Lawyers who handle family law cases spend a significant amount of time in court. When in court, lawyers give their undivided attention to that client, and will have to return your calls at another time. When your time in court comes, you will expect that same treatment. You need to be understanding when your lawyer takes several hours, or maybe even a day or more, to return your call.

When these things happen, talking to the secretary can be a big help. There are many questions that the secretary can answer for you. This enables you to get the information you need without talking to the attorney. You should talk to the secretary whenever possible, and leave information with him or her instead of waiting to talk to your lawyer. Another benefit is that you will not be billed for talking to the secretary.

It is also important that you not become a pest. When you need information from you lawyer or need to pass information to him or her, call. Be organized when you call—get your questions answered, find out what happens next and when you should expect to hear something, and finish your call. Do not make frequent, unnecessary phone calls to your lawyer, as this just runs up your bill and irritates your lawyer. You should also be on time for appointments and court hearings.

Pay your bill on time. The clients who get the most prompt attention are those that pay their bills on time. While you should review your bill carefully and be sure you understand the fee agreement, you should expect to pay for everything the attorney does on your case. This includes more than just going to court for you. You will also be billed for paperwork, letters, and telephone calls.

Even with a lawyer representing you, you will need to provide him or her with the information necessary to prepare the case. While each case is different and will require different evidence, there are some general types of evidence and witnesses that you will need in most contested custody and visitation cases.

You will need to gather this evidence together and provide it to your attorney. For more information on what this evidence is, please review Chapter 8.

Anything you can do to help the attorney do his or her job more effectively and efficiently will not only make the litigation process easier for you, it will also help you reduce the total cost of your attorney's fees. Your attorney is there to help you and to give you advice about how best to handle your case, and these tips should help you navigate the attorney/client relationship with greater ease.

Court Procedures

If you decide to represent yourself, you will be responsible for knowing what all the court rules and procedures are. The court officials and clerks cannot give you legal advice or tell you what documents you need to file or how to prepare them. Once you get to court, the judge cannot tell you how to try your case. This chapter provides you with the basic procedures found in most courts. As always, you need to check for any local rules that apply to the courts in your location.

FILING YOUR PETITION

Before you take your petition to the court, call the clerk and ask what the filing fee is and what forms of payment the court will accept. Then, take your original pleading and several copies to the clerk's office. (In addition to the original for the court clerk, you will need at least one copy for each party and a file-stamped copy for yourself.) Tell the clerk you want to file the petition, and then follow whatever instructions he or she gives you.

In most states, you will need more than just your complaint or petition. Unless you are filing against parties to an existing case and your state allows some other notice procedure, you will need a *summons* form to go with your petition. Most states have their own summons form, so use the one for the state where you will be filing. Often, the court clerk can provide the official summons form.

Many states also have a *cover sheet* that must be filed with each new case. A cover sheet usually just provides the court with statistical information for use by the court in compiling data for budgeting and other internal purposes. These forms are usually provided by the court clerk.

In some states, you will need to file certain *affidavits*. You will need to do some research to find out what is required in your state. Sometimes you will not find out about what else needs to be filed until you try to file your petition. The clerk will tell you what form is missing. You will then need to find a copy of the required form, complete it, and return to the clerk to file your case. Several forms for different situations are provided in Appendix D, with some samples of completed forms in Appendix C. There are three main places to look for forms you need but do not have: 1. the clerk's office; 2. a file in another case at the clerk's office; and, 3. a form book at your local law library.

NOTIFYING OTHERS

When you file a complaint or petition for visitation or custody, there are certain people you must notify. In every case, you must notify the other people with legal relationships to the minor children. In most cases, you will only have to notify the parents. However, if the child welfare authorities are involved, or some other nonparent has been to court and has a court-ordered relationship, those people must all also be notified. This notification procedure is called *service of process*.

Each state has its own rules for how *process* (i.e., court paper) is to be *served* (i.e., delivered). Check with the rules of civil procedure for your state to decide how this is to be accomplished. It may be that a sheriff or constable has to personally deliver the papers to the other party, or you may be able to mail the documents by certified mail. It is important to check these rules carefully. Using a method that is not authorized by your state will mean that the judge cannot hear your case until you have gone back and served the lawsuit properly.

Waiver (form 12)   If you know at the time you file your lawsuit that your case will settle, you may be able to have the other parties sign a notarized **WAIVER** of service. (see form 12, p. 191.) An example of a completed **WAIVER** is included in Appendix C. (see form G, p.154.) One warning—the **WAIVER** must be signed after the original pleading has been filed. A **WAIVER** signed before the lawsuit is filed is invalid. If both parents are willing to sign, have each of them complete a separate form. Complete the **WAIVER** as follows.

⬧ Complete the case style portion according to the instructions in Chapter 3 and Chapter 5.

⬧ Type in the name of your state and county after the words "state of" and "county of."

⬧ On the line in the first paragraph, type in the name of the person (usually one of the parents) who will be signing this form.

⬧ On the first line in the second paragraph, type in the word "Defendant" or "Respondent," whichever applies in your state. Type the address of the person who will be signing this form on the second line of this paragraph, and on the third line type in the title of the complaint or petition ("Complaint for Child Custody," "Petition for Grandparent Visitation," etc.).

⬧ Have the person sign the form before a notary public. This form will then be filed with the court clerk.

Summons   In some states, you will need to arrange for service by the sheriff, and in others, the court clerk will do this. If the clerk arranges for service, he or she will need a copy of the complaint or petition for every person who is going to be served, and you will need one or two copies for yourself.

The form of the *summons*, which is the official notification of the lawsuit that will be attached to your complaint or petition, varies from state to state. In many states, this form will be furnished and prepared by the court clerk. Before you go to the courthouse to file your lawsuit, ask the clerk whether or not you have to provide a summons. If you need to provide one, look in a form book or a pending file and copy the form. Form E in Appendix C is an example of a completed summons, so you can get an idea of what one looks like. (see form E, p.152.) However, you must use the summons form that is acceptable in your state.

After delivering the papers, the sheriff will file a document with the court verifying who was served and when. Anyone being served with a complaint or petition will have a certain number of days in which to file a written response with the court.

Certificate of Service (form 7)

Once the other parties have been legally served with your petition, you will also need to send them copies of any other papers you may file with the court later. This is usually done by regular first-class mail, although you may also hand-deliver them. (However, a subpoena for someone to appear for a hearing or deposition, or to produce documents, must be personally served—do not use a **CERTIFICATE OF SERVICE** form for a subpoena.) To show the court that you have mailed copies of these later papers to the other parties, you need to complete a **CERTIFICATE OF SERVICE**. This can either be at the end of the document you are filing or on a separate sheet of paper. (see form 7, p.181.) Complete the **CERTIFICATE OF SERVICE** as follows.

◈ Complete the case style portion according to the instructions in Chapter 3 and Chapter 5.

◈ Type in the name or title of the papers being sent on the first line in the main paragraph.

◈ Check the appropriate blank for how the papers are being sent ("mailed" or "hand-delivered"), and fill in the date the papers are sent or delivered.

◈ Type in the name, address, and telephone number of the person (or persons) to whom the papers are being sent or delivered (usually the parents or their attorney).

◈   Sign your name on the line marked "signature," and type in your name, address, and telephone number on the appropriate lines below. This form can be attached to whatever form you are sending and filed with the court.

**Notice
of Hearing
(form 10)**

Basically, a **Notice of Hearing** simply includes the case style; the name of the party (or his or her attorney) being notified; the type of hearing being held; and, the date, time, and place of the hearing. (see form 10, p.187.) This form can be used for trial or any other type of hearing. This form may need to be modified to comply with the requirements of your court. An example of a completed form is included in Appendix C. (see form L, p.162.)

In some states, you can simply call the court clerk or the judge's secretary and obtain a hearing date. Then, just mail or deliver a **Notice of Hearing** to the other party (or attorney) and show up at the hearing. In other states, you will need to file a **Motion to Set Hearing**. (see form 28, p.225.) This is simply a more formal way of asking for a hearing. If you need to file a motion, try to get a form either from the court clerk or from a form book at your local law library. If you cannot find one specific for your state, use form 28 in Appendix D. Complete the **Motion to Set Hearing** as follows.

◈   Complete the case style portion according to the instructions in Chapter 3 and Chapter 5.

◈   Type in either "Plaintiff," "Petitioner," or "Movant"—whichever term is used in your state—on the first line in the main paragraph.

◈   Type in either "child visitation" or "child custody" on the second line in the main paragraph.

◈   Type in the date and your name, address, and telephone number on the appropriate lines, then sign on the line marked "signature" and file it with the court clerk. Be sure to mail a copy of this form to the other parties, and complete and file a **Certificate of Service** (see form 7, p.181) showing that you have sent out copies.

WHEN YOU CANNOT LOCATE THE PARENT

The following is a scenario that is not uncommon in today's world.

Example:

Your daughter and her husband have divorced. He left the state three years ago to avoid paying child support, and no one knows where he is now. Your daughter asks you to baby-sit your granddaughter for a few hours while she goes shopping. Your daughter calls two days later to tell you that she cannot take it anymore as a single parent, and she will not be back until she gets her head straight. Plus, she will not tell you where she is. Here you are with your eight-year-old granddaughter, who needs to be enrolled in school. What if she needs medical treatment?

An infinite number of circumstances can result in not knowing the whereabouts of one or both of your grandchild's parents.

If you need to file for custody or visitation and cannot locate one or both of the parents, you will not be able to notify them of your petition by any of the means previously discussed. You will need to use an alternative method of service. In such situations, the law provides for what is known as *service by publication*. This is where you publish a notice of your lawsuit in a newspaper. This can be a very tricky procedure that varies greatly from state to state, so you will need to either consult a lawyer or do some research at your local law library.

DEFAULT JUDGMENTS

Once your complaint or petition has been served correctly, the other parties will have a deadline for filing a response with the court to contest your lawsuit. If the deadline passes and the other parties do not file responses, you will be able to get a default judgment. The usual procedure is for you to file a **MOTION FOR DEFAULT** with the court clerk. (see form 8, p.183.) The clerk then issues a *default* (which may be included in the motion form or may be a separate document), and you submit an order for the judge to sign. Some states may not allow a default in custody or visitation cases, and may require you to set a hearing and present evidence to support what you want. Others may require a short hearing on the default. The court clerk should be willing to tell you what the default procedures are in your court.

Motion for Default (form 8)

A **Motion for Default** form is included in Appendix D. (see form 8, p.183.) This form may need to be modified to comply with the requirements of your court. An example of a completed **Motion for Default** is included in Appendix C. (see form F, p.153.) Complete the **Motion for Default** as follows.

◈ Complete the case style portion according to the instructions in Chapter 3 and Chapter 5.

◈ On the first line in the main paragraph, type in "Plaintiff," "Petitioner," or "Movant," whichever is used in your state. On the second line, type in the name of the Defendant(s) or Respondent(s) you wish to have a default entered against. In other words, if one parent responded to your petition and the other did not, a default may only be entered against the one who did not respond. If neither responded, you would type in both of their names. On the third line, type in the title of your petition or complaint, such as "Complaint for Custody."

◈ Sign the form and fill in the date, as well as your name, address, and telephone number, on the appropriate lines. Take or send this form to the clerk, who will complete the bottom part of the form and return a copy to you. Once you receive the copy signed by the clerk, you may take or send an order to the judge for his or her signature.

If no hearing is necessary, once you receive the default signed by the clerk, you can type the order you want the judge to sign (following the instructions in this chapter and Chapters 3 and 5, and send the original and four or five copies to the court for the judge to sign. You should include a self-addressed, stamped envelope with the order, so signed copies can be returned to you.

If a hearing is required, ask the clerk about the procedures for scheduling hearings on default judgments. Usually, either the clerk or the judge's secretary handles the scheduling of hearings. In most cases, at the hearing, the judge will grant your petition without requiring more than minimal evidence about why your requests should be granted. Usually, your testimony alone will be sufficient for this purpose. If there is something unusual about your case, you can take other witnesses to the hearing or bring documents to show the judge. At the hearing, you should present a proposed order for the judge to sign.

Prepare your order following the instructions related to final orders (see pages 82–86), and adapting either form 13, form 14, form 18, or form 19 for your state. You will also need the last known mailing address for each of the parties, which you can provide to the court using the **CERTIFICATE OF LAST KNOWN ADDRESS**. (see form 29, p.227.) Once the judge has signed your order, your case is completed.

UNCONTESTED CASES VS. CONTESTED CASES

There are two basic ways litigation proceedings can go. If the parties are not able to reach an agreement as to what the outcome of the case will be, the case is *contested*, and a judge or jury makes the final decision. In many cases, however, the parties are able to reach an agreement and the case is *settled*. Many factors influence the decision to settle a case. In most cases, the parties are better off if they can settle. That way, you each have some control over the ultimate result, instead of letting some stranger (the judge or jury) decide what happens with your grandchildren. Obviously, if you do settle, the legal procedures are much simpler.

Contested cases, of course, are much more complex. If you are intervening in an ongoing lawsuit or filing documents in a contested case, be sure you send a copy of whatever you file to all the other attorneys in the case by certified mail (or to the parties themselves if they do not have attorneys). If you are intervening, you will need to check the procedural rules for your state regarding service of process in interventions. Instead of sending copies by certified mail, you may need to serve the parties personally. With all documents, except the original (which you are probably having served by the sheriff), you will need to include a **CERTIFICATE OF SERVICE** at the end of the document or as a separate document. (see form 7, p.181.)

AGREED ORDERS

If you reach an agreement with the other parties, you can finalize the agreement by preparing a final order that sets out the terms of the agreement. Get each of the parties to sign the order before it is presented to the judge. You may or may not be required to schedule a hearing before the judge to get your order signed. The clerk of the court will be able to tell you what procedure you need to follow to get the order signed. Provide several copies of the order to the court when you present it for signature. The clerk may keep two or three copies, and each of the parties will need a copy. The order forms in Appendix D can be adapted as an order pursuant to an agreement, usually by changing the first paragraph to say something similar to, "Pursuant to the agreement of the parties as filed in this action, the court makes the following orders."

Agreement (form 27) You can use the **AGREEMENT** form to spell out your agreement in either visitation or custody situations. (see form 27, p.223.)

◈ Complete the case style portion according to the instructions in Chapter 3 and Chapter 5. The title of this document will be either "Agreement Regarding Child Visitation" or "Agreement Regarding Child Custody."

◈ In the space below the introductory sentence, type in the details of your visitation or custody arrangement.

◈ At the end of the form are places for all parties to sign and fill in their names, addresses, and telephone numbers.

◈ Once this form is signed by all parties, it can be filed with the court clerk, along with an order for the judge to sign. The order must contain the same visitation or custody provisions as the **AGREEMENT**.

MOTIONS

As your case progresses, there may be things that you want the judge to do, such as order a home study in a custody case. This is accomplished by filing a *motion* with the court. Generally, a motion is addressed to the judge and tells him or her what action you want taken and (briefly) why. Several motion forms are provided in Appendix D and are discussed throughout the book.

When you file your motion, you should also supply the clerk with a **NOTICE OF HEARING** (form 10), which will be filled in following the clerk's instructions when your hearing is scheduled. A sample completed **NOTICE OF HEARING** is included in Appendix C. (see form L, p.162.) You will have to notify all the other parties or their attorneys of the time and place of the hearing. This should generally be done by certified mail. After the hearing, if the judge grants your request, you will need to supply an order for the judge to sign, along with several extra copies. The clerk will return the copies to you with the judge's signature or stamp on them. Keep a copy for yourself and send a copy to all the other parties or their attorneys.

Motion for Social Study (and Order) (form 20)

A **MOTION FOR SOCIAL STUDY (AND ORDER)** can be used to ask the judge to have someone, usually a state agency, conduct a *home study*. (see form 20, p.207.) This usually will only be done in custody cases, unless the parents make an issue of conditions in your home in a visitation case. Someone from the agency will visit your home and the home of the parents or anyone else seeking to get or keep custody, and will make a report to the judge of the suitability of each home. In order to complete this form, follow the steps given here.

◈ Complete the case style portion according to the instructions in Chapter 3 and Chapter 5.

◈ Sign and date the form, and type in your name, address, and telephone number on the appropriate lines.

◈ Complete a **CERTIFICATE OF SERVICE** (see form 7, p.181), and mail a copy of your completed form 20 to all of the other parties.

◈ File the original of form 20 and form 7 with the court clerk. The judge will complete the bottom portion of the form, which will be the order.

Motion and Order for Appointment of Guardian Ad Litem (forms 21 and 22)

A **MOTION FOR APPOINTMENT OF GUARDIAN AD LITEM** should be used if you want a *guardian ad litem* (GAL) appointed for the child. (see form 21, p.209.) A *guardian ad litem* is someone appointed by the court to independently and impartially represent the best interest of the child. (Usually, this will only be done in custody cases.) Having an independent person support your contention that giving you custody would be in the child's best interest can help swing the case your way. Of course, if the current custodian is just as suitable as you, you run a very real risk that the guardian ad litem will recommend that custody not be changed. Form 21 is self-explanatory, so just fill in the information required. An **ORDER APPOINTING GUARDIAN AD LITEM** is an order you submit to the court along with your motion. (see form 22, p.211.) All you need to do is fill in the information at the end of the form regarding who should receive copies. For both forms, be sure to complete the case style portion according to the instructions in Chapter 3 and Chapter 5.

In some instances, the guardian ad litem will be an attorney. However, the trend has been away from appointing attorneys to also serve as guardians ad litem. Many times, it will be a specially trained volunteer, often called a *Court Appointed Special Advocate* (CASA), who will be appointed as the guardian ad litem. The CASA volunteer has specific duties to perform—basically, having regular contact with the child and ensuring that the child's best interest is being served by the judicial proceedings.

Courts often also appoint an attorney ad litem or an amicus attorney to represent the child. It is this attorney's job to be the child's lawyer and convey to the court what the child's wishes are.

If your case is complex enough, you may want (or be forced by the court) to have both a guardian ad litem and an attorney ad litem. If so, you can adapt form 21 to ask for one or both of these positions to be filled.

One area where appointment of these positions is routinely seen is when there is an allegation of child abuse, especially in cases filed by the child welfare department. The CASA volunteer keeps in contact with the child, evaluates the appropriateness of the placement of the child (where the child lives during the proceeding), and makes recommendations about changes to the placement and about final arrangements for custody of and access to the child.

The attorney ad litem is responsible for legal representation of the child. This involves filing pleadings in court on behalf of the child, just like the attorneys for the adult parties. The attorney ad litem may or may not agree with the positions taken by the child protective services workers, and can argue for whatever outcome the child and the attorney believe is in the child's best interest. Even if child welfare does not want to terminate a parent's rights, the attorney ad litem can make the request on behalf of the child. If the child wants to live with the grandparents, the attorney ad litem can ask the court to give the grandparents custody because that is the child's wish. Conversely, if child welfare wants to put the child in permanent foster care, and the child wants to be returned to his or her parents, the attorney ad litem can advocate in court for this position.

Obviously, the guardian ad litem and the attorney ad litem are very important people, and it is in your best interest to work with them and be as cooperative as possible. Alienating them will not help you win in court.

Motion and Order for Psychiatric/ Psychological Examination (forms 23 and 24)

A **MOTION FOR PSYCHIATRIC/PSYCHOLOGICAL EXAMINATION** should be used if you think a psychological evaluation would help show that you should have custody. (see form 23, p.213.) (This usually will only apply to custody cases, unless the parents make your psychological health an issue in a visitation case.) To complete this form, check the lines for the items that apply in your situation, date and sign the form, and fill in the name, address, telephone number, and certificate of service section. Then, file form 23 along with form 24, **ORDER FOR PSYCHIATRIC/PSYCHOLOGICAL EXAMINATION**, which is the order for the judge to sign. (see form 24, p.215.) For both forms, be sure to complete the case style portion according to the instructions in Chapter 3 and Chapter 5.

Motion to Proceed In Forma Pauperis (form 25)

If you are unable to pay for the court costs of filing and the fee for personal service, you can file a **MOTION TO PROCEED IN FORMA PAUPERIS**. (see form 25, p.217.) This may be called by various names, depending upon the state. For example, in California it is called an *Application for Waiver of Court Fees and Costs*, and in Illinois it is called an

Application to Sue or Defend as a Poor Person. Be aware that you will need to show a certain degree of poverty to qualify (you will probably have to be able to qualify for food stamps or other welfare benefits). Do not try this just because you would rather not pay the fees. Also, filing this form may not be a good idea if you are seeking custody. In a custody case, the question of your financial ability to care for the child will surely arise. On the other hand, with child support payments from the parents, you may still be better able to care for the child.

Form 25 can be used for this purpose, although be sure to check with the court clerk to see if there is an approved or required form for your court. Fill out the form as follows.

◈ Complete the case style portion according to the instructions in Chapter 3 and Chapter 5.

◈ Fill in all of the financial information required in the form.

◈ Form 25 is in the form of an affidavit, so you will need to sign it before a notary public.

◈ File this form with the clerk. You will be notified if your motion is accepted or if you will need to pay the filing and other fees.

Discovery   In many states, you will have *discovery* devices available to you. Some of these are expensive, while others are available at little or no cost. One inexpensive device is *interrogatories. Interrogatories* are written questions that you send to another party. That party must then answer the questions. This is a way for you to learn who the witnesses are that will testify against you. You may also be able to send *requests for production of documents.* This is a series of categories of documents that you ask another party to supply to you, either to support your case or to learn more about his or her case against you.

Another method of learning about the case against you is by taking a deposition. A *deposition* is when a witness testifies under oath before a certified shorthand reporter. This is a more expensive method because of the expense of the court reporter. Court reporter fees can typically run about $50 per hour for the reporter's time, and several dollars per page for typing up a transcript of the testimony. A one-hour deposition can easily cost $200 in court reporter fees. If you are taking the deposition of an expert witness, such as a doctor or therapist, the witness will also have to be paid for his or her time. You will need to look up the procedural rules for your state to determine what the specific requirements are that govern these discovery devices, and whether or not your state will allow you to use them in this type of a case.

Subpoena (form 9)

When it is time for your trial, you will need to notify your witnesses and tell them when to be present. The safest way to do this is to get a subpoena and have it served on them. While you are not required to have a witness subpoenaed in order for them to testify, it is best to use a subpoena. Otherwise, the judge will probably not give you a continuance if something keeps your unsubpoenaed witnesses from appearing at the trial. A subpoena will also help your witnesses get time off work to testify for you. If you intend to use an expert witness (like a doctor or police officer), you must use a subpoena.

The subpoena is issued by the court clerk, and you should be able to get a form for requesting the subpoena from the clerk. Subpoena forms vary widely from state to state. Although there is a **SUBPOENA** form included in Appendix D, be sure to check the forms for your state. Your court clerk may be able to provide you with the correct subpoena form.

If you want the witness to bring specific documents or other items, you will need to ask for a *subpoena duces tecum*. On the form requesting the subpoena duces tecum, you will need to list the documents or items you want the witness to bring. Be as detailed and specific as necessary to leave no doubt about what is being requested.

Form 9 is a **SUBPOENA** form. However, this may not be sufficient, because most states have their own subpoena forms. (see form 9, p.185.) Be sure to use the approved form for your court. Form 9 is designed to be used as either a subpoena to testify or as a subpoena duces tecum (to bring documents or other things). An example of form 9, completed as a subpoena duces tecum, can be found in Appendix C. (see form K, p.161.) Complete the **SUBPOENA** as follows.

◈ Complete the case style portion according to the instructions in Chapter 3 and Chapter 5.

◈ After the word "to," type in the name and address of the witness.

◈ In the main body of the form, type in the judge's name, the address of the court and courtroom number (or whatever information is required to let the witness know exactly where he or she needs to go to testify), and the date and time of the hearing.

◈ If you want this to be a subpoena duces tecum, type in the words "duces tecum" under the title "subpoena." In the space after the first main paragraph, type in a description of the documents or other items you want the witness to bring to the hearing. Be as specific and detailed as possible, so there is no doubt as to what the person is being asked to bring. See form K in Appendix C for an example.

◈ Type in your name, address, and telephone number on the appropriate lines under the section entitled "Attorney or Party Requesting Subpoena." This is so the witness can contact you if he or she has any questions.

◈ Take the **Subpoena** form to the court clerk, who will fill in the date and sign it. Once it is signed by the clerk, have the **Subpoena** served on the witness by the sheriff or other authorized process server.

Witnesses   When the time for your trial arrives, you should be thoroughly prepared. You should have selected the witnesses who will testify for you and had them served with the subpoenas at least two months before the trial date. You should have located all the documents you intend to use at the trial. Preparation for trial also means that you should know exactly what testimony you need from each witness and have written down the questions you need to ask. Try to be as concise as possible in questioning your witnesses. Do not ask about anything that is not relevant to the issues that the judge is going to be deciding. The judge will want to keep the trial moving and will not be happy if you waste time on unimportant matters.

Before the hearing, you will need to talk to each witness to be sure of what they will say in court. Never make assumptions about this—the surest way to lose your case is to have surprise testimony from a witness. In court, never ask a witness a question to which you do not already know the answer. When you interview the witnesses, be sure to ask them every question you might be asking at the hearing. You should also ask the witnesses to tell you everything they know about your case. This will help you not be surprised in court, and you might learn something you did not know.

It is possible that a witness will tell you one thing in an interview and testify to something entirely different. One way to keep this from happening is to take the witness' deposition. If you decide this is too expensive, consider having the witness prepare a written, signed statement. You can also take a third party with you to the interview to verify the statements made by the witness.

Expert Witnesses

In many cases, you will be using *expert witnesses* to testify on your behalf. A witness is an *expert* if his or her testimony is based on his or her special education, training, or experience—he or she is giving a professional opinion. At the hearing, you will need to ask these witnesses about their education and experience—this is called *qualifying the witness as an expert.* If you are using a doctor as an expert, you will need to talk to him or her several months before the hearing to determine whether he or she will come to court for you. Because of their busy schedules, most doctors prefer to testify by deposition, and they charge high hourly rates to come to court. The other parties will need to approve of using any such deposition for trial testimony. If you are in this situation, ask the doctor questions in the deposition just as though you were in court.

COURTROOM MANNERS

When you go to court, you should always be respectful. Remember, the judge will be making a decision that greatly impacts your relationship with your grandchildren. It is not a good idea to make the judge angry by being disrespectful, either to the judge or to another party.

One of the ways you show respect is by the way you dress. You should always wear nice clothes to court, never shorts or sweat suits.

Always stand up when the judge enters or leaves the courtroom and any time you talk to the judge. Always address the judge as "your Honor," no matter what you hear some of the attorneys in the courtroom say. Many attorneys address the judge as "judge," but this is incorrect. You should never argue with the judge or the other parties or their attorneys. When presenting your position or opposing a request by another party, speak to the judge, not to the other party.

Be sure you listen to the judge when he or she speaks, and follow any instructions that you are given. It is important that you maintain control of your emotions. Displays of anger are never appropriate.

EVIDENTIARY RULES

The judge may give you instructions about what evidence you may or may not use. Before going to court, read the rules of evidence in civil cases for your state (there may be separate rules for criminal cases). These are important rules that you must follow in order to prove your case. For example, there are specific requirements for admitting documents into evidence. If you fail to follow the rules, you may not be able to use your documents.

Hearsay One major rule of evidence you are sure to encounter is the *hearsay rule*. Basically, *hearsay* is something someone told the witness who is testifying. As a general rule, witnesses cannot testify to something that someone else told them. For example, a friend cannot testify about something your grandchild's teacher told her. Instead, the teacher must testify as a witness. Documents can also be excluded under the hearsay rule. For instance, a letter from your grandchild's teacher about your grandchild cannot be used in court because it is hearsay.

There are, however, many exceptions to the hearsay rule, and you need to familiarize yourself with them. Some things that would otherwise be excluded as hearsay (something the grandchild's mother told you is an example) can be used in court under the exception relating to admissions made by parties to the lawsuit. To avoid problems with this rule, try to be sure that your witnesses testify about what they know firsthand—not what they heard from someone else.

Relevancy   You will also encounter the *relevance* rule. Every document you use and every question you ask a witness must be relevant to the things you need to establish in order to win. For example, if your case is based on your grandchild being physically abused by the parent, testimony that the parent refused to let you talk to your grandchild on the telephone may not be relevant.

Documents and Photographs   You will also run into specific rules about how to use documents and photographs. You will need to follow the rules for your state, but you will generally need to have a witness testify about the identity of the document or photo, as well as the person who created the document or photo.

A final tip on the rules of evidence—when questioning a witness, be sure to just ask questions without testifying yourself or making explanations.

Every rule of evidence that might apply in your case cannot be covered in a book like this, so you will also need to check the rules of evidence for your state for more specific information. These rules will be found in the statute books for your state.

TRIAL PROCEDURES

If you represent yourself, the judge may be helpful in guiding you through the trial procedures. If so, just follow his or her lead. Most trials follow the same format. Each party will first be given the chance to make a brief opening statement. The person who initiated the lawsuit (the plaintiff or petitioner) goes first. This is not the time to argue your case or cover all the facts. Just tell the judge what the issues are and what you want the final decision to be.

Once the opening statements are over, the trial begins and witnesses are called. The plaintiff or petitioner goes first again. He or she calls a witness and asks questions of that witness, then the other parties have an opportunity to cross-examine the witness. This process continues until the plaintiff has called all of his or her witnesses. Then, the other parties call their witnesses. When all the parties have finished presenting their cases, the judge will allow each to make a final argument. In your final argument, review your most important points for the judge and ask him or her to do whatever it is you want done. After everyone has made an argument, the judge will announce the decision and tell the parties the outcome. The winning party will then be responsible for drafting the final judgment.

Sample Opening Statement

Assume that you are a widowed paternal grandmother of two. The grandchildren's parents are divorced and the mother has custody. During the six years the parents were married, you saw your grandchildren regularly—in fact, they stayed with you every afternoon after school and at least one Saturday evening a month. However, in the six months since the divorce, the mother has not allowed you to see the grandchildren. You, the mother, and the grandchildren all live in Arkansas. What follows is an opening statement that you might use in this situation.

May it please the Court. My name is Jane Doe, and I am the paternal grandmother of Sam and Sara Doe. I am here today seeking grandparent visitation pursuant to Section 9-13-103 of the Arkansas Statutes. Specifically, I intend to prove that after my son, Robert, and Wanda, the children's mother, divorced, Wanda got custody and has since refused me reasonable visitation with my grandchildren. Robert is in the military and is stationed overseas, and is not able to see the children very often. Because I had a close relationship with these children in the past, I believe my evidence will show that it is in their best interest to continue to see me on a regular basis. In addition, I intend to prove that I had frequent and regular contact with the children for at least twelve months, and that my grandchildren will be harmed by the loss of their relationship with me. I will also show that I have the ability and the willingness to cooperate with Wanda, and I have the capacity—in fact, the very strong desire—to give the children love, affection, and guidance. As I had no success in getting to see my grandchildren any other way, I have come here today to ask you to order the mother, Wanda Doe, to allow me to see the grandchildren and to set a specific schedule for those visits. Thank you.

Sample Closing Statement

Using the same facts, here is a sample closing statement. For your case, you will want to add other significant facts from your hearing.

May it please the Court. Your Honor, my grandchildren are very precious to me, and as you know from the evidence you have heard today, I am very concerned about how the loss of our relationship has damaged them. Up until the time the children's parents divorced, I saw them every day after school and at least one weekend a month. I agree wholeheartedly with the psychologist, Dr. Dan Jones, when he says that maintaining this relationship is important to the emotional well-being of the children, especially during this vulnerable period after the divorce.

I believe that the actions of the mother in keeping my grandchildren and me apart has harmed the children. This is verified by the change in their schoolwork—you can see from the report cards that their grades have been much worse since they quit staying with me after school. The school counselor, Miss Smith, testified about how each of the children has talked to her about missing me and being hurt that their mother did not want them to see me. The mother has not put on any credible evidence to show why I should not see the kids because there is not any reason to keep me away from my grandchildren.

The evidence has clearly shown that Wanda Doe has consistently refused reasonable visitation rights ever since she and my son divorced. Because of her actions, I qualify for visitation under Section 9-13-103 of the Arkansas Statutes. The evidence has overwhelmingly shown that visitation with me is in the children's best interest, and that the rights of the parents are not substantially impaired if visitation is awarded. I, therefore, urge the court to do the right thing for my grandchildren and order regular visitation of at least once a month. Thank you.

FINAL ORDER

Once the judge announces his or her decision, you will need to prepare a final order for the judge to sign. The actual title of this form is different in various states. It may be called a *Judgment, Decree, Final*

Order, or something else. Generally, the final order should reflect the date of the hearing, the parties who were present, and the decision that the judge made. When you submit the final order to the judge to be signed, you should also send copies to the other parties. Before your final order is signed, the judge will give the other parties an opportunity to object to the form of the order. The judge may even require that all of the attorneys (or parties, if they represent themselves) sign the judgment. This is not the time to object to the decision the judge made. The only appropriate objection is that the written judgment does not agree with the decision announced by the judge. Once the final order has been signed and everyone is sent a copy, the case is over, unless there is an appeal.

Generally, the party who wins has the responsibility of preparing the final order. Appendix D contains four final order forms—two for visitation and two for custody. These may need to be modified to comply with the requirements of your particular state or court. (For examples of completed final orders, see form H and form M in Appendix C.)

Once the hearing is complete and the judge has awarded you visitation, your next hurdle is to ensure that the order is properly drafted, so you can enforce your visitation rights if the parents still refuse to cooperate. It is important that the language in the order set the visitation schedule out very specifically and that the parents be ordered to surrender your grandchild to you for your periods of visitation. For example, if the judge has awarded you visitation on every third weekend of the month, the visitation order should read like the one in Appendix C. (see form H, p.155.)

Visitation Order (form 13)

The **Visitation Order** is for use in all states *except* Texas. (see form 13, p.193.) Complete form 13 as follows.

⬥ Complete the case style portion according to the instructions in Chapter 3 and Chapter 5.

⬥ On the line in the first paragraph, type in the date of your court hearing.

⬥ In the "Visitation" paragraph, type your name on the first line, and your grandchildren's names on the second line. In the space after this paragraph, type in the visitation schedule ordered by the judge. Be as specific as possible on such things as days and times, but do not add to (or subtract from) what the judge said.

Be sure to check the rules for your state to see if any other information is required. For example, the warnings on page 2 of the Texas form. (see form 14.)

Decree Granting Grandparent Access (form 14)

The **DECREE GRANTING GRANDPARENT ACCESS** is the visitation order for use in Texas. (see form 14, p.195.) Complete form 14 as follows.

◈ Complete the case style portion according to the instructions in Chapter 3 and Chapter 5.

◈ Fill in the date of your hearing in the first blank, or leave it blank for the judge to complete.

◈ Put your names in the second blank and the parents' names in the next blank, picking the option that applies. The first option is when the parent comes to court for the hearing, the second is when the parent files a **WAIVER**. (see form 12, p.191.)

◈ In the "Findings" section, list the names and statistical information for your grandchildren.

◈ In the section marked "Orders," state very specifically the visitation you are getting.

Custody Order (form 18)

The **CUSTODY ORDER** is for use in all states *except* Texas. (see form 18, p.203.) Some states have specific requirements for final judgments, so be sure to check the statutes for your state. For example, the Texas forms (see form 14 and form 19) have several paragraphs under the heading "Warnings to Parties," which are required to be in all final decrees in Texas. An example of form 18 completed is included in Appendix C. (see form M, p.163.)

Complete the **CUSTODY ORDER** as follows.

◈ Complete the case style portion according to the instructions in Chapter 3 and Chapter 5.

◈ On the line in the first paragraph, type in the date of the final hearing.

◈ On the line in the paragraph under the heading "Custody," type in the name (or names) of who is to have custody. If all went well at the hearing, this will be your name (or your name and your spouse's name). In the space below this paragraph, type in the names of the children.

◈ On the line in the paragraph under the heading "Visitation," type in the name (or names) of the persons who will be receiving visitation rights. If all went well at the hearing, this will be the name of one or both of your grandchildren's parents. Even if you were not successful in obtaining custody at the hearing, you may be able to secure specific visitation rights, which should be spelled out in the final order. In the space below that paragraph, type in the details of the visitation ordered by the judge. Be as specific and detailed as possible, so there is no doubt of exactly when visitation is to be allowed.

◈ If child support has also been ordered, type in this information on the lines in the paragraph under the heading "Child Support." On the first line, fill in the name of the person who was ordered to pay support. On the second and third lines, fill in the amount of support and the period when each payment is owed (such as "week" or "month," etc.).

◈ The paragraph under the heading "Costs" is to designate who was ordered to pay the court costs.

◈ Present the order to the judge for signing (either directly to the judge at the end of the hearing or to the judge's secretary later). Provide enough copies so one can be given or sent to each party.

Decree for Child Custody (form 19)

The **DECREE FOR CHILD CUSTODY** is a custody order specifically for use in Texas. (see form 19, p.205.) Form 19 is very similar to form 14, except that some additional matters relating to custody are included in form 19. Complete the **DECREE FOR CHILD CUSTODY** as follows.

◈   Complete the case style portion according to the instructions in Chapter 3 and Chapter 5.

◈   Follow the instructions on the previous page for form 14, until you get to the heading titled "Conservatorship."

◈   Under the heading "Conservatorship," type in the name (or names) of the person (or persons) who will have custody, and the names of the children.

◈   Under the heading "Possession Order," type in the name of the person (or persons) who will be receiving visitation and the details of when visitation will be allowed.

◈   The paragraph under the heading "Costs" is to designate who was ordered to pay the court costs.

◈   Present the order to the judge (either directly to the judge at the end of the hearing or to the judge's secretary later) for signing. Provide enough copies so that one can be given or sent to each party.

APPEALS

It is possible to appeal a decision made by the judge after a trial. The appeals process, which includes many strict deadlines, is not covered in this book, and you will need to research this independently if it becomes an issue in your case. If you are thinking about an appeal, you should immediately contact a lawyer, because once a deadline is missed, there is usually nothing that can be done and you have lost any chance to appeal.

The one thing you should know about appeals is that you can only appeal an issue of law—not an issue of fact. This means that if a judge finds that the facts of the case do not warrant visitation or custody, there is nothing to appeal. A party gets one day in court, and an appeals court cannot substitute its judgment for that of the trial judge.

What *can* be appealed is if a judge makes an error in interpreting the law. For example, if a judge rules that a law is unconstitutional, or that it does not apply to certain parties when it actually does, you can have an appellate court rule on whether that is a correct interpretation of the law.

Winning an appeal may not grant you any custody or visitation, and may just send you back to the trial court for more hearings. Appeals are extremely expensive, technical, and time-consuming, and a lawyer should be involved.

Evidence You Will Need

When a judge decides a case, it is on the basis of the evidence formally presented in court. Evidence consists of things, such as records and other documents, and testimony from witnesses you call to testify for you. In this chapter, some of the kinds of evidence that might be helpful for you in both visitation and custody cases are discussed.

VISITATION

Obviously, you will need much more extensive evidence in a custody case than in a visitation case. The first step in deciding what evidence you will need for your visitation case is to refer again to the eligibility requirements for your state. For example, say you and your grandchild live in Michigan, and the qualifying ground for visitation that you intend to use is that your grandchild has resided with you for seven months, then returned to live with the parents, and that you are not getting to see the grandchild. In that case, you will need evidence to prove that the grandchild resided with you for the seven months and that you are not getting visitation. Of course, you can testify to these facts, as can other family members who know about either of these situations.

Keep in mind that you must also meet the burdens imposed by *Troxel*, as specified in the laws of your state. While Michigan law is being used as a guide for this example, the information and proof is appropriate and necessary in the other states as well. Therefore, you will need to prove that the decision to deny visitation creates a substantial risk of harm to the child's mental, physical, or emotional health. To show best interest, you will need to address the following factors:

- ✪ the love, affection, and other emotional ties existing between the child and the grandparent;

- ✪ the length and quality of the prior relationship between the child and the grandparent;

- ✪ the role performed by the grandparent;

- ✪ the grandparent's moral fitness;

- ✪ the grandparent's mental and physical health;

- ✪ the child's reasonable preference;

- ✪ the willingness of the grandparent, except in cases of abuse or neglect, to encourage a close relationship between the child and the parent;

- ✪ the effect on the child of hostility between the parent and the grandparent;

- ✪ any history of physical, emotional, or sexual abuse or neglect of any child by the grandparent;

- ✪ whether the parent's decision to deny visitation is related to the child's well-being or is for some other, unrelated reason; and,

- ✪ any other factor relevant to the physical or psychological well-being of the child.

Other sources of proof include testimony from friends, neighbors, fellow church members, or members of clubs to which you belong.

School and medical records are other good sources of proof of your grandchild's residence. You will also need to show that visitation is in your grandchild's best interest. Photographs and videotapes showing you having fun with your grandchild are a good way to help establish the nature of your relationship. Other adults who have seen you interact with your grandchildren make good witnesses for this purpose. You may also want to have a psychologist or therapist testify about the importance of your grandchildren having a relationship with you. You will need to get any testimony available—for example, from your grandchild's school or day care—about how the loss of the relationship has changed the child for the worse.

CUSTODY

All of this same evidence will also be useful in custody cases. Once again, you will first need to look at the laws on custody for your state and tailor your evidence to that law. If child abuse or neglect is involved, you may be able to get evidence or testimony from public agencies like the Department of Human Services, Child Protective Services (or whatever your state's child welfare department is called), the police department, or your grandchild's school. Most of these records are governed by confidentiality rules. If this is the case, you may need either a subpoena or court order to gain access to the records. If you need a court order, prepare a simple motion asking the court to order these records released to you. You can adapt one of the motion forms in Appendix D (such as form 20, 21, or 23). You will also need to prepare an order for the judge to sign. Look at form 22 or form 24 for an example of an order that goes with a motion.

Baby-sitters and day care centers may be another source of evidence. If it is applicable to your case, remember to check with the appropriate alcohol or drug treatment center, family violence crisis center, or rape crisis center. Physicians and their records are also fertile ground for helpful evidence, as are any counselors or therapists that may have seen your grandchild, the parents, or the grandparents.

If your grandchildren are in a bad environment at home or exposed to unsavory characters while with their parents, you will need to locate people with personal knowledge of these facts to testify for you.

Another item that may be helpful to you in a custody case is the *home study*. A home study results from the judge appointing a qualified, neutral third party to make an evaluation of all the parties involved in a case. This person then makes a recommendation to the judge as to who should get custody. If the facts of your case merit it, you can also ask the judge to order drug testing or a psychological evaluation of the parties. These evaluations by neutral third parties carry a great deal of weight with the judge and can be very helpful to your case.

Specific Case Examples

All of the material contained in this book is general in nature and must be adapted to fit the needs of your particular case. In order to give you some guidance, the following section contains some examples of specific, real-life cases. Where possible, the case citation is included. The citation is a set of numbers that tells you where to look up the case so that you can read the judge's opinion for yourself. The first number refers you to the volume in the set of books (called the *reporter*) that contains the case, and the second number is the page number in the book. The number in parentheses is the year in which the case was decided by the court. The middle abbreviation tells you which set of reporters to use. The country is divided into regions, and the regions each have their own reporters. (See page 4 for more information on reporters). As a general rule, the following cases involve grandparents and have been appealed. It is generally the appeals court opinion to which the citations will direct you. First, an examination of visitation cases will be made.

VISITATION

In the case of *Rosemary E.R. v. Michael G.Q.*, 471 A.2d 995 (1984), the maternal grandmother sought visitation with her six-year-old grandchild. The grandmother, who was eighty years old, confined to a wheelchair, and lived with her seventy-five-year-old sister, was found by the court as suitable for visitation and as having a happy relationship with her other grandchildren. Her daughter (the child's mother) was dead and the father had remarried. The father opposed the visits because the child had adjusted well to the new family situation and because the grandmother might not be able to supervise the child. Even though she was found to be suitable for visitation, the judge denied the visitation, saying the grandmother had not proved that visitation was in the child's best interest over the father's objections.

In another New York case, *Emmanuel S. v. Joseph E.*, 577 N.E.2d 27 (1991), the paternal grandparents sought visitation because their relationship with the parents had deteriorated when the grandchild was about three months old, and they no longer saw the grandchild. The judge gave these grandparents six hours of visitation on the second Sunday of every month.

In a third New York case, *Seymour S. v. Glen S.*, 592 N.Y.S. 411 (1993), the paternal grandfather sued for visits over the parents' objections. The court did not give this grandparent visitation because he had not made reasonable efforts to establish contact with the grandchild before he filed suit, had alienated both of his own sons, and had not had any contact with the child's father for two years.

Another case, *Santi v. Santi*, 633 N.W.2d 312 (Iowa 2004), holds a cautionary tale for grandparents, in addition to being the case that declared the Iowa grandparent visitation statute unconstitutional. In this case, the paternal grandparents filed a suit seeking grandparent visitation. The child's parents were still married to each other but were not allowing the grandparents to see the child. According to the court's opinion, the trouble between the parents and the grandparents started when the grandparents reneged on a promised honeymoon cruise for the parents because the grandchild, then an infant, was not going to be left in their care. The family eventually made peace on this issue, and the grandfather began baby-sitting on his days off.

Trouble arose again, however, when the grandparents bought the child's first shoes and took her to see Santa without the parent's permission. Then, other minor issues, like the amount of fast food the child got to eat while with the grandparents, cropped up. Communications got so strained that they all went to counseling. Unfortunately, this did not help. By the time of the trial on the grandparent visitation request, the grandparents were not allowed to see the child at all. The parents' reasoning was that their lives were just less stressful without the interaction with the grandparents. At the conclusion of this case, the grandparents were left with nothing, since the grandparent visitation statute was ruled unconstitutional, and their relationship with the child's parents was so fractured they lost the access they had.

A case from California also shows an area in which grandparents need to carefully weigh what they hope to gain versus what they might lose. In *Punsley v. Ho*, 105 Cal. Reptr. 2d 139 (Cal. App. 4 Dist, 2001), the grandparents filed a visitation request after the death of their son. In that case, the parents were divorced and Ms. Ho had gotten custody of the child. After the divorce, the father died of cancer. For a time, the paternal grandparents continued to see the child regularly. However, the grandparents lived some distance away from the mother and child, and eventually, the grandparents did not get to visit the child. They hired an attorney and attempted to work out a schedule for access. The mother did not agree to their schedule, but offered a more limited one. The grandparents rejected this schedule and went to court.

Although they won in the trial and got visitation on the third Sunday of alternate months, the mother appealed and won on appeal. Because the grandparents had not proved that the mother was unfit, the appeals court overturned the order giving them visitation. One of the factors in the court's decision was the fact that the mother did not discount the value of a relationship between the child and the grandparents and had offered them some visitation.

The overriding lesson offered by the last two cases mentioned is this—if you are getting access to your grandchild, you must always keep in mind that the parents are the primary decision-makers. If they offer you some visitation, it may be extremely difficult to prove that you need more time. If dealing with you and your demands so complicates the parent's lives that it is just not worth the trouble for them, you may end up being left out in the cold.

As these cases show, it is almost always in your best interest to work with the parents as much as you can, and be very wary about how much time you demand with the grandchild. Although it can be hard to cede control in these unhappy family situations, the parents are the parents, and your role as a grandparent is more limited. You should keep these limits in mind when deciding whether or not you should go to court. It helps to be realistic about the situation. Are the parents really being unfair, or are you asking for too much? Are you fulfilling your role as a good grandparent, or are you trying to take the reins and parent the child? Finally, ask yourself if you have explored all the available avenues to resolve the problem without going to court. If you have, then use the information in this book to help you through the process.

CUSTODY

For illustration purposes, a few sample custody cases follow.

In Alaska, the paternal grandparents filed for custody in *Bass v. Bass*, 437 P.2d 324 (1968). The court gave custody to the grandparents because they proved that the mother was emotionally immature, generally neglected the child's physical needs, and did not pay much attention to the health of the child.

Another case in which grandparents got custody is from North Dakota, *Mansukhami v. Pailing*, 318 N.W.2d 748 (1982). In that case, the paternal grandparents had cared for the grandchildren. Their son was deceased and had not provided support or care for the children while alive. During the separation, divorce, and reconciliation between the parents, the grandchildren lived with the grandparents while the parents lived in another town. The mother later remarried and wanted custody. The grandparents got custody because all of the expert witnesses who testified said that giving custody to the mother would be detrimental to the children and because the judge felt that the grandchildren saw the grandparents as their *psychological parents*.

Another case, although it did not involve grandparents, shows how the parental preference can defeat a grandparent's claim for custody. In that case, the nonparent did not get custody, even though the parents had left the child with the nonparent for three years. During that time, the parents did not provide support or have contact with the child. When the father later sued for custody, he won because parents have preference over nonparents. Grandparents will encounter similar problems in states with parental preference.

If you want to read other cases, there will be a list following the statutes relating to grandparent visitation and to custody. It would be a good idea for you to read some of the cases from your state to get an idea of how the judges interpret the laws and what evidence has been successful. As you can see from these examples, cases do not always come out the way you think they will or even the way you think they ought to come out.

If you are confused, and it seems that some of these cases contradict each other, you are beginning to understand the confusing and unpredictable legal system with which you are about to interact.

CONCLUSION

Being a grandparent can be a rich and rewarding experience. It is always sad when family relationships become so strained that you end up in the court system. If you find yourself in that position, this book has given you the basic tools to help you either represent yourself or work more effectively with an attorney.

Glossary

A

amicus attorney. An attorney appointed by the court to represent your grandchild.

attorney at litem. An attorney representative for your grandchild.

B

best interest of the child. Standard used by courts as a part of deciding who should get custody of and visitation with a child.

C

court-appointed special advocate (CASA). A person, usually a specially trained volunteer, who is appointed to monitor the case to be sure the best interest of the child is being protected. This person is not a lawyer representing the child.

case style. The title to a case, it lists the parties involved.

complaint. The document that initiates a lawsuit.

custodial parent. The person with whom the child primarily lives.

custody. The term for the person who has the rights and duties of a parent. Can also refer to physical possession of the child.

G

guardian ad litem. A person appointed by the court to protect the best interest of the child. CASAs often act as guardians ad litem.

J

jurisdiction. The legal ability of the court to hear your case.

N

noncustodial parent. The parent who does not have primary possession of the child.

P

petition. Document that initiates a lawsuit.

petitioner. Person who filed the petition.

pleading. Any document filed in court requesting action by the judge.

plaintiff. Another word for the person who initiates the lawsuit.

S

standing. Term for whether you meet the legal requirements to file a particular kind of lawsuit.

T

***Troxel* rule.** The standards set out by the *Troxel v. Granville* case, which says that a fit parent is presumed to act in the best interest of the child and their decisions must be given special weight.

V

visitation. Time with the child, but not accompanied by parental rights.

State Laws

The following section contains a state-by-state listing of the applicable laws relating to grandparent visitation and custody. While every effort has been made to provide up-to-date information, the law can change at any time. Therefore, it is important for you to consult the current laws for your state to be sure you satisfy all of the legal requirements. Refer back to the section on "Legal Research" in Chapter 1 for more information about researching the law for your state.

– Warning –

Since *Troxel*, many courts have declared their grandparent visitation statutes unconstitutional or have otherwise changed their statutes. Check for recent court decisions in your state before filing for visitation. None of these decisions affect custody cases.

EXPLANATION OF TERMS

The following is an explanation of what information may be found under each of the headings in this appendix.

The law: The first listing directs you to the title of the book where the laws for that state may be found. An abbreviation for the law, which is used in the following sections, is also given. The symbol "§" means "section." For some states, information is also given to try to help you find the specific volume or volumes you will need. For example, a direction to "ignore volume numbers" means the books will give both a volume number and a section or chapter number on the cover. Use the section or chapter number, not the volume number. If the section number is followed by "et seq.," it means the reference begins there and continues in several following sections in sequence.

Grandparent visitation: This listing tells you the various grounds you may use to get grandparent visitation. These are the grounds that should be stated in your complaint or petition for visitation. The statutory provision relating to grandparent visitation is also given. Other information may be given, such as whether other documents are required.

Effect of adoption: The section on effect of adoption tells you whether or not you can still have visitation rights with your grandchild if your child's parental rights have been terminated and the grandchild is adopted by someone else, either a stepparent or a stranger.

Custody statutes: This section tells you where to look for the general laws pertaining to child custody for your state, and gives a summary of what factors are considered. The factors are those used in divorces cases; however, they will also give you an idea of what criteria may be used in your case for grandparent custody.

Parental preference: This section tells you whether or not your state has a parental preference. Remember, the strength of the preference varies from state to state, and you will need to read some of the annotations of your state's law to determine how strong this preference is in your state.

ALABAMA

The law: Code of Alabama (C.A.) Title 30. Ignore volume numbers.

Grandparent visitation: Grandparents may file an original action for visitation if one or both parents are deceased; the marriage of the parents has been dissolved; when a parent has abandoned the child; the child was born out of wedlock; when the child is living with both biological parents who are still married to each other, whether or not there is a broken relationship between either or both parents of the grandchild and the grandparent and either or both parents have used their parental authority to prohibit a relationship between the child and the grandparents. The court must find that visitation is in the best interest of the child. There are statutory factors the court is to consider in deciding best interest: the willingness of the grandparent to encourage a close relationship between the child and the parent; the preference of the child; the mental and physical health of the child and the grandparent; any evidence of domestic violence inflicted by one parent on the other parent or the grandchild; other relevant factors in the particular circumstances, including the wishes of any parent who is living. A visitation request can only be filed one time in any two year period and not during any year in which another custody action has been filed. Once visitation has been granted, the legal custodian or parent may petition for revocation of the visitation for good cause shown; this request can only be file one time in any two year period. Visitation cannot be granted if the parent related to the grandparent seeking visitation has either given up legal custody voluntarily or by court order, or has abandoned the child financially, unless the grandparent has an established relationship with the child and the court finds that the visits are in the child's best interest. See *In Re AMK v. ED*, 826 So.2d 889 (Ala. Civ. App. 2002), Title 30, Chapter 3 (C.A. §30-3-4.1).

Effect of adoption: Natural grandparents may have post-adoption visitation when the child is adopted by a stepparent, another grandparent, brother, sister, half-brother or sister, an aunt or uncle and their respective spouses.

Custody statutes: Factors: (1) moral character of parents; and (2) age and sex of child. C.A. §30-3.

Parental preference: Yes.

ALASKA

The law: Alaska Statutes (A.S.). Ignore volume numbers; look for title numbers. Supplement is in the front of each volume.

Grandparent visitation: Grandparents may be awarded visitation in an action for divorce, legal separation, or for placement of the child; or when both parents have died; if it is in the best interest of the child. Title 25, Section 25.20.150 (A.S. §25.20.150). Grandparents may petition for visitation if the grandparent has established or attempted to establish ongoing personal contact with the child and the visits are in the child's best interest. (See A.S. §25.20.065). After a decree or final order relating to custody is entered under A.S. Sec. 25.20.060 or Sec. 25.20.150 or relating to an adoption, the grandparents may petition only if they did not petition during the pendency of the above action or there has been a change in circumstances relating to the custodial parent or the minor child that justifies reconsideration.

Effect of adoption: Adoption terminates any rights unless the adoption decree specifically provides for visitation between the adopted child and the natural relatives.

Custody statutes: Best interest of the child considering: (1) physical, emotional, mental, religious, and social needs of the child; (2) capability and desire of each party to meet those needs; (3) child's preference; (4) love and affection existing between child and each party; (5) length of time the child has been in a stable, satisfactory environment, and the desirability of maintaining continuity; (6) desire and ability of each party to allow an open and loving frequent relationship between the child and other party; (7) any evidence of domestic violence, child abuse or neglect, or history of violence between the parties; (8) any evidence of substance abuse by a party or other household member that directly affects the child; or, (9) any other relevant factor. A.S. §25.20.150.

Parental preference: Yes.

ARIZONA

The law: Arizona Revised Statutes Annotated (A.R.S.). Ignore volume numbers; look for section numbers.

Grandparent visitation: Either parents' marriage dissolved for at least three months, parent of the child is deceased or missing for at least three months and parent reported missing, or child born out of wedlock. Visitation must be in the best interest of the child, considering the following factors: the historical relationship between the child and the grandparents; the motivation of the grandparents in seeking the visits; the motivation of the person denying the visits; the quantity of time requested and the potential adverse impact visits will have on the child's customary activities; and, if one or both of the parents is deceased, the benefit in maintaining an extended familial relationship. If possible, the court shall order the visits to occur during the time the grandparent's child has access to the grandchild. A.R.S. §25-409. In 2000, after the U.S. Supreme Court decision in *Troxel*, the Arizona courts upheld the grandparent visitation statute in *Jackson v. Tangreen*, 18 P.3d 100 (Az. 2000). This case was appealed to the U.S. Supreme Court, which refused to hear the appeal. You should note that case law imposes a presumption that a fit parent acts in the best interest of the child and that parent's decision about visitation gets special weight. Case law also says that the grandparent visitation order should be as minimally intrusive as possible. See *McGovern v. McGovern*, 33 P.3d 506 (Az. App. 2001).

Effect of adoption: Visitation rights automatically terminate upon placement for adoption unless the adoption is by a stepparent. If the child is removed from placement, visitation may be reinstated.

Custody statutes: Best interest of child considering: (1) parties' wishes; (2) child's wishes; (3) interaction and interrelationship between the child and each parent, siblings, and other significant persons; (4) child's adjustment to home, school, and community; (5) mental and physical health of all persons involved; (6) which parent is more likely to allow frequent and continuing contact with the other parent; (7) if one parent, both parents, or neither parent has provided primary care of the child; (8) the nature and extent of coercion or duress used by a parent in obtaining an agreement regarding custody; and, (9) whether a parent has complied with Chapter 3, Article 5 (the domestic relations education section). A.R.S. §§ 25-401 to 25-414.

Parental preference: Yes.

ARKANSAS

The law: Arkansas Code Annotated (A.C.A.). Look for title or chapter numbers.

Grandparent visitation: Grandparents may seek visitation order: (1) if the parents' marriage is terminated by death, divorce, or legal separation; (2) if the child is in the custody or guardianship of a person other than one or both of his or her natural or adoptive parents; or, (3) if the child is born out-of-wedlock (for paternal grandparents to qualify, paternity must have been legally established). In all cases, the court must determine visitation is in the best interest of the child. An order denying visitation shall be in writing and state the reasons for the denial. Title 9, Chapter 13, Section 9-13-103 (A.C.A. §9-13-103). There is a rebuttable presumption that a custodian's decision denying visitation is in the child's best interest. To rebut this presumption, the grandparents must prove that a significant and viable relationship between the child and the grandparents exists, by showing either (1) that the child resided with the grandparent for at least six consecutive months, with or without the custodian; (2) the grandparent was the child's caregiver for at least six consecutive months; (3) there was frequent and regular contact between the child and the grandparent for at least twelve months; or, (4) other facts that show the loss of the relationship will harm the child. The grandparents must show that they have the capacity to cooperate with the custodian and the capacity to give the child love, affection, and guidance. Once granted, the visitation can be modified by the court.

Effect of adoption: Adoption terminates all rights of grandparents.

Custody statutes: Only statutory provision is that custody is to be determined "without regard to the sex of the parent but solely in accordance with the welfare and best interests of the children." A.C.A. §9-13-101 et seq.

Parental preference: Yes.

CALIFORNIA

The law: Deering's California Codes Annotated, Family Code. Be sure you use the volume marked "Family." [There is also a set called "West's Annotated California Codes," which will contain the same section numbers.]

Grandparent visitation: If a parent is deceased, parents and grandparents of the deceased parent get visitation if in child's best interest. Otherwise, parents must be divorced or currently living separately and apart on a permanent or indefinite basis, one parent absent for over a month and the other parent does not know that parent's whereabouts, one parent must join in the petition with the grandparents, or the child must not be residing with either parent. Court must also find that there is a preexisting relationship between the grandparents and the grandchild such that visitation is in the child's best interest, and the court must balance the interest of the child in having visitation with the parents' right to exercise their parental authority. There is a rebuttable presumption that visitation is not in the best interest of the child if both parents agree that the grandparent should not be granted visitation. Family Code, Section 3100 et seq. (Family Code §3100 et seq.). Although it is not specifically stated in the statute, case law establishes a presumption that a fit parent acts in the child's best interest. See *Punsley v. Ho*, 87 Ca.App.4th 1099, 105 Cal.Rept.2d 139 and *In Re Marriage of Harris*, 96 P.3d 141.

Effect of adoption: Natural grandparents may still get visitation.

Custody statutes: Factors: (1) child's preference (if child is old enough); (2) desire and ability of each parent to allow relationship with other parent; and, (3) child's health, safety, and welfare. Family Code §§3020–3424.

Parental preference: Yes.

COLORADO

The law: West's Colorado Revised Statutes Annotated. (C.R.S.A.).

Grandparent visitation: Any grandparent may seek a court order when there is or has been a child custody case or case concerning the allocation of parental responsibilities concerning the grandchild. This includes cases where a marriage is declared invalid or dissolved by court order or a court ordered legal separation, legal custody of or parental responsibilities allocated to a nonparent or a child is placed outside the home. Grandparents may also petition if they are the parent of a deceased parent of the grandchild (excluding a child who has been legally adopted or has been placed for adoption). When the grandparents file, they must include an affidavit setting forth the facts supporting the requested order and shall give notice and a copy of the affidavit to the person with custody or parental responsibilities. That person may file opposing affidavits. If the application is not opposed, and the court finds that the visits are in the best interest of the child, the court shall enter a visitation order. If any party requests a hearing, or the court feels that a hearing is necessary, the court will hold a hearing. In order to grant visits, court must find the visit in the child's best interest. Title 19, Article 1, Section 19-1-117 (C.R.S.A. §19-1-117 et seq.). Although it is not specified in the statute, there is a case that says the statute is to be interpreted as giving the biological parents' decisions special weight and significance. The parent does not have to prove that the grandparent's visits would be harmful. See *In Re C.M.*, 74 P.3d 342 (Col. App. 2002).

Effect of Adoption: Grandparent visitation rights automatically terminate upon completion of adoption by anyone other than a stepparent.

Custody statutes: Best interest of the child considering: (1) parties' wishes; (2) child's wishes; (3) interaction and interrelationship between child and parties, siblings, and other significant persons; (4) child's adjustment to home, school, and community; (5) mental and physical health of all persons involved; (6) custodian's ability to encourage sharing, love, affection and contact with the other party; (7) evidence of parties ability to cooperate and make joint decisions; (8) evidence of each party's ability to encourage sharing, love, affection, and contact with other party; (9) any history of abuse or neglect; (10) any history of spouse abuse; and, (11) various other factors relating to joint custody. C.R.S.A. § 14-10-123 et seq.

Parental preference: No.

CONNECTICUT

The law: Connecticut General Statutes Annotated (C.G.S.A). Ignore "chapter" numbers; look for "title" numbers.

Grandparent visitation: Upon the court's best judgment of facts of the case and the best interest of the child and subject to the conditions and limitations the court deems equitable. Title 46b, Section 46b-59 (C.G.S.A. §46b-59). Although the statute does not contain any limits, case law states that this statute does not apply to an intact family. See *Costagno v. Wholean*, 684 A.2d 1181, 239 Conn. 336 (1996). There is case law that states that an allegation with proof that the parent's decision to deny visitation will cause harm presents a compelling state interest that permits interference, as long as the grandparent has established a parent-like relationship with the child. This case upheld the validity of grandparent visitation. See *Roth v. Weston*, 789 A.2d 431.

Effect of adoption: Grandparents may still get visitation after their natural grandchild is adopted.

Custody statutes: Best interest of child considering (1) wishes of the child, if of sufficient age and (2) causes of the parents' divorce as they may be relevant to the child's best interest. C.G.S.A. §46b-56.

Parental preference: No.

DELAWARE

The law: Delaware Code Annotated (D.C.A.). Ignore volume numbers; look for "title" numbers.

Grandparent visitation: The court can grant visitation to grandparents. If the parents live together, visitation cannot be granted over the parents' objection. If the paternal grandparents get visitation, their visitation time comes out of the time allotted to the father. If the maternal grandparents get visitation, their time comes out of the time allotted to the mother. 10 Del. Code §1031(7). See *Rosemary E.R. v. Michael G.Q.*, 471 A.2d 995 (1984).

Effect of adoption: Adoption terminates all rights.

Custody statutes: Best interests of the child considering: (1) wishes of the parents and the child; (2) interaction and interrelationship of child with parents, siblings, and other significant persons; (3) child's adjustment to home, school, and community; and, (4) mental and physical health of all persons involved. D.C.A. 13 §721. Must submit affidavit that Petitioner has been advised of the following children's rights: "(1) the right to a continuing relationship with both parents; (2) the right to be treated as an important human being, with unique feelings, ideas, and desires; (3) the right to continuing care and guidance from both parents; (4) the right to know and appreciate what is good in each parent without one parent degrading the other; (5) the right to express love, affection, and respect for each parent without having to stifle that love because of disapproval by the other parent; (6) the right to know that the parents' decision to divorce was not the responsibility of the child; (7) the right not to be a source of argument between the parents; (8) the right to honest answers to questions about the changing family relationships; (9) the right to be able to experience regular and consistent contact with both parents and the right to know the reason for any cancellation of time or change of plans; and (10) the right to have a relaxed, secure relationship with both parents without being placed in a position to manipulate one parent against the other." See 13 D.C.A. §701 and 13 D.C.A. §721 et seq.

Parental preference: Yes.

DISTRICT OF COLUMBIA

The law: District of Columbia Code (D.C.C.).

Grandparent visitation: No statutory provisions for grandparent visitation.

Custody statutes: No mention of grandparents, but following criteria are used in divorce cases: Best interest of the child considering: (1) wishes of the child; (2) wishes of the parties; (3) interaction and interrelationship between the child and parents, siblings, and other significant persons; (4) child's adjustment to home, school, and community; and, (5) mental and physical health of all persons involved. District of Columbia Code, Title 30, Sections 911 & 914 (D.C.C. §§ 30-911 & 30-914).

FLORIDA

The law: Florida Statutes (F.S.). A new set is published every odd-numbered year, with hard-cover supplements every even-numbered year. Ignore volume numbers; look for "chapter" numbers. (There is also a set called "West's Florida Statutes Annotated," which includes supplements in the back of each volume.)

Grandparent visitation: The court shall grant visitation when it is in the best interest of the child if the parents' marriage has been dissolved, a parent has deserted the child, or the child was born out of wedlock, Chapter 752, Section 752.01 (F.S §752.01 et seq.). This version of the statute has been declared unconstitutional in *Sullivan v. Sapp*, 866 So.2d 28 (Fla. 2004). In that case, the court stated that any statute that did not require harm to the child is unconstitutional and that the best interest alone will never be good enough. Therefore, you should check for any legislative amendments before you file a case in Florida.

Effect of adoption: Rights terminate unless the adoption is by a stepparent.

Custody statutes: Best interest of child considering: (1) which party is more likely to allow frequent and continuing contact with the other party; (2) love, affection, and other emotional ties existing between the child and each party; (3) each party's capacity and disposition to provide food, clothing, medical care, or other material needs for the child; (4) length of time the child has been in a stable, satisfactory environment, and the desirability of maintaining continuity; (5) the permanence, as a family unit, of the existing or proposed custodial home; (6) moral fitness of the parties; (7) mental and physical health of the parties; (8) child's home, school, and community record; (9) preference of the child, if of sufficient intelligence, understanding, and experience; and, (10) any other relevant factor. F.S. §61.13(3).

Parental preference: Yes.

GEORGIA

The law: Official Code of Georgia Annotated (C.G.A.). Ignore volume numbers; look for "title" and "chapter" numbers. (This is not the same set as the "Georgia Code," which is a separate set of books with a completely different numbering system. If all you can find is the Georgia Code, look for a cross-reference table to the Official Code of Georgia.)

Grandparent visitation: Any grandparent can file an original action or intervene in any action in which the court has before it a question of custody of the child, divorce of the parents, termination of the parent's rights, other visitation rights regarding the child, or adoption by a blood relative or stepparent. Grandparent may not file when the parents are not separated and the grandchild lives with both parents. The court can grant visitation if it finds that the health or welfare of the child would be harmed unless the visits are granted and also finds that the visits are in the child's best interest. There is no presumption in favor of visitation. The grandparent can only file one time in any two year period and not in any year in which another custody action has been filed. After visits have been granted, the parent can petition for termination for good cause shown, but cannot file more than one time in any two year period. Title 19, Chapter 7, Section 3 (C.G.A. §19-7-3).

Effect of adoption: Rights do not terminate as long as the adoption is by a blood relative of the child or by the child's stepparent.

Custody statutes: No specific factors. Child may choose if at least 14 years of age, unless parent determined to be unfit. C.G.A. §19-9 et seq.

Parental preference: Yes.

HAWAII

The law: Hawaii Revised Statutes (H.R.S.). Ignore volume numbers; look for "title" numbers.

Grandparent visitation: Grandparent may seek visitation if: (1) Hawaii is the home state of the child at the time of commencement of the proceedings and (2) visitation is in the best interest of the child. Title 571, Section 571-46.3 (H.R.S. §571-46.3).

Effect of adoption: Adoption terminates all rights.

Custody statutes: Best interest of child considering: (1) child's wishes, if of sufficient age and capacity to reason and (2) any evidence of family violence. H.R.S. §583-1 et seq.

Parental preference: No.

IDAHO

The law: Idaho Code (I.C.). Ignore volume number.

Grandparent visitation: Visitation may be granted upon a showing that the visitation would be in the best interest of the child. (**Note:** If the grandparent's child who is the parent is also a minor, the grandparent can be ordered to pay child support for the grandchild until the parent is 18 years of age.) Title 32, Section 32-719 (I.C. §32-719).

Effect of adoption: Adoption terminates all rights.

Custody statutes: Best interest of child considering: (1) wishes of parties; (2) wishes of child; (3) interaction and interrelationship between the child and parties, siblings, and other significant persons; (4) adjustment to home, school, and community; (5) mental and physical health of all persons involved; (6) need to promote continuity and stability in the child's life; and, (7) any history of domestic violence. I.C. §32-717.

Parental preference: Yes.

ILLINOIS

The law: West's Smith Hurd Illinois Compiled Statutes Annotated (ILCS).

Grandparent visitation: Grandparents can file for visitation if there is an unreasonable denial of visitation by a parent and at least one of the following conditions exists: one parent is incapacitated as a matter of law or has been sentenced to jail for a term of more than one year; the parents are legally separated from each other during the three month period prior to the filing and at least one parent does not object to the grandparents having visitation (the visitation granted must not diminish the visitation time of the parent not related to the grandparent getting the visitation); a parent's rights have been terminated and the grandparent is the parent of the person whose rights were terminated for reasons other than an adoption (the visitation must not be used to allow the parent whose rights have been terminated to unlawfully visit the child); the child is illegitimate, the parents are not living together, the grandparent is a paternal grandparent, and paternity has been established by a court order. There is a rebuttable presumption that a fit parent's actions and decisions regarding grandparent visitation are not harmful to the child's mental, physical, or emotional health. In order to get visitation, the grandparent must prove that the denial of visitation is harmful to the mental, physical, or emotional health of the child. In making a decision, the court must consider the following factors: the preference of the child; the mental and physical health of the child and the grandparents; the length and quality of the prior relationship between the child and the grandparents; the good faith of the party filing the petition; the good faith of the party denying the visitation; the quantity of time requested and the potential adverse impact visitation would have on the child's customary activities; whether the child resided with the grandparent for at least six consecutive months (with or without the parent); whether the grandparent had frequent or regular contact with the child within the last twelve months; any other factor that shows that the loss of the relationship would harm the mental, physical, or emotional health of the child. Title 750 Illinois Compiled Statutes, Section 5/607 (750 ILCS §5/607).

Effect of adoption: Adoption terminates the rights of the grandparent who is the parent of the person whose rights were terminated.

Custody statutes: Best interest of child considering: (1) wishes of parents and child; (2) interaction and interrelationship between the child and parents, siblings, and other significant persons; (3) adjustment to home, school, and community; (4) mental and physical health of parties and child; (5) any physical threat to child; and, (6) each party's willingness to encourage and facilitate continued contact between the other parent and the child. 750 ILCS §5/602 et seq.

Parental preference: Yes.

INDIANA

The law: West's Annotated Indiana Code (A.I.C.). Look for "title" numbers.

Grandparent visitation: Visitation may be granted if either the child's parent is deceased; the parents' marriage has been dissolved in Indiana; or, if the child was born out of wedlock. (For the paternal grandparents of a child born out of wedlock to obtain visitation, the child's father must have legally established paternity.) If the marriage of the parents was dissolved somewhere other than Indiana, the grandparents may seek visitation if the custody decree does not bind the grandparent under I.C. §31-17-3-12 and if an Indiana court has jurisdiction under I.C. §31-17-3-3 or §31-17-3-14. In all cases, the court must determine that visitation is in the child's best interest, considering whether the grandparent has had, or attempted to have, meaningful contact with the child. Title 31, Chapter 17, Section 5-1 (A.I.C. §31-17-5.1). The law requires the court to make findings when deciding a visitation case, and there is case law that says that, in those findings, the courts should address the presumption that a fit parent's decisions are in the child's best interest, the special weight that the parent's decision must be given, whether the grandparents have proved that visitation is in the child's best interest, and whether the parent has just limited visitation or denied it completely. See *Crafton v. Gibson* 752 N.E.2d 86 (Ind. App. 2001) and *Spaulding v. Williams*, 793 N.E.2d 252.

Effect of adoption: Visitation rights terminate unless the adoption is by the child's stepparent or by a person who is biologically related to the child as a grandparent, sibling, aunt, uncle, niece, or nephew.

Custody statutes: Best interest of child considering: (1) age and sex of child; (2) wishes of parents and child; (3) interaction and interrelationship between the child and parents, siblings, and other significant persons; (4) child's adjustment to home, school, and community; and, (5) mental and physical health of all persons involved. A.I.C. §31-1-11 et seq.

Parental preference: Yes.

IOWA

The law: Iowa Code Annotated (I.C.A.). Ignore volume numbers; look for "section" numbers.

Grandparent visitation: Visitation may be awarded if (1) either the child's parents are divorced; (2) a petition for dissolution of the marriage is pending; (3) the parent who is the child of the petitioning grandparents is deceased; (4) the child has been placed in a foster home; (5) the petitioning grandparents are the parents of the noncustodial parent and the other parent's spouse has adopted the child; (6) the grandparent is the parent of the child's noncustodial parent and the child had been born out of wedlock and paternity was established in court; or, (7) a parent of the minor child unreasonably refuses to allow visits by the grandparent or unreasonably restricts the visitation (this applies, but is not limited to, situations in which the parents are divorced and the parent who is that grandparent's child has custody). The court must also determine that visitation is in the child's best interest, and that the grandparent has established a substantial relationship with the child. Also, visitation can be ordered by the juvenile court as a part of a dispositional or permanency hearing, or in a guardianship proceedings. Iowa Code Annotated, Section 598.35 (I.C.A.

§598.35). There are cases that have held that the Iowa visitation statute is unconstitutional. See *Santi v. Santi*, 633 N.W.2d 312 (2001) and *Howard v. Howard*, 661 N.W.2d 183 (Iowa 2003).

Effect of adoption: Visitation rights terminate unless the adoption is by a stepparent.

Custody statutes: Best interest of child "which will assure the child the opportunity for the maximum continuing physical and emotional contact with both parents." I.C.A. §598.21.

Parental preference: Yes.

KANSAS

The law: Kansas Statutes Annotated (K.S.A.). You may find these either as "Vernon's Kansas Statutes Annotated," or "Kansas Statutes Annotated, Official." Both sets have very poor indexing systems.

Grandparent visitation: Visitation may be granted in a custody order. Kansas Statutes Annotated, Section 60-1616 (K.S.A. §60-1616). Section 38-129 states that, for a grandparent to be granted reasonable visitation, the court must find that the visits would be in the best interest of the child and when a substantial relationship between the child and the grandparent has been established. Case law says that visitation actions under §60-1616 also include the requirements from §38-129, and require the court to find special weight to the fundamental presumption that a fit parent acts in the child's best interest. See *Skov v. Wicker*, 32 P.3d 1122 (Kansas 2001).

Effect of adoption: Adoption terminates rights unless you are the parent of the child's deceased parent and the surviving parent's spouse adopts.

Custody statutes: Best interest of child considering: (1) any agreement of the parties; (2) length of time child has been under actual care and control of any person other than a parent and the circumstances involved; (3) desires of the parties; (4) desires of child; (5) interaction and interrelationship between child and parties, siblings, and other significant persons; (6) child's adjustment to home, school, and community; (7) each party's willingness and ability to respect and appreciate the bond between the child and the other party; (8) any evidence of spousal abuse; and, (9) any other relevant factor. K.S.A. §60-16-1610(a)(3). Four types of custody are recognized, in the following order of preference: (1) joint; (2) sole; (3) divided (if 2 or more children); and, (4) nonparental. K.S.A. §60-1610(a)(3).

Parental preference: Yes.

KENTUCKY

The law: Kentucky Revised Statutes (KRS). Ignore volume numbers; look for "chapter" numbers. These are in a binder, with updates found in the beginning of each volume in a section marked "Current Service."

Grandparent visitation: Visitation may be granted if the court determines that the visitation is in the best interest of the child. A grandparent can get the same visitation as that awarded to a noncustodial parent, if that grandparent's child is deceased and the grandparent has assumed the financial obligation of child support, unless the court finds that this would not be in the child's best interest. Chapter 405, Section 021 (KRS §405.021). Case law says that the courts must consider a broad array of factors in deciding a visitation case, including the nature and stability of the relationship between the child and the grandparents, the amount of time the child and grandparent have spent together, the potential benefits and detriments to the child if visitation is granted, the effect visitation would have on the relationship between the child and the parents, the physical and emotional health of the adults involved, the stability of the child's living and schooling arrangements, and the wishes of the child. The grandparents must prove by clear and convincing evidence that the visits are in the child's best interest. See *Vibbert v. Vibbert*, 144 S.W.3d 292 (Ky. App. 2004).

Effect of adoption: Visitation rights terminate except in the case of a stepparent adoption where there has been no termination of the parental rights of the parent whose parents are seeking visitation. Once a grandparent has been granted visitation rights, those rights will not be adversely affected by the termination of parental rights of that grandparent's child, unless the court determines that it is in the child's best interest to do so.

Custody statutes: Best interest of child considering: (1) wishes of parents and child; (2) interaction and interrelationship between child and parents, siblings, and other significant persons; (3) child's adjustment to home, school, and community; and, (4) mental and physical condition of all persons involved. KRS §405.020 et seq. and §403 et seq.

Parental preference: Yes.

LOUISIANA

The law: Louisiana Statutes Annotated-Revised Statutes (LSA-R.S), Children's Code (Ch. C), and Civil Code (CC). The books containing the laws of Louisiana are one of the more complicated sets of any state. There are several sets of books divided into subjects. All sets have the title of either "Louisiana Statutes Annotated," or "West's LSA," which is followed by the area of law such as Revised Statutes, Civil Code, Civil Procedure, etc. The divorce laws were completely rewritten in 1990, and may be found in a separate soft-cover volume titled "West's Louisiana Statutes Annotated, Civil Code." Look for a subheading titled "Ch.1. The Divorce Action."

Grandparent visitation: When one parent dies, is interdicted, or incarcerated, the parents of the deceased, interdicted, or jailed party may have reasonable visitation if the court finds it to be in the best interest of the child. Louisiana Statutes Annotated-Revised Statutes, Article 9:344 (La.-R.S. 9:344), Children's Code, Article 1264 (Ch. C Art. 1264) et seq., and Civil Code Article 136 (CC Art. 136). Case law has ruled that the *Troxel* rules apply, which means that the court must presume that a fit parent's decision is in the child's best interest and must give that decision special weight. The presumption can be rebutted. *Dickson*, 843 So.2d 1261 (La. App. 2003).

Effect of adoption: The natural parents of a deceased pa solved by death and the parents of a party who has forfeit to the adoption of his child pursuant to Article 1245 of the have limited visitation rights to a minor child who has been

Custody statutes: Joint legal custody is preferred and presumed best for the child. Parties must submit a joint custody plan. A party requesting sole custody must prove it is in the child's best interest considering the following factors: (1) the child's love, affection, and emotional ties with each parent; (2) capacity and disposition of the parties to give love, affection, guidance, education, and religious guidance; (3) capacity and disposition of the parties to give the child food, clothing, medical care, etc.; (4) length of time the child has been in a stable, satisfactory environment, and the desirability for continuity; (5) permanence as a family unit of the existing or proposed home; (6) moral fitness of the parties; (7) mental and physical health of the parties; (8) home, school, and community record of the child; (9) preference of the child, if old enough; (10) willingness of each party to facilitate a relationship between the child and the other spouse; (11) distance between parties residences; and, (12) any other factor the judge decides is proper (except race). LSA-C.C., Art. 131 et seq.

Parental preference: Yes.

MAINE

The law: Maine Revised Statutes Annotated (M.R.S.A.). Ignore volume numbers; look for "title" numbers.

Grandparent visitation: Visitation may be granted if at least one of the child's parents or legal guardians has died or if there is a sufficient existing relationship between the child and grandparent or if a sufficient effort to establish one has been made. The court shall consider any objections by the parent. In all cases, the visitation must be in the child's best interest and not significantly interfere with any parent-child relationship. In determining the child's best interest, the court must consider: (1) the child's age; (2) the relationship of the child with the grandparent, including the amount of previous contact; (3) the preference of the child, if old enough to express a meaningful choice; (4) the duration and adequacy of the child's current living arrangement, and the desirability of maintaining continuity; (5) the stability of the proposed living arrangement; (6) the motivation of the parties and their capacity to give love, affection, and guidance; (7) the child's adjustment to home, school, and community; (8) the capacity of parent and grandparent to cooperate or learn to cooperate in child care; (9) the methods of assisting cooperation and resolving disputes and each person's willingness to learn those methods; (10) the existence of a grandparent's conviction for a sex offense or a sexually violent offense; and, (11) any other factor having a reasonable bearing on the physical and psychological well-being of the child. Title 19A, Maine Revised Statutes Annotated, Section 1801 (19A M.R.S.A. §1801 et seq.). Additional affidavit required.

Effect of adoption: Adoption terminates all rights.

Custody statutes: Best interest of child considering: (1) child's age; (2) child's relationship with each party and other significant persons; (3) preference of child, if of suitable age and maturity; (4) duration and adequacy of child's current living arrangement, and desirability of maintaining continuity; (5) stability of proposed living arrangement; (6) motivation of the parties and their capacity to give love, affection, and guidance; (7) child's adjustment to home, school, and community; (8) each party's capacity to allow and encourage a relationship between the child and the other party; (9) each party's capacity to cooperate in child care; (10) the methods for assisting parental cooperation and resolving disputes, and each party's willingness to use those methods; (11) effect on the child if one party has sole authority regarding upbringing; (12) any history of domestic abuse; and, (13) any other relevant factor. 19A M.R.S.A. §§214 & 752.

Parental preference: Yes.

MARYLAND

The law: Annotated Code of Maryland, Family Law (A.C.M.). Be sure you have the volume marked "Family Law."

Grandparent visitation: An equity court may grant a grandparent's request for reasonable visitation if it is found to be in the child's best interest. Case law sets out the factors to be considered in determining the best interests: (1) the nature and stability of the child's relationship with the parents; (2) the nature and stability of the relationship between the child and the grandparent, taking into account the frequency or contact, regularity of contact, and amount of time spent together; (3) the potential benefits and detriments to the child; (4) the effect visits would have on the child's attachment to the nuclear family; (5) the physical and emotional health of the adults involved; and, (6) the stability of the child's living and schooling arrangements. Article 9, Section 9-102 (A.C.M. Family Law §9-102). Before you file in Maryland, you will need to review case law for your state. There are some cases that find that the statute has been constitutionally applied (see *Herrick v. Wain*, 838 A.2d 1263 (Md. App. 2003)), and some that find it was unconstitutionally applied (see *Brice v. Brice* 754 A.2d 1132 (Md. App. 2000)).

Effect of adoption: All rights terminate upon adoption.

Custody statutes: No statutory factors. Custody discussed at A.C.M. Family Law §9-101 et seq.

Parental preference: Yes.

MASSACHUSETTS

The law: Annotated Laws of Massachusetts (A.L.M.).

Grandparent visitation: Visitation may be granted if the child's parents are divorced, married but living apart under a temporary order or judgment of separate support, one of the parents is deceased, or if the child was born out of wedlock and paternity established by a court or by acknowledgment by the father and the child's parents live apart, if the visitation is in the child's best interest. Chapter 119, Section 39D (A.L.M. Chapter 119 §39D). Must include "care and custody affidavit" with petition. Case law states that the *Troxel* rules apply, which means that there is a rebuttable presumption that the decision of a fit parent is in the child's best interest and that decision must be given special weight. See *Blixt v. Blixt*, 774 N.E.2d 1052 (Mass. 2002).

Effect of adoption: Rights terminate upon adoption by anyone other than a stepparent.

Custody statutes: No specific factors in statute; only general concepts. A.L.M., Chapter 208 §31.

Parental preference: Yes.

MICHIGAN

The law: Michigan Statutes Annotated (M.S.A.), or Michigan Compiled Laws Annotated (M.C.L.A.). Michigan has two separate sets of laws, each by a different publisher. Each set has a cross-reference index to the other set. Ignore volume and chapter numbers; look for section numbers.

Grandparent visitation: Grandparents may seek visitation under one or more of the following circumstances: an action for divorce, separate maintenance, or annulment involving the child's parents is pending before the court; the child's parents are divorced, separated under a judgment of separate maintenance, or have had their marriage annulled; the child's parent who is a child of the grandparents is deceased; the child's parents have never been married, they are not residing in the same household, and paternity has been established by the completion of an acknowledgment of paternity or by court order; legal custody of the child has been given to a person other than the child's parent or the child is placed outside of and does not reside in the home of a parent; in the year preceding the commencement of the visitation action, the grandparent provided an established custodial environment for the child, whether or not the grandparent had custody under a court order. It is presumed that a fit parent's decision to deny visitation does not create a substantial risk of harm to the child's mental, physical, or emotional health. To rebut the presumption, the grandparent must prove that the decision to deny visitation creates a substantial risk of harm to the child's mental, physical, or emotional health. The court must also find that the visitation is in the child's best interest, considering the following factors: the love, affection, and other emotional ties existing between the child and the grandparent; the length and quality of the prior relationship between the child and the grandparent, and the role performed by the grandparent; the grandparent's moral fitness; the grandparent's mental and physical health; the child's reasonable preference; the effect on the child of hostility between the grandparent and the parent; the willingness of the grandparent, except in cases of abuse and neglect, to encourage a close relationship between the child and the parents; any history of physical, emotional, or sexual abuse or neglect of any child by the grandparent; whether the parent's decision to deny visitation is related to the child's well being or is for some other unrelated reason; or, any other factor relevant to the physical and psychological well-being of the child. A grandparent may not file more than once every two years, absent a showing of good cause. The court may not modify visitation unless if finds, based on facts that have arisen since the entry of the visitation order, that a change in circumstances has occurred and that a modification or termination of the visitation order is necessary to avoid creating a substantial risk of harm to the mental, physical, or emotional health of the child. If two fit parents sign an affidavit that they both oppose an order for visitation, the court shall dismiss the complaint or motion seeking grandparent visitation; however, this provision does not apply if one of the parents is a stepparent who adopted the child. Michigan Statutes Annotated, Section 25.312(7b) (M.S.A. §25.312(7b)). This is same as Michigan Compiled Laws Annotated, §722.27b. Additional affidavit required.

Effect of adoption: Visitation rights terminate upon adoption unless the adoption is by a stepparent.

Custody statutes: Best interest of child considering: (1) love, affection, and other emotional ties existing between the parties and the child; (2) the capacity and disposition of each to give love, affection, guidance, and continuation of education and raising the child in its religion; (3) the capacity and disposition of each to provide food, clothing, and medical care; (4) length of time the child has lived in a stable, satisfactory environment, and the desirability of maintaining continuity; (5) permanence as a family unit of the existing or proposed custodial home; (6) moral fitness of the parties; (7) mental and physical health of the parties and child; (8) home, school, and community record of the child; (9) preference of the child, if of suitable age; (10) willingness and ability of the parties to facilitate and encourage a relationship between the child and the other parent; and, (11) any other relevant factor. M.S.A. §25.312(3); M.C.L.A. §722.23. Grandparent or other third party may only get custody if: (1) child's biological parents were never married; (2) the parent with custody dies or is missing and the other parent has not been granted custody; and, (3) the person seeking custody is related within the 5th degree by marriage, blood, or adoption (grandparent or great-grandparent qualifies). M.S.A. §25.312(6c)–(6e); M.C.L.A. §§722.26c-722.26e.

Parental preference: Yes.

MINNESOTA

The law: Minnesota Statutes Annotated (M.S.A.). Ignore volume numbers; look for "section" numbers.

Grandparent visitation: Visitation may be granted: (1) if the grandparents are the parents of a deceased parent of the child or (2) during or after proceedings for divorce, custody, legal separation, annulment, or paternity. In both situations, it must be determined that visitation is in the child's best interest and will not interfere with the parent-child relationship. When the minor child has resided with the grandparents for a period of twelve months or more and is subsequently removed from the home by the child's parents, the grandparents may request visitation if it is found to be in the best interest of the child and found not to interfere with the parent-child relationship. The court may not deny visitation based on interference with the parent-child relationship unless the court determines by a preponderance of the evidence that the interference would occur. M.S.A. §257C.08.

Effect of adoption: Visitation rights terminate upon adoption by anyone other than a stepparent or grandparent.

Custody statutes: Factors: (1) wishes of the parties; (2) preference of the child, if of sufficient age; (3) child's primary caretaker; (4) intimacy of the relationship between child and each party; (5) interaction and interrelationship between child and the parties, siblings, and other significant persons; (6) child's adjustment to home, school, and community; (7) length of time in a stable, satisfactory environment, and desirability of maintaining continuity; (8) permanence, as a family unit, of the existing or proposed home; (9) mental and physical health of all persons involved; (10) each party's capacity and disposition to give love, affection, and guidance, and to continue educating and raising the child in the child's culture and religion, if any; (11) child's cultural background; (12) effect of any domestic violence on the child; and, (13) any other relevant factor. M.S.A. §518.17. See M.S.A. §518.179 for list of criminal acts that prohibit custody.

Parental preference: No.

MISSISSIPPI

The law: Mississippi Code Annotated 1972 (M.C.).

Grandparent visitation: When a Mississippi court enters a decree awarding custody or terminating the rights of a parent, or when a parent dies, the parents of the noncustodial parent or the deceased parent can be awarded visitation. A grandparent who does not qualify as above can petition for visitation if there is a viable relationship between the child and the grandparent, and the grandparent is unreasonably denied access, and the visits are in the child's best interest. A viable relationship is defined as providing financial support, in whole or in part, for six months; or frequent visits, including overnight, for at least one year. The time granted to grandparents should be less than that given to a parent. By case law, the factors the court must consider are: the amount of disruption extensive visits will have, the suitability of the grandparent's home, the age of the grandchild, the age and health of the grandparent, the emotional ties between the grandparent and the grandchild, the moral fitness of the grandparent, the distance from the grandparent's home to the grandchild's home, any undermining of the parent's general discipline, any employment of the grandparent and the responsibility associated with it, and the willingness of the grandparent to accept that the rearing of the child is the parent's responsibility and they are not to interfere. See *Martin v. Coop,* 693 So.2d 912 (Miss. 1997) Title 93, Section 93-16-1 (M.C. §93-16-1 et. seq.). See *Stacy v. Ross*, 798 So.2d 1275 (Miss. 2001).

Effect of adoption: Visitation rights terminate upon adoption by anyone other than a stepparent or if one of the child's adopted parents was related to the child by blood or marriage before the adoption.

Custody statutes: No statutory factors. Child may choose if at least 12 years of age. Court may require a custody plan from the parties. M.C. §93-13-1 et seq. and 93-23-1 et seq.

Parental preference: Yes.

MISSOURI

The law: Vernon's Annotated Missouri Statutes (A.M.S.). Ignore volume numbers; look for "section" numbers.

Grandparent visitation: Visitation may be granted when the parents of the child have filed for dissolution of their marriage, when one parent of the child is deceased and the surviving parent denies reasonable visitation, when a grandparent is unreasonably denied visitation with the child for a period of more than ninety days, or when a child is adopted by a stepparent, another grandparent, or other blood relative. The court must find that the visitation is in the child's best interest. Chapter 452, Section 452.402 (A.M.S. §452.402). When the parents are living together there is a rebuttable presumption that the parents know what is best for the child. See *Blakely v. Blakely*, 83 S.W.3d 537 (Mo. Banc).

Effect of adoption: The right of a grandparent to seek or maintain visitation may terminate upon the adoption of the child by someone other than a stepparent, another grandparent, or other blood relative.

Custody statutes: Best interest of child considering: (1) wishes of the parties; (2) wishes of the child; (3) interaction and interrelationship between child and parties, siblings, and other significant persons; (4) child's adjustment to home, school, and community; (5) mental and physical health, and any abuse history, of all persons involved; (6) child's needs for continuing relationship with both parties, and the ability and willingness of each to actively perform their duties as mother and father for the needs of the child; (7) any intention of either party to relocate outside the state; (8) which party is more likely to allow frequent and meaningful contact between the child and the other party; and, (9) any other relevant factor. A.M.S. §452.375 et seq.

Parental preference: Yes.

MONTANA

The law: Montana Code Annotated (M.C.A.). Ignore volume numbers; look for "title" numbers.

Grandparent visitation: Visitation may be granted when the court finds that the visitation would be in the child's best interest, including but not limited to a child who is the subject of a disposition made under Title 41. Title 40, Chapter 9, Section 40-9-101 (M.C.A. §40-9-101 et seq.).

Effect of adoption: Visitation rights terminate on adoption by anyone other than a stepparent or a grandparent.

Custody statutes: Factors: (1) parties' wishes; (2) child's wishes; (3) interaction and interrelationship between child and parties, siblings, and other significant persons; (4) child's adjustment to home, school, and community; (5) mental and physical condition of all persons involved; (6) any physical abuse, or threat of physical abuse, against a party or the child; (7) any chemical dependency or abuse of either party; (8) the continuity and stability of care; (9) the developmental needs of the child; (10) any adverse effects of the visits on the child; and, (11) any other relevant factor. M.C.A. §40-4-212.

Parental preference: Yes.

NEBRASKA

The law: Revised Statutes of Nebraska 1943 (R.S.N.). Ignore volume numbers; look for "chapter" numbers.

Grandparent visitation: Visitation may be granted if at least one of the child's parents is deceased, the marriage of the parents has been dissolved or a petition for dissolution is pending, or if the child's parents have never been married but paternity has been legally established. The court must find that there is a significant beneficial relationship between the grandparents and grandchild and that it would be in the best interest of the child to allow the relationship to continue. The visitation cannot adversely interfere with the parent-child relationship. The grandparent must prove these things by clear and convincing evidence, which is a higher standard of proof than in most civil cases. Chapter 43, Section 43-1801 (R.S.N. 1943 §43-1801 et seq.). See *Nelson v. Nelson*, 674 N.W.2d 473 (Neb. 2004).

Effect of adoption: Adoption terminates all rights.

Custody statutes: Best interest of child considering: (1) relationship of child and each party; (2) reasonable desires of the child; and, (3) general health, welfare, and social behavior of child. R.S.N. 1943 §42-364.

Parental preference: Yes.

NEVADA

The law: Nevada Revised Statutes Annotated (N.R.S.A.). Ignore volume numbers; look for "chapter" numbers.

Grandparent visitation: If child's parents are separated or divorced or if one parent is deceased or has relinquished his or her parental rights or had them terminated or has never been married to the other parent but has cohabited with the other parent and is deceased or separated from the other parent, the grandparents and great-grandparents may get visitation if in the best interest of the child. The statute lists specific factors that are to be considered in determining the best interest of the child. Chapter 125C, Section 125C.050 (N.R.S.A. 125C.050). The court must find that the parent has denied or unreasonably restricted visitation between the grandparent and child. There is a rebuttable presumption that the granting of visitation is not in the best interest of the child. To rebut this presumption, the party seeking visitation must prove by clear and convincing evidence that visitation is in the child's best interest. In deciding whether the presumption has been rebutted, the court must consider the following factors: the love, affection, and other emotional ties between the grandparent and the child; the capacity and disposition of the grandparent to give the child love, affection, and guidance and serve as a role model for the child, cooperate in providing the child food, clothing, and other material needs during visitation, and cooperate in providing the child with health care or alternative care recognized and permitted under Nevada law in lieu of health care; the prior relationship between the child and the grandparent, including whether the child resided with the grandparent and was included in holidays and family gatherings with the grandparent; the moral fitness of the grandparent; the mental and physical health of the grandparent; the reasonable preference of the child; the willingness and ability of the grandparent to facilitate and encourage a close and continuing relationship between the child and the parents and between the child and other relatives; the medical and other health needs of the child; the support provided by the party seeking visitation; and, any other factor arising solely from the facts and circumstances of the particular dispute that specifically pertains to the need for granting visitation against the wishes of the parent.

Effect of adoption: Grandparents can get visitation with a grandchild placed for adoption if the petition for visitation is filed with the court before the date on which the parental rights have been terminated and if the court finds that the visitation would be in the best interest of the child.

Custody statutes: Best interest of the child considering: (1) which party is more likely to allow frequent association and a continuing relationship with the other party; (2) wishes of the child, if of sufficient age and intelligence; (3) "any nomination by a parent of a guardian for the child"; and, (4) whether either party has engaged in act of domestic violence against the child, the other party, or other person residing with the child. N.R.S.A. §125.480. See N.R.S.A. §125.510 for required language in decree relating to custody. N.R.S.A. §125.450 et seq.

Parental preference: Yes.

NEW HAMPSHIRE

The law: New Hampshire Revised Statutes Annotated (N.H.R.S.A). Ignore "title" numbers; look for "chapter" numbers.

Grandparent visitation: Visitation may be granted if there is or has been a proceeding under Chapter 458 (for example, for divorce or separation) or if one of the parents is deceased or has had his or her parental rights terminated, and if the visitation is in the best interest of the child. The best interest is to be determined by using the factors set out in the statute. Grandparents may also be awarded visitation if the child is born out-of-wedlock, provided the child has been legitimated. The court must consider the following factors: whether the visits would interfere with any parent-child relationship or with a parent's authority over the child, the best interest of the child, the nature of the relationship between the grandparent and the child including but not limited to the frequency of contact and whether the child has lived with the grandparent and the length of time of such residence, and when there is no reasonable cause to believe that the child's physical or emotional health would be endangered by such visitation or lack of it, and the grandparent and the parent including friction between the parent and grandparent and the effect such friction would have on the child, the circumstances resulting in the absence of a nuclear family, any recommendation by a court appointed guardian ad litem, and the preference of the child. Chapter 458, Section 458:17-d (N.H.R.S.A. 458:17-d).

Effect of adoption: All rights terminate.

Custody statutes: Factors: (1) preference of child and (2) any domestic violence. In divorce cases, joint custody is presumed in child's best interest, unless abuse is shown. Decree must state reasons if joint custody is not ordered. N.H.R.S.A. §458:17.

Parental preference: No.

NEW JERSEY

The law: New Jersey Statutes Annotated (N.J.S.A.). Ignore "article" numbers.

Grandparent visitation: Visitation may be granted if in the best interest of the child, considering: (1) the relationship between the child and the grandparent; (2) the relationship between the parent and the grandparent; (3) the time elapsed since the last contact between the child and the grandparent; (4) the effect visitation will have on the relationship between the child and the custodial parent; (5) if the parents are divorced, the time sharing arrangement between the parents regarding the child; (6) the good faith of the grandparent in filing for visitation; (7) any history of physical, emotional, or sexual abuse or neglect by the grandparent; and, (8) any other relevant factor. If the grandparent had in the past been a full-time caretaker for the child, that is prima facie evidence that the visits are in the child's best interest. Title 9, Chapter 2, Section 9:2-7.1 (N.J.S.A. §9:2-7.1). See *Moriarty v. Bradt*, 827 A.2d 203 (N.J. 2003).

Effect of adoption: All rights terminate unless the adoption is by a stepparent.

Custody statutes: Best interest of the child, considering the following factors: (1) parents' ability to agree, communicate, and cooperate in matters relating to the child; (2) parents' willingness to accept custody and facilitate visitation;

(3) interaction and interrelationship between the child and parents and siblings; (4) any history of domestic violence; (5) preference of child, if of suitable age; (6) needs of child; (7) stability of home environment offered; (8) quality and continuity of education; (9) fitness of parents; (10) geographical proximity of the parties' homes; (11) extent and quality of time with the child before and after separation; (12) employment responsibilities; and (13) age and number of children. Judge must follow the parties agreement, unless he or she determines it is not in the child's best interest. When parties do not agree, judge may require each party to submit a proposed custody plan. N.J.S.A. §§2A:34-23 & 9:2-1 et seq.

Parental preference: Yes.

NEW MEXICO

The law: New Mexico Statutes 1978 Annotated (N.M.S.A.). Ignore "volume" numbers; look for "chapter" numbers.

Grandparent visitation: Visitation may be granted as part of or subsequent to a judgment of dissolution of the parent's marriage, legal separation, or paternity; if one of the parents is deceased; if the child resided with the grandparent for at least three months and the child was less than six years of age at the beginning of the three month period and was subsequently removed from the grandparent's home; or if the child has resided with the grandparent for a period of at least six months when the child is over the age of six at the beginning of the six month period and the child was subsequently removed from the grandparent's home. Court must consider statutory provisions relating to the best interest of the child. Chapter 40, Section 40-9-1 (N.M.S.A. §40-9-1). In determining best interest, the court should consider the prior interaction between the parents and grandparents, the present relationship between the parents and grandparents, the time sharing or visitation arrangements in place prior to the filing of the grandparent visitation action, any prior convictions of the grandparent for abuse or neglect, and whether the grandparent has been a previous caregiver for the child. See *Gutierrez v. Connick*, 87 P.3d 552 (N.M. App. 2003).

Effect of adoption: Grandparents may obtain visitation after adoption by a stepparent, a relative of the grandchild, a person designated to care for the grandchild in the provisions of a deceased parent's will, or a person who sponsored the grandchild at a baptism or confirmation conducted by a recognized religious organization.

Custody statutes: Best interest of the child, considering: (1) wishes of parties; (2) wishes of child; (3) interaction and interrelationship between the child and parties, siblings, and other significant persons; (4) child's adjustment to home, school, and community; and, (5) mental and physical condition of all persons involved. Other factors are also listed in considering joint custody between parents. N.M.S.A. §40-4-9 et seq.

Parental preference: Yes.

NEW YORK

The law: McKinney's Consolidated Laws of New York Annotated, Domestic Relations Law (C.L.N.Y., D.R.L.). Be sure you use the volumes marked "Domestic Relations."

Grandparent visitation: Visitation may be granted when at least one of the child's parents is deceased or when circumstances show that conditions exist that equity would see fit to intervene. Visitation must also be in the best interest of the child. *Note:* There are some court cases that say courts do not generally permit grandparent visitation over the objections of both parents. C.L.N.Y., D.R.L. §72. It may be possible for grandparents to get visitation even in situations when the nuclear family is intact and over the objections of the parents. See *Wilson v. McGlinchey*, 811 N.E.2d 526 (N.Y. App. 2004).

Effect of adoption: Visitation can be continued after adoption.

Custody statutes: Best interest of child. No statutory factors. C.L.N.Y., D.R.L. §240.

Parental preference: Yes.

NORTH CAROLINA

The law: General Statutes of North Carolina. (G.S.N.C.). Ignore "volume" numbers; look for "chapter" numbers.

Grandparent visitation: Visitation may be granted as a part of any order determining custody of the child. Chapter 50, Section 50-13.2 (G.S.N.C. §50-13.2).

Effect of adoption: Visitation rights terminate unless the adoption is by a stepparent or a relative of the child and a substantial relationship exists between the grandparent and the child.

Custody statutes: No statutory factors other than best interest of child. G.S.N.C. §50-13 et seq.

Parental preference: Yes.

NORTH DAKOTA

The law: North Dakota Century Code Annotated (N.D.C.C.). Ignore "volume" numbers; look for "title" numbers.

Grandparent visitation: A grandparent may be granted reasonable visitation rights upon a finding that visitation would be in the best interest of the child and would not interfere with the parent/child relationship. The court must consider the amount of personal contact that has occurred between the grandparent and the child and the parent. Title 14, Chapter 14-09, Section 14-09-05.1 (N.D.C.C. §14-09-05.1).

Effect of adoption: If a grandparent already has visitation rights prior to the adoption, those rights can be terminated upon adoption if found to be in the child's best interest.

Custody statutes: Factors: (1) love, affection, and emotional ties between child and each party; (2) each party's capacity and disposition to give love, affection, and guidance, and to continue the child's education; (3) each party's disposition to provide food, clothing, medical care, and other material needs; (4) length of time the child has been in a stable, satisfactory environment, and the desirability of maintaining continuity; (5) the permanence, as a family unit, of the existing or proposed custodial home; (6) moral fitness of the parties; (7) mental and physical health of the parties; (8) child's home, school, and community record; (9) the reasonable preference of the child, if of sufficient intelligence, understanding, and experience; (10) any existence of domestic violence; (11) the interaction and interrelationship between the child and parties, siblings, and other significant persons; and, (12) any other relevant factor. N.D.C.C. §§14-05-22 and 14-09 et seq.

Parental preference: Yes.

OHIO

The law: Page's Ohio Revised Code Annotated (O.R.C.).

Grandparent visitation: Visitation may be granted as a part of or subsequent to the parents' divorce, dissolution of marriage, legal separation, annulment, or child support proceeding if grandparent has an interest in welfare of child and visitation would be in child's best interest. Also if the child's parents were never married to each other. If one of the child's parents is deceased, the parent of that parent may seek visitation. Title 31, Section 3109.051 (O.R.C. §§3109.051 and 3109.11). In deciding whether or not to grant visitation, the court should consider the following factors: the prior interaction and interrelationships between the child, the parents, and the grandparent; the respective geographical locations; the available time for the child and the parents; the age of the child; the child's adjustment to home, school, and community; the wishes of the child; the mental and physical health of all the parties; the willingness of the parties to reschedule missed time; any child abuse or neglect convictions; the wishes and concerns of the parents as expressed to the court; and, any other factors relevant to the best interest of the child. See *Harrold v. Collier*, 2005 Ohio LEXIS 2241.

Effect of adoption: Visitation rights terminate upon adoption unless the adoption is by a stepparent.

Custody statutes: Best interest of the child, considering: (1) wishes of parties; (2) child's wishes, if interviewed by judge; (3) interaction and interrelationship between child and parents, siblings, and other significant persons; (4) child's adjustment to home, school, and community; (5) mental and physical condition of all persons involved; (6) party more likely to honor and facilitate visitation; (7) compliance with any child support orders; (8) any history of abuse or neglect; (9) any history of visitation denial; and, (10) whether a party intends to make his or her residence outside of Ohio. O.R.C. §3109 et seq.

Parental preference: Yes.

OKLAHOMA

The law: Oklahoma Statutes Annotated (O.S.A.).

Grandparent visitation: A grandparent may seek visitation if it is in the best interest of the child **and** there is a showing of parental unfitness or unsuitability or that the child would suffer harm or potential harm without the visits *and* an action for divorce, separate maintenance, or annulment is pending or an order in one of these types of cases has been entered; the grandparent is the parent of a deceased parent of the child; if legal custody has been given to persons other than the parent or if the child does not reside with a parent; if the grandparent had custody of the child and there is a strong, continuous relationship between the grandparent and the child; the child's parent has deserted the other parent for more than one year and there is a strong, continuous relationship between the grandparent and child; if the parental rights have been terminated and there is a strong, continuous relationship between the grandparent and child; or any other time and for any reason the court deems is in the best interest. Title 10, Section 5 (10 O.S.A. § 5). See *O'Neal v. Ogle*, 91 P.3d 646 (Okla. 2004).

Effect of adoption: If a parent's parental rights have been terminated, the parent of that parent may seek visitation (1) if there is a previous relationship between the grandparent and the grandchild and (2) if the visits are in the child's best interest.

Custody statutes: Factors: (1) physical, mental, and moral welfare of child and (2) child's preference. It is presumed against child's best interest for party guilty of domestic violence to have custody. 43 O.S.A. §112 et seq.

Parental preference: Yes.

OREGON

The law: Oregon Revised Statutes Annotated (O.R.S.). Ignore "volume" numbers; look for "chapter" numbers.

Grandparent visitation: Grandparents may seek visitation if there is a strong, emotional tie or an ongoing personal relationship between the grandparent and the child. There is a presumption that a fit parent acts in the best interest of the child, and the person seeking visitation must rebut that presumption. Factors the court should consider: if the grandparent has been a primary caretaker; if circumstances detrimental to the child would result is the visitation is not granted; if the parent has fostered, encouraged, or consented to the relationship; if granting the visitation would not substantially interfere with the custodial relationship; or, if the parent has unreasonably denied or limited contact between the child and the grandparent Chapter 109, Section 109.119 (O.R.S. § 109.119).

Effect of adoption: Visitation rights terminate upon adoption.

Custody statutes: Factors: (1) emotional ties between the child and other family members; (2) each party's interest in and attitude toward the child; (3) desirability of continuing existing relationships; and, (4) any abuse of one party by the other. Conduct and lifestyle are only considered if it is causing or may cause emotional or physical damage to the child (this will require strong proof). O.R.S. §§107.105 & 107.137.

Parental preference: Yes.

PENNSYLVANIA

The law: Purdon's Pennsylvania Consolidated Statutes Annotated (Pa.C.S.A.).

Grandparent visitation: Visitation may be granted when at least one of the parents of the child is deceased, when the parents' marriage is dissolved or the parents have been separated for six months or more, or when the child has resided with the grandparents for twelve months or more and is subsequently removed from the home by the parents. The court must find that the visitation is in the best interest of the child and will not interfere with the parent-child relationship and must consider the amount of personal contact between the child and the grandparent prior to the application. If the visitation is based on a deceased parent, only the parents of the deceased parent qualify. If access is sought under the provision in which the child has lived with the grandparent for twelve months, the grandparent can seek partial custody. Title 23, Section 5311 (23 Pa.C.S.A. § 5311 et seq.).

Effect of adoption: Visitation rights terminate unless the child is adopted by either a stepparent or grandparents.

Custody statutes: Best interest of child based upon which party is more likely to encourage and allow frequent and continuing contact with the other parent. A grandparent can seek custody if it is in the best interest of the child not to be in the custody of either parent and is in the best interest of the child for the grandparent to have custody because the grandparent has either assumed the parenting role for at least twelve months or because the child is at substantial risk because of parental abuse, neglect, alcohol or drug abuse, or mental illness. 23 Pa.C.S.A. §5300 et seq.

Parental preference: Yes.

RHODE ISLAND

The law: 1988 Reenactment of the General Laws of Rhode Island 1956 (G.L.R.I.). Ignore "title" and "chapter" numbers; look for "section" numbers.

Grandparent visitation: Visitation may be granted if the court finds that it is in the best interest of the child for the grandparent to be given visitation, that the grandparent is a fit and proper person to have visitation, that the grandparent has repeatedly attempted to visit the grandchild during the six months immediately preceding the filing of the application and was not allowed to visit as a direct result of the actions of either or both of the parents, that there is no other way the grandparent is able to visit the child, and that the grandparent by clear and convincing evidence has successfully rebutted the presumption that the parent's decision to refuse the grandparent visitation was reasonable. Visitation may also be granted if the grandparent's child is deceased or if the child's parents are divorced. G.L.R.I. §15-5-24.1 et seq.

Effect of adoption: Adoption terminates all rights.

Custody statutes: Best interest of child. No statutory factors. G.L.R.I. §15-5-16 et seq.

Parental preference: Yes.

SOUTH CAROLINA

The law: Code of Laws of South Carolina 1976 (C.L.S.C.). Ignore "volume" numbers; look for "title" numbers.

Grandparent visitation: A grandparent may be awarded visitation if one of the parents is deceased or the parents are divorced or separated. The court must make a written finding that the visits are in the child's best interest and will not interfere with the parent-child relationship. The court must consider the nature of the relationship between the child and the grandparents prior to the filing of the request for visitation. Title 20, Section 20-7-420 (C.L.S.C. §20-7-420). Case law creates a presumption that a fit parent acts in the best interest of the child, and there is a case that goes on to say that it is seldom in the child's best interest for grandparents to have visitation when the grandparent's child who is the parent of the grandchild has access to the grandchild. Parental unfitness must be shown by clear and convincing evidence. See *Latimer v. Farmer*, 602 S.E.2d 32 (SC 2004) and *Camburn v. Smith*, 586 S.E.2d 565 (SC 2003).

Effect of adoption: Adoption terminates all rights.

Custody statutes: Determined "...as from the circumstances of the parties and the nature of the case and the best spiritual as well as other interests of the children as may be fit, equitable and just." C.L.S.C. §20-3-160.

Parental preference: No.

SOUTH DAKOTA

The law: South Dakota Codified Laws (S.D.C.L.). Ignore "volume" numbers; look for "title" numbers.

Grandparent visitation: A court may grant visitation to grandparents if it is in the best interest of the child and will not significantly interfere with the parent-child relationship or if the parent has denied or prevented a reasonable opportunity for the grandparent to visit the child. See *Currey v. Currey*, 650 N.E.2d 272 (S.D. 2003).

Effect of adoption: Visitation rights terminate upon adoption unless the adoption is by a stepparent or grandparent.

Custody statutes: Only statutory reference is that custody is to be determined "as may seem necessary and proper." S.D.C.L. §25-4-45.

Parental preference: Yes.

TENNESSEE

The law: Tennessee Code Annotated (T.C.A.). Ignore "volume" numbers; look for "section" numbers.

Grandparent visitation: The statute provides: (1) If one parent is deceased, then the parent of the deceased parent can get visitation; (2) if the parents are divorced or legally separated, any grandparent may request visitation; (3) if the child's parent is missing for at least six months, the parents of the missing parent can seek visitation; (4) if a court in another state has ordered grandparent visitation, those grandparents may seek visitation; (5) the child resided in the home of the grandparents for twelve months or more and was subsequently removed by the parent; and, (6) the child and the grandparent maintained a significant existing relationship for a period of twelve months or more immediately preceding the severance of the relationship, and the relationship was severed by the parent for reasons other than abuse or the presence of a danger of substantial harm to the child, and severance is likely to cause substantial emotional harm. In considering a petition for grandparent visitation, the court must first determine the presence of a danger of substantial harm to the child. Such a finding may be based on the cessation of the relationship between the child and the grandparent, upon proof that (1) the child had such a significant existing relationship with the grandparent that the loss of the relationship is likely to occasion severe emotional harm to the child; (2) the grandparent functioned as a primary caregiver, such that cessation of the relationship could interrupt the provision of the daily needs of the child and thus occasion physical or emotional harm; or, (3) the child has a significant existing relationship with the grandparent and the loss of the relationship presents a danger of other direct and substantial harm to the child. A significant relationship is defined as (1) the child lived with the grandparent for six consecutive months; (2) the grandparent was a full-time caretaker for six consecutive months; or, (3) the grandparent had frequent visits for a period of at least one year. The court must find visitation is in the child's best interest, considering the following factors: (1) the length and quality of the prior relationship between the child and the grandparents; (2) the existing emotional ties of the child to the grandparents; (3) the preference of the child; (4) the effect of hostility between the grandparents and parents of the child, manifested before the child, and the willingness of the grandparents, except in cases of abuse, to encourage a close relationship between the child and the parents; and, (5) the good faith of the grandparents in filing for visitation; (6) with a divorce or separation, the time sharing arrangements between the parents and the child; or, (7) if one parent is deceased or missing, the fact that the grandparents are the parent of the deceased or missing parent of the child. If the child has been removed from the parents' home, the grandparents must also prove that they would adequately protect the child and that they are not implicated in certain specified acts against the child. Title 36, Sections 36-6-302 to 36-6-307 (T.C.A. §§36-6-302 to 36-6-307). See *In re B.E.D.*, 2004 Tenn. App. Lexis 177.

Effect of adoption: Visitation rights terminate upon adoption unless the adoption is by a stepparent or other relative of the child.

Custody statutes: Best interest of child "as the welfare and interest of the child or children may demand." T.C.A. §36-6-101 et seq.

Parental preference: Yes.

TEXAS

The law: Vernon's Texas Codes Annotated (V.T.C.A.).

Grandparent visitation: The court shall order reasonable visitation if at the time the visitation is requested, at least one biological or adoptive parent has not had that parent's parental rights terminated; the grandparent requesting the visitation overcomes the presumption that a parent acts in the best interest of the child by proving that denial of visitation would significantly impair the child's physical health or emotional well-being; and, the grandparent requesting visitation is a parent of a parent of the child who (1) has been incarcerated during the three month period preceding the filing of the petition; (2) has been found by a court to be incompetent; (3) is dead; or, (4) does not have actual or court-ordered possession of or access to the child. V.T.C.A., Family Code §153.433.

Effect of adoption: If the child has been adopted by anyone other than a stepparent, then grandparents cannot petition the court for access to the child.

Custody statutes: Factors: (1) qualifications of the parents and (2) any evidence of intentional use of abusive force against spouse or any person under age 18 within the past two years. V.T.C.A., Family Code. §14.01.

Parental preference: Yes.

UTAH

The law: Utah Code Annotated (U.C.). Ignore "volume" numbers; look for "title" numbers.

Grandparent visitation: Grandparents can bring suit in accordance with this section or during a pending divorce or other proceeding involving custody or visitation issues. There is a rebuttable presumption that a parent's decision in regard to grandparent visitation is in the child's best interest. In determining whether or not the grandparents have rebutted this presumption, the court shall consider relevant factors, including whether the grandparent is a fit and proper person to have visitation with the child; visitation with the child has been denied or unreasonably limited; the parent is unfit or incompetent; the grandparent has acted as the child's custodian or caregiver, or otherwise has had a substantial relationship with the child, and the loss or cessation of that relationship is likely to cause harm to the grandchild; the grandparent's child who is a parent of the grandchild has died or has become a noncustodial parent through divorce or legal separation or has been missing for an extended period of time; visitation is in the best interest of the child; or, the wishes of the child. Title 30, Chapter 5, Section 30-5-2 (U.C. §30-5-2). (See also U.C. §30-3-5.)

Effect of adoption: Adoption terminates visitation rights unless the adoption is by a stepparent or if the court finds that a relationship has been established with the grandparent and continued contact is in the best interest of the child.

Custody statutes: Best interest of child considering (1) past conduct and demonstrated moral standards of the parties; (2) child's wishes; (3) which party is most likely to act in the child's best interest, including allowing contact with the other party; and, (4) any other relevant factor. U.C. §30-3-10.

Parental preference: Yes.

VERMONT

The law: Vermont Statutes Annotated (V.S.A.). Ignore "chapter" numbers; look for "title" numbers.

Grandparent visitation: Visitation may be granted when an action for custody or visitation is or has been considered by the court, or if the grandparent's child is dead, physically or mentally incompetent, or has abandoned the child. The court must find that the visitation is in the child's best interest after considering the statutory factors relating to best interest. The court shall grant visitation upon a finding that it is in the best interest of the child. Factors in determining best interest are: the love, affection, and other emotional ties between the grandparent and the child; the capacity and disposition of the parties involved to give the child love and affection and guidance; the nature of the relationship between the grandparent and the child and the desirability of maintaining that relationship; the moral fitness of the parties; the mental and physical health of the parties; the reasonable preference of the child; the willingness of the grandparents to facilitate and encourage a close and continuing relationship between the child and the parents; or, any other factor the court considers relevant. There is a Vermont Supreme Court case that ruled that this statute was unconstitutionally applied and further ruled that a parental decision must be given a presumption of validity. Title 15, Section 1011 et seq. (15 V.S.A. §§1011 et seq.) See *Glidden v. Conley*, 820 A.2d 197 (Vt. 2003).

Effect of adoption: Visitation rights terminate unless the child is adopted by a stepparent or a relative of the child.

Custody statutes: Best interest of the child considering: (1) relationship of the child and each party, and each party's ability and disposition to provide love, affection, and guidance; (2) ability and disposition to provide food, clothing, medical care, other material needs, and a safe environment; (3) ability and disposition to meet the child's present and future developmental needs; (4) quality of the child's adjustment to present housing, school, and community, and potential effect of a change; (5) ability and disposition to foster a continuing relationship with the other party; (6) quality of the child's relationship with the primary caregiver; (7) child's relationship to other significant persons; and, (8) ability and disposition of the parties to make joint decisions. 15 V.S.A. §665.

Parental preference: Yes.

VIRGINIA

The law: Code of Virginia 1950 Annotated (C.V.). Ignore "chapter" numbers; look for "title" and "section" numbers.

Grandparent visitation: In any case in which custody is an issue, the court can, after giving due regard to the primacy of the parent/child relationship, find upon a showing by clear and convincing evidence that the best interest of the child would be served by awarding visitation to any nonparent with a legitimate interest. (C.V. § 20-124.2B) See *Yipp v. Hodges*, 598 S.E.2d 760 (Va. App. 2004).

Effect of adoption: Adoption terminates all rights.

Custody statutes: Best interest of child considering: (1) age, physical, and mental condition of the child and parties; (2) relationship between the child and each party; (3) needs of the child; (4) the role each party played, and will play, in the child's upbringing and care; (5) any history of family abuse; and, (6) any other relevant factor. C.V. §20-1-7.2. 20-107.2.

Parental preference: Yes.

WASHINGTON

The law: West's Revised Code of Washington Annotated (R.C.W.A.).

Grandparent visitation: A grandparent may petition for visitation at any time in a pending dissolution, legal separation, or modification of parenting plan proceeding if the grandparent can show by clear and convincing evidence that a significant relationship with the child exists and that the visitation is in the child's best interest. In determining best interest, the court may consider the following factors: the strength of the relationship between the child and the grandparent; the relationship between each of the child's parents and the grandparent; the nature and reason for either parent's objection to the visitation; the effect that granting visitation will have on the relationship between the child and the parents; the residential time sharing arrangements between the parents; the good faith of the grandparent; any criminal history or history of physical, emotional, or sexual abuse or neglect by the grandparent; or, any other factor relevant to the child's best interest. The Washington Supreme Court has ruled this statute unconstitutional. Title 26, Chapter 26.09, Section 26.09.240 (R.C.W.A. §26.09.240). See *Appel v. Appel*, 109 P.3d 405 (Wash. 2005).

Effect of adoption: Adoption terminates all rights.

Custody statutes: (1) Each party's relative strength, nature, and stability of the relationship with the child, including which party has taken greater responsibility for the child; (2) any agreement of the parties; (3) each party's past and potential for future performance of parenting functions; (4) child's emotional needs and development; (5) the child's relationship with siblings and any other significant adults, and involvement in his or her physical surroundings, school, and other activities; (6) the wishes of the parties and the child; and, (7) each party's employment schedule. The greatest weight is given to factor (1). R.C.W.A. §26.09.187. See also §26.10 for provisions applicable to custody for nonparents.

Parental preference: Yes.

WEST VIRGINIA

The law: West Virginia Code (W.V.C.). Ignore "volume" numbers; look for "chapter" numbers.

Grandparent visitation: Grandparents may petition for visitation whether or not the parents are married. The court must consider the following factors: the age of the child, the relationship between the child and the grandparent, the relationship between the grandparent and the parent, the amount of time since the last contact between the child and the grandparent, the effect the visits will have on the parent-child relationship, any custody or visitation agreements, the time available to the child and the parent, the good faith of the grandparent, any history of abuse, whether the child has lived with the grandparent in the past or the grandparent has been a caretaker of the child, and the preferences of the parent as to visits. If the grandparent's petition is filed as part of a divorce, custody, separation, annulment, or paternity proceeding, the grandparent must prove that the visits are in the child's best interest and that the grandparent's child has failed to appear or their whereabouts are unknown. If the petition is not filed as part of one of the above proceedings, and the grandparent's child has custody or visitation that would allow grandparents visitation if it were allowed by the parent, there is a rebuttable presumption against visitation. (W.V.C. §48-10-101 et seq.). See *State ex rel Brandon L. v. Moats*, 551 S.E.2d 674 (W.Va. 2001).

Effect of adoption: Adoption terminates all rights.

Custody statutes: No statutory factors. Presumption in favor of primary caretaker. W.V.C. §48-2-15.

Parental preference: Yes.

WISCONSIN

The law: West's Wisconsin Statutes Annotated (W.S.A.). Ignore "chapter" numbers; look for "section" numbers.

Grandparent visitation: Visitation may be granted if the grandparent has maintained a relationship with the child similar to the parent-child relationship. The court is to consider the best interest of the child and the wishes of the child. Visitation may also be granted to grandparents if one of the child's parents is deceased and the court finds that the visitation is in the child's best interest. The court must also find that the grandparent has not acted contrary to decisions made by the parent. Conviction of certain listed crimes will disqualify a grandparent from visitation. W.S.A. §§880.155 and 767.245. Case law requires the court to give presumptive weight to a parent's decision about visitation. See *In Re Paternity of Roger D.H.*, 641 N.W.2d 440 (Wi. App. 2002).

Effect of adoption: Adoption has no effect on the grandparent's rights if the adoption is by the stepparent.

Custody statutes: Referred to as "legal custody and physical placement." Best interest of the child considering: (1) wishes of parties; (2) wishes of child; (3) interaction and interrelationship between child and the parties, siblings, and any other significant person; (4) child's adjustment to home, school, and community; (5) mental and physical health of all parties involved; (6) availability of public or private child care services; (7) whether one party is likely to unreasonably interfere with the child's continuing relationship with the other party; (8) any evidence of child abuse; (9) any evidence of interspousal battery or domestic abuse; (10) whether either party has had a significant problem with alcohol or drug abuse; and, (11) any other relevant factor. W.S.A. §767.24.

Parental preference: Yes.

WYOMING

The law: Wyoming Statutes Annotated (W.S.A.). Ignore "volume" numbers; look for "title" numbers.

Grandparent visitation: Visitation may be granted if it is in the child's best interest and the rights of the child's parents are not substantially impaired. Title 20, Chapter 7, Section 20-7-101 (W.S.A. §20-7-101).

Effect of adoption: Right terminates upon adoption if neither adopting parent is a natural parent of the child.

Custody statutes: Custody to be determined "...as appears most expedient and beneficial for the well-being of the children. The court shall consider the relative competency of both parents and no award of custody shall be made solely on the basis of gender of the parent." No other statutory factors. W.S.A. §20-2-201 et seq.

Parental preference: Yes.

Resources

While this book serves as a thorough legal guide to the rights of grand-parents, you may find additional resources helpful in your situation. There are social issues that can interfere with the relationship between you and your children or your grandchildren. This appendix of websites, organizations, and hotlines identifies problems that families may face, and what may result in legal action. Use this appendix to help your family deal with these issues without having to go to court.

WEBSITES:

Adoption:

http://naic.acf.hhs.gov/general/nad/index.cfm
Directory listed by state of adoption organizations

http://relative.adoption.com
Information and considerations for relatives considering adoption

http://parenting.adoption.com/parents/grandparents-as-parents.html
Information for adopting Grandparents, including legal options

Child Abuse:

www.childhelpusa.org
Information on helping abused children, including counseling and how to report abuse

www.helpguide.org
Links to information on understanding and coping with child abuse

http://nccanch.acf.hhs.gov
Information on identifying, preventing, and reporting child abuse

Crime:
http://prisonerswithchildren.org/pubs/gpmanual/visit.htm
Answers to legal questions and information on grandparent visitation rights

Death and Grief:
www.helpguide.org
Information and strategies on how to cope with grief

Divorce:
www.divorcehq.com/grandparent.html
Information on grandparents' rights to visitation after divorce, links to divorce attorneys listed by state

www.divorcelinks.com
Divorce laws organized by state

www.divorcenet.com
Specific information on state laws and finding a lawyer

www.divorcesource.com/info/grandparents/grandparents.shtml
Information for grandparents on legal procedures for enforcing visitation and issues between parents and grandparents

Domestic Violence (including Sexual Abuse):
www.allaboutcounseling.com/domestic_violence.htm
Answers questions dealing with domestic violence

www.allaboutcounseling.com/sexual_abuse.htm
Answers questions dealing with sexual abuse

www.helpguide.org
Links to information for understanding and coping with domestic violence

www.ncjfcj.org/content/view/20/94
Information for helping victims of domestic violence

www.tameside.gov.uk/leavingcare/domesticviol.htm
Information about obtaining court orders for custody of children of domestic violence

Grandparents Raising Children:
www.aarp.org
Guidance for relationships between grandparents and grandchildren

www.acf.hhs.gov/index.html
Information for families dealing with social issues (adoption, drug abuse, etc.)

www.brookdalefoundation.org
Partners with community organizations to ensure grandparents obtain information about services associated with assuming a parental role

www.familymanagement.com/facts/english/grandparents_kids.html
Information and articles for grandparents raising grandchildren, with links to sections addressing children's issues (i.e., sexual abuse, depression, adoption)

www.grandparentagain.com
Information about raising grandchildren, including stories about court experiences and advice on reporting child abuse

www.grandparenting.org
Open forum for grandparent concerns; includes articles

www.grandparentsrights.org
Nonprofit organization for grandparents' rights

http://nccanch.acf.hhs.gov/topics/prevention/supporting/tips_resources/grandparents.cfm
Tips for grandparents raising grandchildren

Legal Issues:

www.abanet.org
American Bar Association—Resource to finding a lawyer

www.abanet.org/aging/chapter/home.html
American Bar Association—Grandparents' rights to visitation, details about legal procedures

www.aoa.gov/prof/notes/notes_grandparents.asp
Links to legal information for grandparents raising children

www.cyberparent.com/gran
Link to information and articles for grandparents raising children, including visitation rights after divorce and going to court

www.expertlaw.com/library/child_custody/grandparents_rights.html
Discusses arguments for and against grandparent rights

www.fullcirclecare.org/grandparents/grandlegal.htm
Guide through the court system for grandparents raising grandchildren

www.grandparenting.org/Grandparent%20Visitation.htm
Current information on grandparent visitation laws and state statutes

www.infoline.org/InformationLibrary/Documents/Custodial%20Grandparents%20pt.asp
Explanation and definitions of grandparent guardianship, termination of parental rights, and adopting grandchildren

www.grandsplace.com
Link to legal resources on custody and visitation, specific state statutes included

www.firstgov.gov/Topics/Grandparents.shtml
Links to other websites and resources for grandparent guidance

http://prisonerswithchildren.org/pubs/gpmanual/visit.htm
#terminated
Answers questions about visitation rights of grandparents

www.raisingyourgrandchildren.com/Legal_Issues.htm
Links to information on legal and financial assistance for grandparents

Mental Health Disorders:

www.aacap.org
American Academy of Child & Adolescent Psychiatry

www.helpguide.org
Links to information for understanding and coping with children who have mental health issues

Rape and Sexual Abuse:

www.voices-action.org
International organization providing assistance to victims of sexual abuse and rape

Runaway and Exploited Children:

www.nrscrisisline.org
Provides information about parenting teenagers, as well as information for teenagers and runaways

Substance and Drug Abuse:

www.aarp.org/families/grandparents/raising_grandchild/a2004-09-01-grandparents-addiction.html
Information and resources for grandparents dealing with drug abusing children

www.drugfreeinfo.org/aparents.html
Links to websites with information on drug and substance abuse prevention

www.helpguide.org
Links to information for understanding and coping with drug abuse

ORGANIZATIONS:

Adoption:

Association of Administrators of the Interstate Compact for the Placement of Children (ICPC)
American Public Human Services Association
810 First Street NE
Suite 500
Washington, DC 20002-4267
202-682-0100
http://icpc.aphsa.org
Guide through the procedures of children placement in adoptive, foster, or relative homes

National Adoption Information Clearinghouse
330 C Street, SW
Washington, DC 20447
703-352-3488
888-251-0075
http://naic.acf.hhs.gov
Directory listed by state of adoption organizations

Child Abuse:

Administration for Children and Families
370 L'Enfant Promenade, SW
Washington, DC 20447
www.acf.hhs.gov
(see website for phone contact specific to region)
Government organization for child welfare

National Association of Child Care Resource and Referral Agencies (NACCRRA)
3101 Wilson Boulevard
Suite 350
Arlington, VA 22201
703-341-4100
www.naccrra.net
Directory for communities to assist in finding child care

National Clearinghouse on Child Abuse and Neglect Information
330 C Street, SW
Washington, DC 20447
703-385-7565
800-394-3366
http://nccanch.acf.hhs.gov
Information on identifying, preventing, and reporting child abuse

Divorce:

American Association for Marriage and Family Therapy
112 South Alfred Street
Alexandria, VA 22314-3061
703-838-9808
www.aamft.org
Information to assist in family relationships

American Association for Geriatric Psychiatry (AAGP)
7910 Woodmont Avenue
Suite 1050
Bethesda, MD 20814-3004
301-654-7850
www.aagpgpa.org/p_c/marriage.asp
Discusses effects of divorce later in life

Grandparenting Support:

AARP Grandparent Information Center (GIC)
601 E Street NW
Washington, DC 20049
888-OUR-AARP (687-2277)
www.aarp.org
Addresses issues facing grandparents raising grandchildren

Brookdale Foundation Relatives as Parents Program (RAPP)
950 Third Avenue
19th Floor
New York, NY 10022
212-308-7355
www.brookdalefoundation.org
Partners with community organizations to ensure grandparents obtain information about services associated with assuming a parental role

Center for Family Connections (CFFC)
350 Cambridge Street
Cambridge, MA 02141
617-547-0909
800-KINNECT (546-6328)
www.kinnect.org
Information for families affected by adoption, foster care, kinship, and guardianship

Children's Defense Fund (CDF)
25 E Street NW
Washington, DC 20001
202-628-8787
www.childrensdefense.org
Information and resources on the well-being of children raised by relatives

Grandparents Rights Organization
100 West Long Lake Road
Suite 250
Bloomfield Hills, MI 48304
248-646-7177
www.grandparentsrights.org
Nonprofit organization supporting grandparents' rights

Legal Issues:

Center for Communication and Consumer Services
U.S. Administration on Aging
Washington, DC 20201
202-619-0724
www.aoa.gov
Links to legal information for grandparents raising children

Generations United
1333 H Street, NW
Suite 500
Washington, DC 20005
202-289-3979
www.gu.org
Organization promoting intergenerational unity, with link to information for relatives caring for children

National Committee of Grandparents for Children's Rights, Inc.
School of Social Welfare
HSC
Level 2
Room 093
Stony Brook University
Stony Brook, NY 11794-8231
866-624-9900
http://grandparentsforchildren.org
Grandparents concerned with their relationship with their grandchildren, with information about visitation rights

Mental Health Disorders:

National Mental Health Association
2001 North Beauregard Street
12th Floor
Alexandria, Virginia 22311
703-684-7722
800-969-NMHA (6642)
www.nmha.org
Nonprofit organization supporting mental health and mental illnesses

Federation of Families for Children's Mental Health
1101 King Street
Suite 420
Alexandria, VA 22314
703-684-7710
www.ffcmh.org
Network of family organizations to assist in raising mentally ill children

Substance and Drug Abuse:

American Council on Alcoholism (ACA)
1000 East Indian School Road
Phoenix, AZ 85014
800-527-5344
www.aca-usa.org
Promotes education of the effects and treatment of alcohol abusers

National Council on Alcoholism and Drug Dependence, Inc.
22 Cortlandt Street
Suite 801
New York, NY 10007-3128
212-269-7797
www.ncadd.org
HOPE LINE: 800/NCA-CALL (24-hour affiliate referral)
Information for the public about alcoholism and drug abuse

National Families in Action
2957 Clairmont Road NE
Suite 150
Atlanta, Georgia 30329
404-248-9676
www.nationalfamilies.org
Information on drug abuse prevention for children

The Family
555 SW 148th Avenue
Sunrise, FL 33325
800-41-SOBER
800-417-6237
www.thefamilyrecovery.com
Drug rehabilitation center with information on intervention and recovery

Violence—Criminal, Domestic, and Sexual:

Criminal Justice Center
Minnesota Program Development, Inc.
2104 4th Avenue
Suite B
Minneapolis, MN 55404
612-824-8768
Criminal justice system addressing domestic violence

National Coalition Against Domestic Violence
P.O. Box 18749
Denver, CO 80218-0749
303-839-1852
www.ncadv.org
Information and support for community-based programs for women and children who are victims of domestic violence

HOTLINES:

Adoption:

American Adoption
800-ADOPTION

Independent Adoption Center
800-877-6736

National Adoption Center
800-TO-ADOPT

Child Abuse:

ChildHelp USA National Child Abuse Hotline
800-4-A-CHILD
800-2-A-CHILD (TDD for hearing impaired)

Department of Social Services
Adoption/Children's programs: 800-345-KIDS
Child Abuse Hotline: 800-342-3720
National Child Abuse Hotline: 800-25-ABUSE

Youth Crisis Hotline
800-HIT-HOME (448-4663)

Crime:

National Center for Victims of Crime
800-FYI-CALL (394-2255)

National Victim Center
800-FYI-CALL (394-2255)

WAVE (Working Against Violence Everywhere)
888-960-9600

Death and Grief:

National Grief Recovery Help Line
800-848-9595

National Depression Association
800-826-3632

Divorce:

Divorce—Dealing with Parents' Divorce
Boys Town Hotline (for Girls AND Boys)
800-448-3000

Domestic Violence:

Domestic Violence Hotline
800-829-1122

Family Violence Prevention Fund
800-313-1310

National Domestic Violence/Child Abuse/Sexual Abuse
800-799-SAFE (7233)
800-787-3224 (TDD)
800-942-6908 (Spanish)

National Resource Center on Domestic Violence
800-537-2238

Mental Health Disorders:

Alzheimer's Association Hotline
800-621-0379

CHADD—Children & Adults with Attention Deficit/Hyper-activity Disorder
800-233-4050

Mental Health InfoSource
800-447-4474

National Institute of Mental Health
888-ANXIETY (269-4389)

National Mental Health Association
800-969-6642

National Center for Learning Disabilities
888-575-7373

National Respite Locator Service
800-773-5433

Rape and Sexual Abuse:

Rape, Abuse, and Incest National Network (RAINN)
800-656-4673

Stop It Now!
888-PREVENT (773-8368)

Sexual Assault Hotline
800-656-4673

Society's League Against Molestation
800-491-WATCH

Voices in Action
800-7-VOICE-8 (786-4238)

Runaway and Exploited Children:

Child Find of America Hotline
800-I-AM-LOST (426-5678)
800-A-WAY-OUT (292-9688)

Child Quest International Sighting Line
888-818-HOPE (4673)

Missing Children Network
800-235-3535

National Child Safety Council Childwatch
800-222-1464

National Hotline for Missing and Exploited Children
800-843-5678

National Runaway Switchboard
800-621-4000

Operation Lookout National Center for Missing Youth
800-LOOKOUT (566-5688)

Parent Abduction Hotline
800-292-9688

Runaway Hotline
800-231-6946

Substance and Drug Abuse:

Al-ateen
800-352-9996

Al-Anon Family Group Headquarters
800-356-9996

Alcohol Abuse and Crisis Intervention
800-234-0246

Alcohol and Drug Abuse Assessment and Treatment
800-234-0420

Alcohol Hotline Support & Information
800-331-2900

Be Sober Hotline
800-BE-SOBER

Cocaine Help Line
800-COCAINE (262-2463)

Drug Help National Helplines
800-378-4435

National Association for Children of Alcoholics
888-55-4COAS (554-2627)

National Drug Information Treatment and Referral Hotline
800-662-HELP (4357)

Marijuana Anonymous
800-766-6779

Sample, Completed Forms

The forms in this appendix have been filled in for a fictional case. The purpose is to give you some idea of how the forms look after they have been completed. Not all of the forms in Appendix D are included here.

TABLE OF FORMS

The following is a list of the forms included in this appendix. These forms have been given letter designations in order to distinguish them from the blank forms in Appendix D, which have been given a numerical designation. If a form is based on a form from a particular state, the name of the state appears in parentheses after the title of the form.

FORM A: COMPLAINT FOR GRANDPARENT VISITATION 145

FORM B: COMPLAINT FOR GRANDPARENT VISITATION
(MASSACHUSETTS) 147

FORM C: PETITION OF GRANDPARENT(S) FOR INTERVENTION
IN SUIT AFFECTING THE PARENT-CHILD RELATIONSHIP
(TEXAS— VISITATION—EXISTING CASE) 148

FORM D: ORIGINAL PETITION FOR GRANDPARENT ACCESS
(TEXAS—VISITATION—NEW CASE) 150
FORM E: SUMMONS...152
FORM F: MOTION FOR DEFAULT 153
FORM G: WAIVER...154
FORM H: DECREE GRANTING GRANDPARENT ACCESS
(TEXAS—VISITATION)......................................155
FORM I: PETITION FOR CHILD CUSTODY 157
FORM J: ORIGINAL PETITION IN SUIT AFFECTING THE PARENT-CHILD
RELATIONSHIP (TEXAS—CUSTODY—NEW CASE) 159
FORM K: SUBPOENA DUCES TECUM 161
FORM L: NOTICE OF HEARING....................................162
FORM M: CUSTODY DECREE 163

IN THE CIRCUIT COURT OF THE THIRD JUDICIAL CIRCUIT
IN AND FOR DOUGLAS COUNTY, NEBRASKA

JOHN DOE and JANE DOE

      Petitioners,

VS.   CASE NO._____

ROBERT DOE and WANDA DOE

      Respondents.

COMPLAINT FOR GRANDPARENT VISITATION

_____ JOHN DOE and JANE DOE _____ [hereinafter called the
_____ Petitioners _____] for his/her/their _____ Complaint for Grandparent
Visitation _____ against _____ ROBERT DOE and WANDA DOE _____
_____ [hereinafter called the _____ Respondents _____], allege(s) and
state(s):

1.   Parties.

The _____ Petitioners _____ is/are _____ paternal grandparents _____,
and reside(s) at 176 Cornhusker St., Omaha, NE _____.

The _____ Respondents _____ is/are _____ parents _____,
and reside(s) at 123 Aksarben Way, Omaha, NE _____.

The child(ren) is/are _____ SARA DOE and SAM DOE _____,
and reside(s) at 123 Aksarben Way, Omaha, NE _____.

2.   Grounds.

In support of this request for grandparent visitation, _____ Petitioners _____
allege(s) and show(s) the Court as follows: A petition for dissolution of the
Respondents' marriage is pending, visitation would be in the best interest of the
children and would not interfere with the parent-child relationship _____.

3.   The _____ Petitioners _____ is/are not aware of any other court decision, order, or proceeding concerning the custody or visitation of the child(ren) in this state or any other, except:

4.   Relief Requested.

The _____ Petitioners _____ request(s) the following relief from the Court:
Visitation with the children from noon to 6:00 p.m., on the third Sunday of each
month, outside of the Respondents' residence.   .

DATED: _____ May 19, 2006 _____

John Doe
Signature

Jane Doe
Signature

Name: __ John Doe _____   Name: __ Jane Doe _____

Address: 176 Cornhusker St. _____   Address: 176 Cornhusker St. _____

        Omaha, NE 68108 _____   Omaha, NE 68108 _____

Telephone: (402) 555-5555 _____   Telephone: (402) 555-5555 _____

Commonwealth of Massachusetts
The Trial Court
_____ Division Probate and Family Court Department Docket No._____

COMPLAINT FOR GRANDPARENT VISITATION

_____JOHN DOE AND JANE DOE_____ ,
Plaintiffs
v.
_____ROBERT DOE AND WANDA DOE_____ ,
Defendants

1. Now come the plaintiffs in this action seeking to obtain visitation rights with their grandchildren, namely:

| Sam Doe | Date of Birth: 04/01/98 |
| Sara Doe | Date of Birth: 01/12/01 |

who are unmarried minors and who reside at: _____123 Tea Party Way, Boston, MA 02109_____ .

2. Plaintiffs are the _____paternal_____ grandparents who reside at _____1776 Revolution St., Boston, Suffolk County, MA 021109_____ .

3. The defendant, _____Wanda Doe_____ , who resides at _____123 Tea Party Way, Boston, _____Suffolk____ County, ____Massachusetts 02109____ , and the defendant, _____Robert Doe_____ , who resides at ____1812 Overture Cir., Boston, Suffolk_____ County, ____Massachusetts 02109___ , are the parents of the children.

4. Please check and complete ONLY ONE of the following sections:

   a.   On _____October 1, 2002_____ , the defendants were divorced by judgment of the Court. The judgment did not provide for visitation rights for the above-named grandparents.

   b.   On _____ , the defendant father was adjudicated by judgment to be the father of the child(ren). The adjudicated father and mother of the child do not reside together. The judgment/order did not provide for visitation rights for the above-named grandparents.

   c.   On _____ , the defendants signed an acknowledgment of parentage which was approved by the Court. The parents of the child do not reside together. The order/judgment did not provide for visitation for the above-named grandparents.

   d.   The defendants are married but living apart and subject to a temporary order or judgment of separate support. The order/judgment did not provide for visitation for the above-named grandparents.

   e.   On _____ , _____ died leaving _____ as the surviving parent.

   f.   On _____ , _____ died and on _____ , _____ died. The children currently _____ _____ (explain legal status of children).

5. The plaintiffs allege that it is in the best interest of the minor children that they be granted visitation with the said children.

WHEREFORE, plaintiffs request that the Court enter a judgment that provides them with visitation rights.

Date: _____May 23, 2006_____

John Doe
_____
Plaintiff

John Doe
_____
Print Name

Jane Doe
_____
Plaintiff

Jane Doe
_____
Print Name

1776 Revolution St.
_____
Street address

Boston, MA 02109
_____
City or town

Tel. No. (617) 555-5555
_____

NO.   94-11111

IN THE MATTER OF	*	IN THE DISTRICT COURT
THE MARRIAGE OF	*	
ROBERT DOE		
AND		___99th___ JUDICIAL DISTRICT
WANDA DOE		
AND IN THE INTERESTS OF		
SAM DOE and SARA DOE,		
MINOR CHILDREN		___BEXAR___ COUNTY, TEXAS

PETITION OF GRANDPARENT(S) FOR INTERVENTION IN SUIT AFFECTING THE PARENT-CHILD RELATIONSHIP

This petition in intervention is brought by _____JOHN DOE and JANE DOE_____.
In support, Intervenors show:

1.   Parties

This suit is brought by _____JOHN DOE_____, whose age is __65__ years and _____JANE DOE_____, whose age is __57__ years. Petitioners, who are the _____paternal_____ grandparents of the children the subject of this suit, reside at _1836 Alamo St., San Antonio, TX 78284_. Petitioners have standing to bring this suit under section 153.432 of the Texas Family Code.

2.   Jurisdiction

No court has continuing jurisdiction of this suit or of the children the subject of this suit.

3.   Children

The following children are the subject of this suit:

NAME: SAM DOE

SEX: Male

BIRTHPLACE: San Antonio, TX

BIRTH DATE: April 1, 1998

PRESENT RESIDENCE: 123 Sam Houston Dr., San Antonio, TX 78284

NAME: SARA DOE

SEX: Female

BIRTHPLACE: Houston, TX

BIRTH DATE: January 12, 2001

PRESENT RESIDENCE: 123 Sam Houston Dr., San Antonio, TX 78284

4.   Mother

The mother of the children is _____WANDA DOE_____, whose age is over 21 years and whose residence is ___123 Sam Houston Dr., San Antonio, TX 78284_.

5. <u>Father</u>

The father of the children is _____ROBERT DOE_____ , whose age is over 21 years and whose residence is _____181 Lone Star, San Antonio, TX 78284_____ .

6. <u>Court-Ordered Relationships</u>

There are no persons having a court-ordered relationship with the children.

7. <u>Property</u>

A full description and statement of value of all property owned or possessed by the children is as follows.

No property is owned by the children.

8. <u>Access</u>

It is in the best interest of the children that Petitioners be granted reasonable access to the children by order of this Court.

Denial of visitation would significantly impair the child's physical health or emotional well-being.

At the time this relief is requested, Petitioners allege the parents of the children are biologic or adoptive parents.

A suit for the dissolution of the parents' marriage is pending.

The father has been incarcerated during the three-month period preceding the filing of this petition.

Other statutory grounds: _____ .

Petitioners request the Court to enter its order for access to the children as follows: Grandparents _____ROBERT DOE and JANE DOE_____ are to have possession of the children from <u>12:00 noon to 5:00 p.m., on the third Sunday of each month</u>.

9. <u>Prayer</u>

Petitioners prays that citation and notice issue as required by law. Petitioners pray that the Court grant relief in accordance with the foregoing allegations. Petitioners pray for general relief.

Respectfully submitted,

BY: *John Doe*
Name: John Doe
BY: *Jane Doe*
Name: Jane Doe
Address: 1836 Alamo St.
San Antonio, TX 78284
Telephone: (512) 555-5555

CERTIFICATE OF SERVICE

I certify that a true copy of the above was served on Robert Doe, 181 Lone Star, San Antonio, TX 78284; and Wanda Doe, 123 Sam Houston Dr., San Antonio, TX 78283 ,
in accordance with the Texas Rules of Civil Procedure on _____May 19, 2006_____ .

John Doe

NO. 06-0383

IN THE INTEREST OF	§	IN THE DISTRICT COURT
	§	
MARY ANN DOE,	§	__99th__ JUDICIAL DISTRICT
	§	
A CHILD	§	__BEXAR__ COUNTY, TEXAS

ORIGINAL PETITION FOR GRANDPARENT ACCESS

1. Discovery Level

Discovery in this case is intended to be conducted under level 2 of rule 190 of the Texas Rules of Civil Procedure.

2. Parties

This suit is brought by ____MARTHA DOE____, whose age is __68__ years. Petitioner, who is the paternal grandparent of the child the subject of this suit, resides at ____155 Happy Family Way, Wholesome, Texas____. Petitioner has standing to bring this suit as more fully detailed below.

3. Jurisdiction

No court has continuing jurisdiction of this suit or of the child the subject of this suit.

4. Child

The following child is the subject of this suit:

Name: __Mary Ann Doe__

Sex: __Female__

Birthplace: __Anyplace, Texas__

Birth date: __12/25/95__

Present residence: __1812 Warrior Dr., Wholesome, Texas__

5. Mother

The mother of the child the subject of this suit is__Jane Ann Doe__, who is __30__ years of age and resides at ____1812 Warrior Dr. Wholesome, Texas 77777____.

Process should be served at that address.

The father of the child the subject of this suit is __John Doe__, who is __30__ years of age and resides at ____100 Lost Canyon, Someplace, Texas____.

Process should be served at that address.

6. Court-Ordered Relationships

There are no court-ordered conservatorships, court-ordered guardianships, or other court-ordered relationships affecting the child the subject of this suit. Or list the court-ordered conservatorships or relationships.

7. Property

There has been no change of consequence in the status of the property of the child the subject of this suit since the prior order was rendered.

8. Access

It is in the best interest of the child the subject of this suit that Petitioner be granted reasonable access to the child by order of this Court.

Denial of visitation would significantly impair the child's physical health or emotional well-being.

At the time this relief is requested, Petitioner alleges the parent of the child is a biological or adoptive parent. Neither parent has had their parental rights terminated. Petitioner further would show the court that the child's parents are divorced, and that access between Petitioner and the child is in the best interest of the child.

Petitioner requests the Court to enter its order for access to the child as follows: __The second weekend of each month from 6:00 p.m. on Friday until 12:00 noon on Saturday__ .

9. Statement on Alternative Dispute Resolution

Petitioner has signed a statement on alternative dispute resolution, which is attached as Exhibit 1.

10. Prayer

Petitioner prays that citation and notice issue as required by law. Petitioner prays that the Court grant relief in accordance with the allegations of this petition.

Petitioner prays for attorney's fees and other costs.

Petitioner prays for general relief.

Respectfully submitted,

Martha Doe

Martha Doe
155 Happy Family Way
Wholesome, Texas 77777
999/555-1234
999/555-1235(fax)
Pro Se petitioner

EXHIBIT 1

STATEMENT CONCERNING ALTERNATIVE DISPUTE RESOLUTION

I AM AWARE THAT IT IS THE POLICY OF THE STATE OF TEXAS TO PROMOTE THE AMICABLE AND NONJUDICIAL SETTLEMENT OF DISPUTES INVOLVING CHILDREN AND FAMILIES. I AM AWARE OF ALTERNATIVE DISPUTE RESOLUTION METHODS INCLUDING MEDIATION. WHILE I RECOGNIZE THAT ALTERNATIVE DISPUTE RESOLUTION IS AN ALTERNATIVE TO AND NOT A SUBSTITUTE FOR A TRIAL AND THAT THIS CASE MAY BE TRIED IF IT IS NOT SETTLED, I REPRESENT TO THE COURT THAT I WILL ATTEMPT IN GOOD FAITH TO RESOLVE CONTESTED ISSUES IN THIS CASE BY ALTERNATIVE DISPUTE RESOLUTION WITHOUT THE NECESSITY OF COURT INTERVENTION.

MARTHA DOE

IN THE CIRCUIT COURT FOR ANNE ARUNDEL COUNTY, MARYLAND

JOHN DOE and JANE DOE,

Plaintiffs,

VS.   **CASE NO.** 06-2749

ROBERT DOE and WANDA DOE,

Defendants.

SUMMONS

TO: Each Sheriff of the State of Maryland

YOU ARE COMMANDED to serve this summons and a copy of the complaint in this action on the Defendant(s):

> Robert Doe and Wanda Doe
> 123 Chesapeake Rd.
> Annapolis, MD 21401

The Defendant(s) is/are required to serve written defenses to the complaint on the Plaintiff(s):

> John Doe and Jane Doe
> 493 Naval Academy Lane
> Annapolis, MD 21401

Within 20 calendar days after this Summons is served on the Defendant(s), exclusive of the day of service, and to file the original of the defenses with the clerk of this court either before service on the Plaintiff(s) or immediately thereafter. If the Defendant fails to do so, a default will be entered against the Defendant for the relief demanded in the complaint.

DATED on _____, _____.

Clerk of the Court

By _____

FAYETTE COUNTY CIRCUIT COURT, KENTUCKY

JOHN SMITH and JANE SMITH,

        Petitioners,

VS.   CASE NO. 06-12345

BOB SMITH and SUSAN SMITH,

        Respondents.

MOTION FOR DEFAULT

The undersigned _____ Petitioners _____ hereby moves for the entry of a default against ____ the Respondents, Bob and Susan Smith ____ for failure to serve or file a timely response to the _____ Petition for Grandparent Visitation _____ as required by law.

DATED: ____ June 23, 2006 ____

                                   John Smith
                           Signature

                           Name _John Smith_

                           Address _123 Horse Park Circle_

                                 Lexington, KY 40511

                           Telephone No. _(606) 555-5555_

DEFAULT

A default is entered in this action against the _____ for failure to serve or file a response as required by law.

DATED: _____

                           CLERK OF THE COURT

                           By: _____

IN THE CIRCUIT COURT FOR JEFFERSON COUNTY, ALABAMA

JOHN SMITH and JANE SMITH,
                Plaintiffs,

vs.   Case No. 06-0383

ROBERT SMITH and MARY SMITH,
                Defendants.

WAIVER

STATE OF ALABAMA   )

COUNTY OF   JEFFERSON   )

BEFORE ME, the undersigned authority, on this day personally appeared __ROBERT SMITH__
_____, who, by me duly sworn, made the following statements and swore that they were true:

I, _____ROBERT SMITH_____, am the ___Defendant___ in the above-entitled and numbered cause. My mailing address is __1421 Jackson Avenue,_____ __Birmingham, AL 35203_____.

I have been given a copy of the __Complaint for Grandparent Visitation_____ _____ that has been filed in this cause, and I have read it and understand it. I hereby enter my appearance in this cause for all purposes and waive the issuance and service of process. I agree that the cause may be taken up and considered by the Court without further notice to me. I further waive the making of a record of testimony in this cause.

I further agree that the cause may be heard by the presiding Judge of the Court or by a duly appointed master, hearing officer, or referee of the Court.

                                          Robert Smith
_____

SIGNED under oath before me on _____September 1, 2006_____.

                                        C. U. Sine
_____
C.U. Sine
Notary Public
My commission expires: January 1, 2009

NO. 06-0383

IN THE INTEREST OF	*	IN THE DISTRICT COURT

SAM DOE
AND   99th   DISTRICT
SARAH DOE

CHILDREN   BEXAR   COUNTY, TEXAS

DECREE GRANTING GRANDPARENT ACCESS

On _____ August 12, 2006 _____, hearing was held in this cause.

Appearances

Petitioners, _____ JOHN DOE and JANE DOE _____, appeared in person.
Respondents, _____ ROBERT DOE _____, appeared in person and through their attorney of record, __ LEE GIL BEIGEL _____.
_____ WANDA DOE _____ waived issuance and service of citation by waiver duly filed herein and did not otherwise appear.

Jurisdiction

The Court, having examined the pleadings and heard the evidence and argument of counsel, finds that it has jurisdiction of this cause and of all the parties and that no other court has continuing, exclusive jurisdiction of this cause.

Findings

A jury was waived, and all matters in controversy, including questions of act and of law, were submitted to the Court. All persons entitled to citation were properly cited. The making of a record of testimony was waived by the parties with the consent of the Court.

The Court finds that the children the subject of this suit are:
NAME: SAM DOE
SEX: Male
BIRTHPLACE: San Antonio, TX
BIRTH DATE: April 1, 1998
PRESENT RESIDENCE: 123 Sam Houston Dr., San Antonio, TX 78284
HOME STATE: Texas
NAME: SARA DOE
SEX: Female
BIRTHPLACE: Houston, TX
BIRTH DATE: Jan. 12, 2001
PRESENT RESIDENCE: 123 Sam Houston Dr., San Antonio, TX 78284
HOME STATE: Texas

Orders

The Court finds that the following orders are in the best interest of the children:
IT IS ORDERED AND DECREED that _ JOHN DOE and JANE DOE _ are granted access to the children as follows: Grandparents _ JOHN DOE and JANE DOE _ are to have possession of the children from 12:00 noon to 8:00 p.m., on the third of each month, beginning on the third Sunday of September, 2006 _____.

Surrender of Child. _____ ROBERT DOE and WANDA DOE _____ are each ORDERED AND DECREED to surrender the child to __ JOHN DOE and JANE DOE __
_____ at the beginning of each period of _____
_____ JOHN DOE and JANE DOE _____ 's possession at the residence of
_____ WANDA DOE _____.

Return of Child. _____ JOHN DOE and JANE DOE _____ ARE ORDERED AND DECREED to surrender the child to _____ WANDA DOE _____
_____ at the end of each period of
_____ WANDA DOE _____ 's possession at the residence of
_____.

Personal Effects. Each party is ORDERED AND DECREED to return with the child the personal effects that the child brought at the beginning of the period of possession.

Designation of Competent Adult. Each party may designate any competent adult to pick up and return the child, as applicable. IT IS ORDERED AND DECREED that a conservator or a designated competent adult be present when the child is picked up or returned.

Location

Each party is ORDERED AND DECREED to keep the other party and the Court fully and promptly informed of his or her current street address of residence, home telephone number, name of employer, place of employment, and work telephone number and of the address of the children's school or day-care center. Each party who intends a change of place of residence is ORDERED AND DECREED to give written notice of the intended date of change, new telephone number, and new street address of residence to the Clerk of this Court and every other party who has possession of or access to the children on or before the 60th day before the change of residence or, if the party did not know and could not have known of the change or if the required information is not available within the 60-day period, on or before the fifth day after the day the party knew or should have known of the change or of the related information.

Notice may be given to the other party by delivering a copy of the notice to the party either in person or by registered or certified mail, return receipt requested, to the party's last known address. Notice may be given to the Court by delivering a copy of the notice either in person to the Clerk of the Court or by registered or certified mail addressed to the Clerk.

WARNINGS TO PARTIES

FAILURE TO OBEY A COURT ORDER FOR CHILD SUPPORT OR FOR POSSESSION OF OR ACCESS TO A CHILD MAY RESULT IN FURTHER LITIGATION TO ENFORCE THE ORDER, INCLUDING CONTEMPT OF COURT. A FINDING OF CONTEMPT MAY BE PUNISHED BY CONFINEMENT IN JAIL FOR UP TO SIX MONTHS, A FINE OF UP TO $500 FOR EACH VIOLATION, AND A MONEY JUDGMENT FOR PAYMENT OF ATTORNEY'S FEES AND COURT COSTS.

FAILURE OF A PARTY TO MAKE A CHILD-SUPPORT PAYMENT TO THE PLACE AND IN THE MANNER REQUIRED BY A COURT ORDER MAY RESULT IN THE PARTY'S NOT RECEIVING CREDIT FOR MAKING THE PAYMENT.

FAILURE OF A PARTY TO PAY CHILD-SUPPORT DOES NOT JUSTIFY DENYING THAT PARTY COURT-ORDERED POSSESSION OF OR ACCESS TO A CHILD. REFUSAL BY A PARTY TO ALLOW POSSESSION OF OR ACCESS TO A CHILD DOES NOT JUSTIFY FAILURE TO PAY COURT-ORDERED CHILD SUPPORT TO THAT PARTY.

EACH PERSON WHO IS A PARTY TO THIS ORDER OR DECREE IS ORDERED TO NOTIFY THE CLERK OF THIS COURT WITHIN 10 DAYS AFTER THE DATE OF ANY CHANGE IN THE PARTY'S CURRENT RESIDENCE ADDRESS, MAILING ADDRESS, HOME TELEPHONE NUMBER, NAME OF EMPLOYER, ADDRESS OF PLACE OF EMPLOYMENT, OR WORK TELEPHONE NUMBER. ALL NOTICES SHALL BE IN WRITING AND SHALL STATE THE NEW INFORMATION AND THE EFFECTIVE DATE OF THE CHANGE. THE DUTY TO FURNISH THIS INFORMATION TO THE CLERK OF THE COURT CONTINUES AS LONG AS ANY PERSON, BY VIRTUE OF THIS ORDER OR DECREE, IS UNDER AN OBLIGATION TO PAY CHILD SUPPORT OR IS ENTITLED TO POSSESSION OF OR ACCESS TO A CHILD. FAILURE TO OBEY THE ORDER OF THIS COURT TO PROVIDE THE CLERK WITH THE CURRENT MAILING ADDRESS OF A PARTY MAY RESULT IN THE ISSUANCE OF A CAPIAS FOR THE ARREST OF THE PARTY IF THAT PARTY CANNOT BE PERSONALLY SERVED WITH NOTICE OF A HEARING AT AN ADDRESS OF RECORD.

Costs

Costs of court are to be borne by the party by whom such costs were incurred.

Date of Judgment

SIGNED on _____, _____ .

_____

JUDGE PRESIDING

APPROVED AS TO FORM ONLY: APPROVED AND CONSENTED TO AS TO
                                             BOTH FORM AND SUBSTANCE:

_____   _____

Attorney for

                                             _____

_____

_____

SUPERIOR COURT OF CALIFORNIA, COUNTY OF ORANGE

JOHN SMITH and JANE SMITH,

        Petitioners,

VS.   CASE NO.06-3481

BOB SMITH and SUSAN SMITH,

        Respondents.

PETITION FOR CHILD CUSTODY

_____ JOHN SMITH and JANE SMITH _____ (hereinafter called the ___ Petitioners ___) for ~~his/her~~/their _____ Petition for Child Custody _____ against _____ BOB SMITH and SUSAN SMITH _____ (hereinafter called the ___ Respondent ___), allege(s) and state(s):

1.   <u>Parties.</u>

The ___ Petitioners ___ ~~is~~/are _____ the maternal grandparents _____ , and reside(s) at _6789 Big Sur Drive, Santa Ana, CA 96734_ .

The ___ Respondents ___ ~~is~~/are _____ the parents _____ , and reside(s) at _241 Fault Line Blvd., Santa Anna CA_ .

The child(ren) is/are _ANN SMITH (DOB 12/12/99 in Dallas, TX), and TOMMY SMITH (DOB 3/5/01 in Lone Pine, CA)_ and reside at _241 Fault Line Blvd., Santa Anna CA_ .

2.   <u>Grounds.</u> In support of this request for physical custody, ___ Petitioners ___ allege(s) and show(s) the Court as follows: _The children's current environment presents a serious threat to the children's physical health and welfare as the Respondents are leaving the children without supervision for extended periods of time and are not providing the children with adequate medical and dental care_ .

3.   The Petitioner(s)~~is~~/are not aware of any other court decision, order, or proceeding concerning the custody or visitation of the child(ren) in this state or any other, except:

4.   Relief Requested. The _____ Petitioners _____ request(s) the following relief from the Court: _That Petitioners be awarded physical custody of the children_ _____

_____

_____

_____.

DATED: _September 6, 2006_

John Smith _____

Signature

Name _John Smith_ _____

Jane Smith _____

Signature

Name _Jane Smith_ _____

Address _6789 Big Sur Drive_ _____

Santa Ana, CA 92711 _____

Telephone No. _(714) 555-5555_ _____

NO.   06-0383

IN THE INTEREST OF	*	IN THE DISTRICT COURT
	*	
SAM DOE	*	
AND	*	_____99th_____ DISTRICT
SARAH DOE	*	
	*	
CHILDREN	*	_____BEXAR_____ COUNTY, TEXAS

ORIGINAL PETITION IN SUIT
AFFECTING THE PARENT-CHILD RELATIONSHIP

1.   Petitioner.
This suit is brought by _____JOHN DOE and JANE DOE_____,
Petitioner(s), who ~~is/~~are over 21 years of age and who reside(s) at
1836 Alamo Street, San Antonio, TX 78284_____.

Petitioners are the grandmother and grandfather of the children the subject of this suit.

Petitioners have standing to bring this suit in that Petitioners would show the court that the child's present environment presents a serious and immediate question concerning the child's physical health or welfare.

2.   Jurisdiction.
No court has continuing jurisdiction of this suit or of the children the subject of this suit.

3.   Children.
The following children are the subject of this suit:

NAME: SAM DOE_____
SEX: Male_____
BIRTHPLACE: San Antonio, TX_____
BIRTH DATE: April 1, 1998_____
PRESENT RESIDENCE: 123 Sam Houston Dr., San Antonio, TX 78284

NAME: SARA DOE_____
SEX: Female_____
BIRTHPLACE: Houston, TX_____
BIRTH DATE: January 12, 2001_____
PRESENT RESIDENCE: 123 Sam Houston Dr., San Antonio, TX 78284

4.   Persons Entitled to Citation.
The mother of the child(ren) is _____ WANDA DOE _____, who is over 21 years of age and who resides at 123 Sam Houston Dr., San Antonio, TX 78284 .
Process should be served at that address.
The father of the child(ren) is _____ ROBERT DOE _____, who is over 21 years of age and who resides at 181 Lone Star, San Antonio, TX 78284 .
Process should be served at that address.
There are no court-ordered conservatorships, court-ordered guardianships, or other court-ordered relationships affecting the children the subject of this suit.

5.   Property.
No property is owned or possessed by the children the subject of this suit.

6.   Conservatorship.
The parents of the children are or will be separated. It is in the best interest of the children that the Petitioner be appointed sole managing conservator of the children.

7.   Support.
_____ ROBERT DOE and WANDA DOE _____, Respondents, are obligated to support the children and should be ordered by the Court to make payments for the support of the children in the manner specified by the Court.

8.   Prayer.
Petitioner prays that citation and notice issue as required by law and that the Court enter its orders in accordance with the foregoing allegations.
Petitioner prays for attorney's fees, expenses, and costs.
Petitioner prays for general relief.

Respectfully submitted,

John Doe
Signature

Name John Doe

Jane Doe
Signature

Name Jane Doe

Address 1836 Alamo St.

San Antonio, TX 78284

Telephone No. (512) 555-5555

IN THE CIRCUIT COURT OF THE THIRD JUDICIAL DISTRICT
COOK COUNTY, ILLINOIS

PAULA SMITH and PETER SMITH
                    Petitioners,
VS.   CASE NO. 06-32946
ROBERT JONES and REBA JONES,
                    Respondents.

SUBPOENA
DUCES TECUM

TO: ED U. KATER
             Northside Elementary School
             1427 Northside Blvd.
             Chicago, IL 60607

YOU ARE HEREBY COMMANDED to appear before the Honorable ___Barry D.___

__Hatchett_____, Judge of the Court, at _____Courtroom C,_____

_Cook County Courthouse, 251 Michigan Ave., Chicago, IL_____,

on _____October 18_____, _2006_, at __9:00__ o'clock _a_.m., to testify in this
action. You are also commended to bring with you the following:

Any and all report cards, grade books, or other school records relating to
Robert Jones, Jr.

If you fail to appear, you may be in contempt of court.

You are subpoenaed to appear by the attorneys or parties designated below, and unless
excused from this subpoena by these attorneys or parties, or the court, you shall respond
to this subpoena as directed.

DATED:_____

Attorney or Party Requesting Subpoena   CLERK OF THE COURT

Name: _Paula Smith_____

Address: _6932 Lakeshore Cir._____

     _Chicago, IL 60607_____   By: _____

Telephone No: _(312) 555-5515_____   Deputy Clerk

STATE OF MINNESOTA DISTRICT COURT
COUNTY OF HENNEPIN, FIRST JUDICIAL DISTRICT

GEORGE BROWN,

         Petitioner,

vs.   CASE NO. 06-2393

GEORGE BROWN, JR., and SUSAN BROWN,

         Respondents.

NOTICE OF HEARING

TO: GEORGE BROWN, JR. and SUSAN BROWN
               6693 Martin Rd.
               Minneapolis, MN 55401

PLEASE TAKE NOTICE that the above-entitled matter will be called on for hearing on ___the Petition for Grandparent Visitation___
on ___Tuesday___, the __16th__ day of _____March_____, _2006_, at __1:30__ o'clock _p_.m., before the Honorable _____I. M. deJudge_____, Judge, in _his chambers at the Hennepin County Courthouse, 417 Oak Street,_ _4th Floor, Minneapolis, MN_ .

George Brown
Signature

Name __George Brown__

Address _4435 S. Mountain View Ave._

        Minneapolis, MN 55401

Telephone No. _(612) 555-5155_

CIRCUIT COURT OF RALEIGH COUNTY, WEST VIRGINIA

JOHN DAVIS and BARBARA DAVIS,
Plaintiffs,

vs.   CASE NO. 06-8392

SAM DAVIS and GAIL DAVIS,
Defendants.

CUSTODY DECREE

This action for child custody was heard before the Court on _____ May 10, 2006 _____.
All interested parties appearing were given the opportunity to be heard and to present evidence. On the evidence presented, the Court makes the following findings and orders:

Jurisdiction

The Court, having examined the pleadings and heard the evidence and argument of the parties, finds that it has jurisdiction of this cause and of all the parties and that no other court has continuing, exclusive jurisdiction of this cause. All persons entitled to notice of this action and final hearing were properly given notice.

Custody

IT IS ORDERED that _____ the Plaintiffs, JOHN DAVIS and BARBARA DAVIS _____
shall have physical custody of the following child(ren):

Sam Davis, Jr., DOB: 2/14/97

The court finds that Defendant's home environment is not in the best interest of the minor child at the present time, due to the alcohol addiction of Defendant Sam Davis, and recent incidents of domestic violence, which led to proceedings being initiated pursuant to W.V.C. §48-2A-1. The court further finds that a transfer of custody to the Plaintiffs is in the best interest of the child, and Plaintiffs are the child's paternal grandparents, have developed a significant relationship with the child, and can offer a suitable home environment as indicated by the home study conducted in this matter.

Visitation

IT IS ORDERED that _____ the Defendants, SAM DAVIS and GAIL DAVIS _____
shall have visitation with the child(ren) as follows:

alternative Saturdays, from 9:00 a.m. to 6:00 p.m., provided that another adult be present during all visitation periods.

Child Support

IT IS ORDERED that _____ the Defendants, SAM DAVIS and GAIL DAVIS _____
shall pay child support in the amount of $_____ 55.00 _____ per _____ week _____,
to _____ the Plaintiffs, JOHN DAVIS and BARBARA DAVIS _____.

Costs

Costs of court are to be borne by _____ the Plaintiffs _____.

Other Provisions

This matter may be reviewed after a period of ninety days, upon motion of the
Defendants, or upon Defendant Sam Davis having successfully completed a licensed
alcohol treatment program, whichever occurs first.

ORDERED on _____, _____ .

_____
Judge

Blank Forms

The following forms are included in this appendix. These forms are of a general nature, except where a specific state is noted. Therefore, you may need to modify these forms for use in your state. These forms are not in any particular order, and you will not need to use all of the forms in this appendix.

NOTE: *Refer to Chapter 3 and Chapter 5 for an example of how to complete the* ***case style***.

TABLE OF FORMS

FORM 1: **COMPLAINT/PETITION FOR GRANDPARENT VISITATION** 167

FORM 2: **PETITION FOR GRANDPARENT VISITATION (FLORIDA)** 169
   NOTE: *This form may no longer be valid. Check with the Clerk of Court for any correct form for grandparent visitation.*

FORM 3: **COMPLAINT FOR GRANDPARENT VISITATION (MASSACHUSETTS)** 173

FORM 4: **ORIGINAL PETITION FOR GRANDPARENT ACCESS (TEXAS—VISITATION—NEW CASE)** 175

FORM 5: PETITION OF GRANDPARENT(S) FOR INTERVENTION IN SUIT AFFECTING THE PARENT-CHILD RELATIONSHIP (TEXAS—VISITATION—EXISTING CASE). 177

FORM 6: UNIFORM CHILD CUSTODY JURISDICTION AND ENFORCEMENT ACT AFFIDAVIT 179

FORM 7: CERTIFICATE OF SERVICE 181

FORM 8: MOTION FOR DEFAULT 183

FORM 9: SUBPOENA 185

FORM 10: NOTICE OF HEARING. 187

FORM 11: REQUEST FOR MEDIATION (AND ORDER) (MISSOURI) 189

FORM 12: WAIVER 191

FORM 13: VISITATION ORDER 193

FORM 14: DECREE GRANTING GRANDPARENT ACCESS (TEXAS—VISITATION) 195

FORM 15: COMPLAINT/PETITION FOR CUSTODY 197

FORM 16: ORIGINAL PETITION IN SUIT AFFECTING THE PARENT-CHILD RELATIONSHIP (TEXAS—CUSTODY—NEW CASE). 199

FORM 17: PETITION OF GRANDPARENT(S) FOR INTERVENTION IN SUIT AFFECTING THE PARENT-CHILD RELATIONSHIP (TEXAS—CUSTODY—EXISTING CASE) 201

FORM 18: CUSTODY ORDER 203

FORM 19: DECREE FOR CHILD CUSTODY (TEXAS—CUSTODY) 205

FORM 20: MOTION FOR SOCIAL STUDY (AND ORDER) 207

FORM 21: MOTION FOR APPOINTMENT OF GUARDIAN AD LITEM 209

FORM 22: ORDER APPOINTING GUARDIAN AD LITEM 211

FORM 23: MOTION FOR PSYCHIATRIC/PSYCHOLOGICAL EXAMINATION. 213

FORM 24: ORDER FOR PSYCHIATRIC/PSYCHOLOGICAL EXAMINATION. 215

FORM 25: MOTION TO PROCEED IN FORMA PAUPERIS 217

FORM 26: FINANCIAL AFFIDAVIT 219

FORM 27: AGREEMENT 223

FORM 28: MOTION TO SET HEARING 225

FORM 29: CERTIFICATE OF LAST KNOWN ADDRESS 227

[CASE STYLE]

COMPLAINT/PETITION FOR GRANDPARENT VISITATION

_____ [hereinafter called the

_____] for his/her/their _____

_____ against _____

_____[hereinafter called the _____], alleges

and states:

1. <u>Parties</u>.

The _____ is/are _____,

and reside(s) at _____.

The _____ is/are _____,

and reside(s) at _____.

The child(ren) is/are _____,

and reside(s) at _____.

2. <u>Grounds</u>.

In support of this request for grandparent visitation, _____

allege(s) and show(s) the Court as follows: _____

_____

_____.

3. The _____ is/are not aware of any other court decision, order, or proceeding concerning the custody or visitation of the child(ren) in this state or any other, except:

4.   <u>Relief Requested</u>.

The _____ request(s) the following relief from the Court:

_____

_____

_____

_____.

DATED: _____

_____   _____
Signature   Signature

Name: _____   Name: _____

Address: _____   Address: _____

_____   _____

Telephone: _____   Telephone: _____

IN THE CIRCUIT COURT OF THE _____ JUDICIAL CIRCUIT,
IN AND FOR _____ COUNTY, FLORIDA

Case No.: _____
Division: _____

_____ ,

_____ ,

Grandparent(s),

and

_____ ,

_____ ,

Respondent(s).

PETITION FOR GRANDPARENT VISITATION

I/We, {full legal name(s)}_____ ,
being sworn, certify that the following information is true:

1. This is a request for grandparent(s) visitation, under chapter 752, Florida Statutes.

2. The minor grandchild(ren) has (have) been living in the State of Florida within the jurisdiction of this Court.

3. I/We desire visitation with the following minor grandchild(ren).

Name	Birth date	Age	Sex

4. The [√ one only] (   ) mother (   ) father of my (our) grandchild(ren) is my (our) [√ one only] (   ) son (   ) daughter. A copy of the my (our) child's (respondent's) birth certificate is attached.

5. [√ all that apply]:
____   a. The (   ) mother (   ) father of the grandchild(ren) has (have) died.
____   b. The mother and father of the grandchild(ren) are divorced.
____   c. The (   ) mother (   ) father of the grandchild(ren) has (have) deserted the grandchild(ren).
____   d. The parents were not married when the grandchild(ren) was (were) born and did not marry after the grandchild(ren)'s birth, and paternity has been established.

6. I/We are requesting the following visitation: {explain} _____
_____
_____

Florida Family Law Form 12.905, Petition for Grandparent Visitation (2/98)

7. It is in the best interests of the grandchild(ren) that the grandparent(s) be allowed reasonable rights of visitation with the grandchild(ren). This is in the grandchild(ren)'s best interests because: {explain}

_____
_____
_____
_____
_____
_____

I understand that I am swearing or affirming under oath to the truthfulness of the claims made in this petition and that the punishment for knowingly making a false statement includes fines and/or imprisonment.

Dated: _____   _____
                                        Signature of Grandparent
                                        Printed Name: _____
                                        Address: _____
                                        City, State, Zip: _____
                                        Telephone Number: _____
                                        Fax Number: _____

STATE OF FLORIDA
COUNTY OF _____

Sworn to or affirmed and signed before me on _____ by _____.

                                        _____
                                        NOTARY PUBLIC—STATE OF FLORIDA

                                        _____
                                        [Print, type, or stamp commissioned name of notary.]

____   Personally known
____   Produced identification
       Type of identification produced _____

IF A NONLAWYER HELPED YOU FILL OUT THIS FORM, HE/SHE MUST FILL IN THE BLANKS BELOW: [✍ fill in all blanks]

I, {full legal name and trade name of nonlawyer}_____,
a nonlawyer, located at {street}_____, {city} _____,
{state} _____, {phone} _____, helped {name} _____,
who is the (one of the) petitioner(s), fill out this form.

   I understand that I am swearing or affirming under oath to the truthfulness of the claims made in this petition and that the punishment for knowingly making a false statement includes fines and/or imprisonment.

Dated: _____

Signature of Grandparent

Printed Name: _____

Address: _____

City, State, Zip: _____

Telephone Number: _____

Fax Number: _____

STATE OF FLORIDA
COUNTY OF _____

Sworn to or affirmed and signed before me on _____ by _____.

NOTARY PUBLIC—STATE OF FLORIDA

_____
[Print, type, or stamp commissioned name of notary.]

____ Personally known
____ Produced identification
     Type of identification produced _____

IF A NONLAWYER HELPED YOU FILL OUT THIS FORM, HE/SHE MUST FILL IN THE BLANKS BELOW: [✍ fill in all blanks]

I, {full legal name and trade name of nonlawyer}_____,
a nonlawyer, located at {street}_____, {city} _____,
{state} _____, {phone} _____, helped {name} _____,
who is the (one of the) petitioner(s), fill out this form.

This page intentionally blank.

Commonwealth of Massachusetts
The Trial Court
_____ Division Probate and Family Court Department Docket No. _____

COMPLAINT FOR GRANDPARENT VISITATION

_____ ,
Plaintiffs
v.

_____ ,
Defendants

1. Now come the plaintiffs in this action seeking to obtain visitation rights with their grandchildren, namely:

who are unmarried minors and who reside at: _____ .

2. Plaintiffs are the _____ grandparents who reside at _____
_____ .

3. The defendant, _____ , who resides at _____
_____ County, _____ , and the defendant, _____ ,
who resides at _____ County, _____ , are the
parents of the children.

4. Please check and complete ONLY ONE of the following sections:

    a.   On _____ , the defendants were divorced by judgment of the Court. The judgment did not provide for visitation rights for the above-named grandparents.

    b.   On _____ , the defendant father was adjudicated by judgment to be the father of the child(ren). The adjudicated father and mother of the child do not reside together. The judgment/order did not provide for visitation rights for the above-named grandparents.

    c.   On _____ , the defendants signed an acknowledgment of parentage which was approved by the Court. The parents of the child do not reside together. The order/judgment did not provide for visitation for the above-named grandparents.

    d.   The defendants are married but living apart and subject to a temporary order or judgment of separate support. The order/judgment did not provide for visitation for the above-named grandparents.

    e.   On _____ , _____ died leaving _____ as the surviving parent.

    f.   On _____ , _____ died and on _____ , _____ died. The children currently _____ _____ (explain legal status of children).

5. The plaintiffs allege that it is in the best interest of the minor children that they be granted visitation with the said children.

WHEREFORE, plaintiffs request that the Court enter a judgment that provides them with visitation rights.

Date: _____

_____   _____
Plaintiff   Plaintiff

_____   _____
Print Name   Print Name

    _____
    Street address

    _____
    City or town

    Tel. No. _____

This page intentionally blank.

NO._____

IN THE INTEREST OF	§	IN THE DISTRICT COURT
	§	
_____	§	_____ JUDICIAL DISTRICT
	§	
A CHILD	§	_____ COUNTY, TEXAS

ORIGINAL PETITION FOR GRANDPARENT ACCESS

1. Discovery Level

Discovery in this case is intended to be conducted under level 2 of rule 190 of the Texas Rules of Civil Procedure.

2. Parties

This suit is brought by _____, whose age is ___ years. Petitioner, who is the maternal/paternal grandparent of the child the subject of this suit, resides at _____. Petitioner has standing to bring this suit as more fully detailed below.

3. Jurisdiction

No court has continuing jurisdiction of this suit or of the child the subject of this suit.

4. Child

The following child is the subject of this suit:

Name: _____

Sex: _____

Birthplace: _____

Birth date: _____

Present residence: _____

5. Mother

The mother of the child the subject of this suit is _____, who is ____ years of age and resides at _____.

Process should be served at that address.

The father of the child the subject of this suit is _____, who is ____ years of age and resides at _____.

Process should be served at that address.

6. Court-Ordered Relationships

There are no court-ordered conservatorships, court-ordered guardianships, or other court-ordered relationships affecting the child the subject of this suit. Or list the court-ordered conservatorships or relationships.

7. Property

There has been no change of consequence in the status of the property of the child the subject of this suit since the prior order was rendered.

8. Access

It is in the best interest of the child the subject of this suit that Petitioner be granted reasonable access to the child by order of this Court.

At the time this relief is requested, Petitioner alleges the parent of the child is a biological or adoptive parent.

[Set out the ground from the statute, such as the parents of the child are divorced.]

Petitioner requests the Court to enter its order for access to the child as follows: _____ _____.

9. Attorney's Fees

It was necessary for Petitioner to secure the services of _____, a licensed attorney, to preserve and protect the child's rights. Respondents _____ and _____ should be ordered to pay a reasonable attorney's fee, and judgment should be rendered in favor of this attorney and against Respondents or, in the alternative, reasonable attorney's fees should be taxed as costs and should be ordered paid directly to the undersigned attorney.

10. Statement on Alternative Dispute Resolution

Petitioner has signed a statement on alternative dispute resolution, which is attached as Exhibit 1.

11. Prayer

Petitioner prays that citation and notice issue as required by law. Petitioner prays that the Court grant relief in accordance with the allegations of this petition.

Petitioner prays for attorney's fees and other costs.

Petitioner prays for general relief.

Respectfully submitted,

_____

NAME
ADDRESS
PHONE NUMBER
FAX NUMBER
Pro Se petitioner

EXHIBIT 1

STATEMENT CONCERNING ALTERNATIVE DISPUTE RESOLUTION

I AM AWARE THAT IT IS THE POLICY OF THE STATE OF TEXAS TO PROMOTE THE AMICABLE AND NONJUDICIAL SETTLEMENT OF DISPUTES INVOLVING CHILDREN AND FAMILIES. I AM AWARE OF ALTERNATIVE DISPUTE RESOLUTION METHODS INCLUDING MEDIATION. WHILE I RECOGNIZE THAT ALTERNATIVE DISPUTE RESOLUTION IS AN ALTERNATIVE TO AND NOT A SUBSTITUTE FOR A TRIAL AND THAT THIS CASE MAY BE TRIED IF IT IS NOT SETTLED, I REPRESENT TO THE COURT THAT I WILL ATTEMPT IN GOOD FAITH TO RESOLVE CONTESTED ISSUES IN THIS CASE BY ALTERNATIVE DISPUTE RESOLUTION WITHOUT THE NECESSITY OF COURT INTERVENTION.

Petitioner's name _____

IN THE MATTER OF   *   IN THE DISTRICT COURT

THE MARRIAGE OF   *

AND   _____ JUDICIAL DISTRICT

AND IN THE INTERESTS OF

MINOR CHILDREN   _____ COUNTY, TEXAS

PETITION OF GRANDPARENT(S) FOR INTERVENTION IN SUIT AFFECTING THE PARENT-CHILD RELATIONSHIP

This petition in intervention is brought by _____.
In support, Intervenors show:

1.   <u>Parties</u>

     This suit is brought by _____, whose age is _____ years and _____ , whose age is _____ years. Petitioners, who are the _____ grandparents of the children the subject of this suit, reside at _____.
Petitioners have standing to bring this suit under section 153.432 of the Texas Family Code.

2.   <u>Jurisdiction</u>

     No court has continuing jurisdiction of this suit or of the children the subject of this suit.

3.   <u>Children</u>

     The following children are the subject of this suit:

     NAME: _____

     SEX: _____

     BIRTHPLACE: _____

     BIRTH DATE: _____

     PRESENT RESIDENCE: _____

     NAME: _____

     SEX: _____

     BIRTHPLACE: _____

     BIRTH DATE: _____

     PRESENT RESIDENCE: _____

4.   <u>Mother</u>

     The mother of the children is _____ , whose age is over 21 years and whose residence is _____.

5.   Father

The father of the children is _____ , whose age is over 21 years and whose residence is _____.

6.   Court-Ordered Relationships

There are no persons having a court-ordered relationship with the children.

7.   Property

A full description and statement of value of all property owned or possessed by the children is as follows.

8.   Access

It is in the best interest of the children that Petitioners be granted reasonable access to the children by order of this Court.

Denial of visitation would significantly impair the child's physical health or emotional well-being.

At the time this relief is requested, Petitioners allege the parents of the children are biologic or adoptive parents.

A suit for the dissolution of the parents' marriage is pending.

The father has been incarcerated during the three-month period preceding the filing of this petition.

Other statutory grounds: _____.

Petitioners request the Court to enter its order for access to the children as follows: Grandparents _____ are to have possession of the children from _____.

9.   Prayer

Petitioners prays that citation and notice issue as required by law. Petitioners pray that the Court grant relief in accordance with the foregoing allegations. Petitioners pray for general relief.

Respectfully submitted,

BY: _____

Name: _____

BY: _____

Name: _____

Address: _____

_____

Telephone: _____

CERTIFICATE OF SERVICE

I certify that a true copy of the above was served on _____
_____,
in accordance with the Texas Rules of Civil Procedure on _____.

[CASE STYLE]

UNIFORM CHILD CUSTODY JURISDICTION AND ENFORCEMENT ACT AFFIDAVIT

1. The name and present address of each child (under 18) in this case is:

2. The places where the child(ren) has/have lived within the last 5 years are:

3. The name(s) and present address(es) of custodians with whom the child(ren) has/have lived within the past 5 years are:

4. I do not know of, and have not participated (as a party, witness, or in any other capacity) in, any other court decision, order, or proceeding (including divorce, separate maintenance, child neglect, dependency, or guardianship) concerning the custody or visitation of the child(ren) in this state or any other state, except: [specify case name and number and court's name and address]

5. I do not have information of any pending proceeding (including divorce, separate maintenance, child neglect, dependency, or guardianship) concerning the custody or visitation of the child(ren), in this state or any other state except: [specify case name and number and court's name and address]

      That proceeding ____is continuing   ____has been stayed by the court.

      ____ Temporary action by this court is necessary to protect the child(ren) because the child(ren) has/have been subjected to or threatened with mistreatment or abuse or is/are otherwise neglected or dependent.
      Attach explanation.

6. I do not know of any person who is not already a party to this proceeding who has physical custody of, or who claims to have custody or visitation rights with, the child(ren), except: [state name(s) and address(es)]

7. The child(ren)'s "home state" is _____ ["Home State" means the state in which the child(ren) immediately preceding the time involved lived with his or her parents, a parent, or a person acting as a parent, for at least 6 consecutive months, and, in the case of a child less than 6 months old, the state in which the child lived from birth with any of the persons mentioned. Periods of temporary absence of the named persons are counted as a part of the 6 month or other period.]

I acknowledge a continuing duty to advise this court of any custody or visitation proceeding (including dissolution of marriage, separate maintenance, child neglect, or dependency) concerning the child(ren) in this state or any other state about which information is obtained during this proceeding.

DATED: _____

                                    _____
                                    Signature of Affiant

                                    Name _____

                                    Address _____

                                    _____

                                    Telephone No. _____

Acknowledged before me on _____, by _____
_____, who is personally known to me or produced _____
as identification, and who did take an oath.

                                    _____
                                    NOTARY PUBLIC
                                    My Commission Expires:

[CASE STYLE]

CERTIFICATE OF SERVICE

I HEREBY CERTIFY that a true copy of _____

_____

was: _____mailed _____hand delivered to the parties listed below, this _____ day of

_____, _____.

Name _____   Name _____

Address _____   Address _____

_____   _____

Telephone No. _____   Telephone No. _____

_____

Signature of Party serving document

Name _____

Address _____

_____

Telephone No. _____

This page intentionally blank.

[CASE STYLE]

MOTION FOR DEFAULT

The undersigned _____ hereby moves for the entry of a default against _____ for failure to serve or file a timely response to the _____ as required by law.

DATED: _____

                                                  _____

                                                  Signature

                                                  Name _____

                                                  Address _____

                                                  _____

                                                  Telephone No. _____

DEFAULT

A default is entered in this action against _____ for failure to serve or file a response as required by law.

DATED: _____

                                                  CLERK OF THE COURT

                                                  By: _____

This page intentionally blank.

[CASE STYLE]

SUBPOENA

TO:

YOU ARE HEREBY COMMANDED to appear before the Honorable _____
_____, Judge of the Court, at _____
_____,
on _____, _____, at _____ o'clock ___.M., to testify in this
action.

You are also commended to bring with you the following:

If you fail to appear, you may be in contempt of court.

You are subpoenaed to appear by the attorneys or parties designated below, and unless
excused from this subpoena by these attorneys or parties, or the court, you shall respond
to this subpoena as directed.

DATED: _____

Attorney or Party Requesting Subpoena   CLERK OF THE COURT

Name: _____

Address: _____   By: _____

_____

Telephone No: _____

This page intentionally blank.

[CASE STYLE]

NOTICE OF HEARING

TO:

PLEASE TAKE NOTICE that the above-entitled matter will be called on for hearing on

_____

on _____, the _____ day of _____, _____, at _____

o'clock _____.M., before the Honorable _____,

Judge, at _____

_____.

_____

Signature

Name _____

Address _____

_____

Telephone No. _____

This page intentionally blank.

_____

VS.   CASE NO. _____

_____

REQUEST FOR MEDIATION

This Request for Mediation is brought by _____,
_____. In support, _____ shows:

There is a reasonable expectation that the dispute in this case may be resolved by the use of mediation.

_____ requests the Court to refer this dispute for resolution by mediation.

_____ prays that the Court grant this Request for Mediation.

_____
SIGNATURE

_____
NAME

_____
ADDRESS

_____
TELEPHONE NUMBER

ORDER ON REQUEST FOR MEDIATION

On _____, the Court considered the Request for Mediation of _____, _____, and finds that the Request should be granted.

IT IS THEREFORE ORDERED that the Request for Mediation of _____ _____, _____, is GRANTED.

IT IS ORDERED that the pending dispute be referred to mediation.

SIGNED on _____, _____.

_____
Judge

This page intentionally blank.

[CASE STYLE]

WAIVER

STATE OF   )

COUNTY OF   )

    BEFORE ME, the undersigned authority, on this day personally appeared _____, who, by me duly sworn, made the following statements and swore that they were true:

    I, _____, am the _____ in the above-entitled and numbered cause. My mailing address is _____ _____.

I have been given a copy of the _____ _____

that has been filed in this cause, and I have read it and understand it. I hereby enter my appearance in this cause for all purposes and waive the issuance and service of process. I agree that the cause may be taken up and considered by the Court without further notice to me. I further waive the making of a record of testimony in this cause.

    I further agree that the cause may be heard by the presiding Judge of the Court or by a duly appointed master, hearing officer, or referee of the Court.

_____

SIGNED under oath before me on _____.

_____
Notary Public
My commission expires:

This page intentionally blank.

[CASE STYLE]

VISITATION ORDER

This action for child custody was heard before the Court on _____.
All interested parties appearing were given the opportunity to be heard and to present evidence. On the evidence presented, the Court makes the following findings and orders

Jurisdiction: The Court, having examined the pleadings and heard the evidence and argument of the parties, finds that it has jurisdiction of this cause and of all the parties and that no other court has continuing, exclusive jurisdiction of this cause. All persons entitled to notice of this action and final hearing were properly given notice.

Visitation:

IT IS ORDERED that _____
shall have visitation with the children, _____
as follows:

Costs: Costs of court are to be borne by _____.

ORDERED on _____, _____.

_____
Judge

This page intentionally blank.

NO. _____

IN THE INTEREST OF	*	IN THE DISTRICT COURT
	*	
	*	
	*	_____ DISTRICT
	*	
	*	
CHILDREN	*	_____ COUNTY, TEXAS

DECREE GRANTING GRANDPARENT ACCESS

On _____, hearing was held in this cause.

Appearances

Petitioners, _____, appeared in person.

Respondents, _____, appeared in person and through their attorney of record, _____.

_____ waived issuance and service of citation by waiver duly filed herein and did not otherwise appear.

Jurisdiction

The Court, having examined the pleadings and heard the evidence and argument of counsel, finds that it has jurisdiction of this cause and of all the parties and that no other court has continuing, exclusive jurisdiction of this cause.

Findings

A jury was waived, and all matters in controversy, including questions of act and of law, were submitted to the Court. All persons entitled to citation were properly cited. The making of a record of testimony was waived by the parties with the consent of the Court.

The Court finds that the children the subject of this suit are:

NAME: _____

SEX: _____

BIRTHPLACE: _____

BIRTH DATE: _____

PRESENT RESIDENCE: _____

HOME STATE: _____

NAME: _____

SEX: _____

BIRTHPLACE: _____

BIRTH DATE: _____

PRESENT RESIDENCE: _____

HOME STATE: _____

Orders

The Court finds that the following orders are in the best interest of the children:

IT IS ORDERED AND DECREED that _____ are granted access to the children as follows: Grandparents _____ are to have possession of the children from _____

_____.

Surrender of Child. _____ are each ORDERED AND DECREED to surrender the child to _____ _____ at the beginning of each period of _____ _____'s possession at the residence of

_____.

Return of Child. _____ ARE ORDERED AND DECREED to surrender the child to _____ _____ at the end of each period of _____'s possession at the residence of

_____.

Personal Effects. Each party is ORDERED AND DECREED to return with the child the personal effects that the child brought at the beginning of the period of possession.

Designation of Competent Adult. Each party may designate any competent adult to pick up and return the child, as applicable. IT IS ORDERED AND DECREED that a conservator or a designated competent adult be present when the child is picked up or returned.

Location

Each party is ORDERED AND DECREED to keep the other party and the Court fully and promptly informed of his or her current street address of residence, home telephone number, name of employer, place of employment, and work telephone number and of the address of the children's school or day-care center. Each party who intends a change of place of residence is ORDERED AND DECREED to give written notice of the intended date of change, new telephone number, and new street address of residence to the Clerk of this Court and every other party who has possession of or access to the children on or before the 60th day before the change of residence or, if the party did not know and could not have known of the change or if the required information is not available within the 60-day period, on or before the fifth day after the day the party knew or should have known of the change or of the related information.

Notice may be given to the other party by delivering a copy of the notice to the party either in person or by registered or certified mail, return receipt requested, to the party's last known address. Notice may be given to the Court by delivering a copy of the notice either in person to the Clerk of the Court or by registered or certified mail addressed to the Clerk.

WARNINGS TO PARTIES

FAILURE TO OBEY A COURT ORDER FOR CHILD SUPPORT OR FOR POSSESSION OF OR ACCESS TO A CHILD MAY RESULT IN FURTHER LITIGATION TO ENFORCE THE ORDER, INCLUDING CONTEMPT OF COURT. A FINDING OF CONTEMPT MAY BE PUNISHED BY CONFINEMENT IN JAIL FOR UP TO SIX MONTHS, A FINE OF UP TO $500 FOR EACH VIOLATION, AND A MONEY JUDGMENT FOR PAYMENT OF ATTORNEY'S FEES AND COURT COSTS.

FAILURE OF A PARTY TO MAKE A CHILD-SUPPORT PAYMENT TO THE PLACE AND IN THE MANNER REQUIRED BY A COURT ORDER MAY RESULT IN THE PARTY'S NOT RECEIVING CREDIT FOR MAKING THE PAYMENT.

FAILURE OF A PARTY TO PAY CHILD-SUPPORT DOES NOT JUSTIFY DENYING THAT PARTY COURT-ORDERED POSSESSION OF OR ACCESS TO A CHILD. REFUSAL BY A PARTY TO ALLOW POSSESSION OF OR ACCESS TO A CHILD DOES NOT JUSTIFY FAILURE TO PAY COURT-ORDERED CHILD SUPPORT TO THAT PARTY.

EACH PERSON WHO IS A PARTY TO THIS ORDER OR DECREE IS ORDERED TO NOTIFY THE CLERK OF THIS COURT WITHIN 10 DAYS AFTER THE DATE OF ANY CHANGE IN THE PARTY'S CURRENT RESIDENCE ADDRESS, MAILING ADDRESS, HOME TELEPHONE NUMBER, NAME OF EMPLOYER, ADDRESS OF PLACE OF EMPLOYMENT, OR WORK TELEPHONE NUMBER. ALL NOTICES SHALL BE IN WRITING AND SHALL STATE THE NEW INFORMATION AND THE EFFECTIVE DATE OF THE CHANGE. THE DUTY TO FURNISH THIS INFORMATION TO THE CLERK OF THE COURT CONTINUES AS LONG AS ANY PERSON, BY VIRTUE OF THIS ORDER OR DECREE, IS UNDER AN OBLIGATION TO PAY CHILD SUPPORT OR IS ENTITLED TO POSSESSION OF OR ACCESS TO A CHILD. FAILURE TO OBEY THE ORDER OF THIS COURT TO PROVIDE THE CLERK WITH THE CURRENT MAILING ADDRESS OF A PARTY MAY RESULT IN THE ISSUANCE OF A CAPIAS FOR THE ARREST OF THE PARTY IF THAT PARTY CANNOT BE PERSONALLY SERVED WITH NOTICE OF A HEARING AT AN ADDRESS OF RECORD.

Costs

Costs of court are to be borne by the party by whom such costs were incurred.

Date of Judgment

SIGNED on _____, _____ .

_____
JUDGE PRESIDING

APPROVED AS TO FORM ONLY:

APPROVED AND CONSENTED TO AS TO BOTH FORM AND SUBSTANCE:

_____   _____

Attorney for

_____   _____

_____

[CASE STYLE]

COMPLAINT/PETITION FOR CUSTODY

_____ (hereinafter called
the _____) for his/her/their _____
against _____ (hereinafter
called the _____), allege(s) and state(s):

1.   Parties.

The _____ is/are _____,
and reside(s) at _____.

The _____ is/are _____,
and reside(s) at _____.

The child(ren) is/are _____,
and reside(s) at _____.

2.   Grounds.

In support of this request for physical custody, _____
allege(s) and show(s) the Court as follows: _____
_____
_____.

3.   The _____ is/are not aware of any other court decision, order, or proceeding concerning the custody or visitation of the child(ren) in this state or any other, except:

4. <u>Relief Requested</u>.

The _____ request(s) the following relief from the Court:

_____

_____

_____

_____.

DATED: _____

_____

Signature

Name: _____

_____

Signature

Name: _____

Address: _____

_____

Telephone: _____

NO. _____

IN THE INTEREST OF	*	IN THE DISTRICT COURT
	*	
	*	
	*	_____ DISTRICT
	*	
	*	
CHILDREN	*	_____ COUNTY, TEXAS

ORIGINAL PETITION IN SUIT
AFFECTING THE PARENT-CHILD RELATIONSHIP

1.   <u>Petitioner</u>.
       This suit is brought by _____,
Petitioner(s), who is/are over 21 years of age and who reside(s) at _____
_____.

       Petitioners are the grandmother and grandfather of the children the subject of this suit.

       Petitioners have standing to bring this suit in that Petitioners would show the court that the child's present environment presents a serious and immediate question concerning the child's physical health or welfare.

2.   <u>Jurisdiction</u>.
       No court has continuing jurisdiction of this suit or of the children the subject of this suit.

3.   <u>Children</u>.
       The following children are the subject of this suit:

       NAME: _____
       SEX: _____
       BIRTHPLACE: _____
       BIRTH DATE: _____
       PRESENT RESIDENCE: _____

       NAME: _____
       SEX: _____
       BIRTHPLACE: _____
       BIRTH DATE: _____
       PRESENT RESIDENCE: _____

4.   <u>Persons Entitled to Citation</u>.

      The mother of the child(ren) is _____, who is over 21 years of age and who resides at _____.

      Process should be served at that address.

      The father of the child(ren) is _____, who is over 21 years of age and who resides at _____.

      Process should be served at that address.

      There are no court-ordered conservatorships, court-ordered guardianships, or other court-ordered relationships affecting the children the subject of this suit.

5.   <u>Property</u>.

      No property is owned or possessed by the children the subject of this suit.

6.   <u>Conservatorship</u>.

      The parents of the children are or will be separated. It is in the best interest of the children that the Petitioner be appointed sole managing conservator of the children.

7.   <u>Support</u>.

      _____, Respondents, are obligated to support the children and should be ordered by the Court to make payments for the support of the children in the manner specified by the Court.

8.   <u>Prayer</u>.

      Petitioner prays that citation and notice issue as required by law and that the Court enter its orders in accordance with the foregoing allegations.

      Petitioner prays for attorney's fees, expenses, and costs.

      Petitioner prays for general relief.

                                  Respectfully submitted,

                                  BY: _____

                                  Name _____

                                  BY: _____

                                  Name _____

                                  Name _____

                                  Address _____

                                  _____

                                  Telephone No. _____

NO. _____

IN THE INTEREST OF	*	IN THE DISTRICT COURT
	*	
	*	
	*	_____ DISTRICT
	*	
	*	
CHILDREN	*	_____ COUNTY, TEXAS

PETITION OF GRANDPARENT(S) FOR INTERVENTION
IN SUIT AFFECTING THE PARENT-CHILD RELATIONSHIP

1.   <u>Petitioner</u>.

This suit is brought by _____,
Petitioner(s), who is/are over 21 years of age and who reside(s) at _____
_____.

Petitioners are the grandmother and grandfather of the children the subject of this suit.

Petitioners have standing to bring this suit in that Petitioners would show the court that the child's present environment presents a serious and immediate question concerning the child's physical health or welfare.

2.   <u>Jurisdiction</u>.

No court has continuing jurisdiction of this suit or of the children the subject of this suit.

3.   <u>Children</u>.

The following children are the subject of this suit:

NAME: _____
SEX: _____
BIRTHPLACE: _____
BIRTH DATE: _____
PRESENT RESIDENCE: _____

NAME: _____
SEX: _____
BIRTHPLACE: _____
BIRTH DATE: _____
PRESENT RESIDENCE: _____

4.   Persons Entitled to Citation.
        The mother of the child(ren) is _____, who is over 21 years of age and who resides at _____.
        Process should be served at that address.
        The father of the child(ren) is _____, who is over 21 years of age and who resides at _____.
        Process should be served at that address.
        There are no court-ordered conservatorships, court-ordered guardianships, or other court-ordered relationships affecting the children the subject of this suit.

5.   Property.
        No property is owned or possessed by the children the subject of this suit.

6.   Conservatorship.
        The parents of the children are or will be separated. It is in the best interest of the children that the Petitioner be appointed sole managing conservator of the children.

7.   Support.
        _____, Respondents, are obligated to support the children and should be ordered by the Court to make payments for the support of the children in the manner specified by the Court.

8.   Prayer.
        Petitioner prays that citation and notice issue as required by law and that the Court enter its orders in accordance with the foregoing allegations.
        Petitioner prays for attorney's fees, expenses, and costs.
        Petitioner prays for general relief.

                              Respectfully submitted,

                              BY: _____

                              Name _____

                              BY: _____

                              Name _____

                              Name _____

                              Address _____

                              _____

                              Telephone No. _____

[CASE STYLE]

CUSTODY ORDER

This action for child custody was heard before the Court on _____.
All interested parties appearing were given the opportunity to be heard and to present evidence. On the evidence presented, the Court makes the following findings and orders:

<u>Jurisdiction</u>

The Court, having examined the pleadings and heard the evidence and argument of the parties, finds that it has jurisdiction of this cause and of all the parties and that no other court has continuing, exclusive jurisdiction of this cause. All persons entitled to notice of this action and final hearing were properly given notice.

<u>Custody</u>

IT IS ORDERED that _____
_____ shall have physical custody of the following children:

<u>Visitation</u>

IT IS ORDERED that _____
_____shall have visitation with the children as follows:

Child Support

IT IS ORDERED that _____
shall pay child support in the amount of $_____ per _____, to
_____.

Costs

Costs of court are to be borne by _____.

Other Provisions

ORDERED on _____, _____.

_____
Judge

NO. _____

In the Interest of	*	In the District Court
	*	
_____,	*	_____ JUDICIAL DISTRICT
	*	
A CHILD	*	_____ COUNTY, TEXAS

DECREE FOR CHILD CUSTODY

On _____, hearing was held in this cause.

<u>Appearances</u>

Petitioners, _____appeared in person.

Respondents, _____appeared in person.

<u>Jurisdiction</u>

The Court, having examined the pleadings and heard the evidence and argument of the parties, finds that it has jurisdiction of this cause and of all the parties and that no other court has continuing, exclusive jurisdiction of this cause.

<u>Findings</u>

A jury was waived, and all questions of fact and of law were submitted to the Court. All persons entitled to citation were properly cited. The making of a record of testimony was:

> waived by the parties with the consent of the Court

> duly reported by_____.

The Court finds that the following children are the subject of this suit:

NAME: _____
SEX: _____
BIRTHPLACE: _____
BIRTH DATE: _____
HOME STATE: _____
SOCIAL SECURITY NO: _____
DRIVER'S LICENSE NO: _____

NAME: _____
SEX: _____
BIRTHPLACE: _____
BIRTH DATE: _____
HOME STATE: _____
SOCIAL SECURITY NO: _____
DRIVER'S LICENSE NO: _____

Conservatorship

The Court finds the following orders are in the best interest of the children:

IT IS ORDERED AND DECREED that _____ shall have physical custody of the following children: _____

_____.

Possession Order

IT IS ORDERED AND DECREED that _____ shall have access to the children as follows: _____

_____

_____

_____.

Costs

Costs of court are to be borne by _____.

Relief Not Granted

IT IS ORDERED AND DECREED that all relief requested in this cause and not expressly granted is denied.

Date of Judgment

SIGNED on _____, _____.

_____

JUDGE PRESIDING

[CASE STYLE]

MOTION FOR SOCIAL STUDY

The undersigned, hereby move(s) this Court to order that a social study be conducted into the circumstances and condition of the child(ren) and of the homes of all parties seeking custody of, or visitation with, the child(ren) to determine the best interest of the child(ren) regarding custody and visitation.

Dated: _____

_____
Signature

Name: _____

Address: _____

_____

Telephone: _____

ORDER FOR SOCIAL STUDY

IN CONSIDERATION of the foregoing Motion for Social Study, and the Court being fully advised in the premises;

IT IS HEREBY ORDERED that _____

_____ shall conduct a social study into the circumstances and conditions of the child(ren) and of the homes of all persons seeking custody of, or visitation with, said child(ren), and shall file written findings and conclusions of the social study with the Court on or before _____.

ORDERED on _____.

_____
Judge

This page intentionally blank.

[CASE STYLE]

MOTION FOR APPOINTMENT OF GUARDIAN AD LITEM

The undersigned movant requests this court appoint a guardian ad litem and states:

1. This matter is before the Court on the undersigned movant's complaint/petition for custody of/visitation with the following minor child(ren):

    Child(ren)
    <u>Name(s)</u>   <u>Date Of Birth</u>   <u>Age</u>   <u>Sex</u>   <u>Presently residing with</u>

2. A guardian ad litem is necessary to protect the best interests of the child(ren).

3. Other court-ordered social investigations are:
    ___ Home study
    ___ Other (specify)_____

4. Payment of attorney's fees for guardian ad litem, at the reasonable rate of $_____/hr. shall be:
    ___waived [indigence affidavit(s) filed].
    ___paid by _____.
    ___determined and allocated by court at conclusion of case.

5. The issues in this case require immediate action. It is requested that the guardian ad litem promptly complete the investigation and file the report with the court and serve copies on parties or counsel by _____.
    (date)

DATED: _____   _____
                                     Signature

                                     Name: _____

                                     Address: _____

                                     _____

                                     Telephone: _____

This page intentionally blank.

[CASE STYLE]

ORDER APPOINTING GUARDIAN AD LITEM

IN CONSIDERATION of the Motion to Appoint Guardian Ad Litem, and the Court being fully advised in the premises; the Court finds that it is in the best interests of the minor child(ren) in this case, that a guardian ad litem be appointed. Therefore, it is

ORDERED that

1. _____

[Name, address, telephone number]

is hereby appointed guardian ad litem for the minor child(ren) in this matter. Counsel for the parties, or pro se parties should contact the guardian ad litem immediately.

2.   <u>Authority of guardian ad litem</u>. Upon presentation of this order to any agency, hospital, organization, school, person, or office, public and private health facilities, medical and mental health professionals, including doctors, nurses, pediatricians, psychologists, psychiatrists, counselors and staff, and law enforcement agencies, the individual designated by this order is hereby authorized to inspect and copy any records relating to the child(ren), without the consent of the child(ren) or the parents of the child(ren).

3.   <u>Confidentiality</u>. The guardian ad litem shall maintain any information received from any such source as confidential, and will not disclose the same except in reports to the court and other parties to this cause.

4.   <u>Attendance at all proceedings</u>. The guardian ad litem shall attend all depositions, hearings, and all proceedings scheduled in this case and shall assure proper representation of the child(ren)'s best interests at such proceedings.

5.   <u>Notification</u>. The guardian ad litem shall be notified of any depositions, hearings, investigations, or other proceedings, and shall be notified prior to any action which may affect the child(ren).

6.   <u>Duties of guardian ad litem</u>. The guardian ad litem, in addition to attendance at all proceedings, shall meet with the parties, their counsel, and the child(ren); may contact psychologists/counselors, family members, friends, neighbors, or school personnel, and shall conduct such other investigation as would assist the court in its determination of the best interests of the child(ren).

7.   <u>Consultation prior to agreement</u>. The guardian ad litem shall be consulted prior to any agreement or plan being entered into which affects the welfare of the child(ren).

8.   <u>Report</u>. The guardian ad litem shall file and serve upon counsel or pro se parties a report of court appointed guardian ad litem at least 1 week prior to the final hearing in this matter.

9.   <u>Payment for services of guardian ad litem</u>. An affidavit of indigence __has __has not been filed. Therefore, the guardian ad litem

      ___shall serve pro bono

      ___shall not serve pro bono and shall be paid for fees and costs incurred.

      The fees and costs shall be

      ___ paid by _____

      ___determined at conclusion of case.

DATED: _____   _____

                                          JUDGE

Attorney for Petitioner or Petitioner   Attorney for Respondent or Respondent

Name _____   Name _____

Address _____   Address _____

_____   _____

Telephone No. _____   Telephone No. _____

Guardian ad litem

Name _____

Address _____

_____

Telephone No. _____

[CASE STYLE]

MOTION FOR PSYCHIATRIC/PSYCHOLOGICAL EXAMINATION

The movant(s), _____, respectfully request(s) that the court order psychiatric or psychological evaluation of the parties and minor child(ren) in this case, and states:

____ 1.   The psychological condition of the party(ies) is at issue in this case and good cause therefore exists for psychological evaluation of:

_____ Mother   _____ Father   _____ Child(ren)   _____ Movant(s)

_____ Other (specify): _____

____ 2.   <u>Payment for psychological evaluations.</u>

____Movant(s) is/are unable to pay and an affidavit of indigence in this case ___has ___has not been filed.

____Father ____Mother of the child(ren) is/are gainfully employed and well able to pay the costs of such evaluations.

____Father ____Mother ____Movant(s) are well able to contribute to the costs of evaluation, and movant(s) request the court order costs of evaluations be equitably divided between them.

DATED: _____   _____
                                      Signature

I HEREBY CERTIFY THAT I have
___mailed
___hand delivered
a copy of this Motion on
_____ to:
Attorney for Opposing Party or Party
Name _____
Address _____
        _____
Telephone No. _____

Attorney for Moving Party or Party
Name _____
Address _____
        _____
Telephone No. _____

This page intentionally blank.

[CASE STYLE]

ORDER FOR PSYCHIATRIC/PSYCHOLOGICAL EXAMINATION

THE COURT having considered the motion for psychological evaluation, it is hereby:

ORDERED AND ADJUDGED that:

1.   The following psychologist/psychiatrist shall conduct a psychological evaluation of the parties and the children as soon as is expediently possible:

       Name _____

       Address _____

       Telephone No. _____

2.   The evaluation shall concentrate on the following issues:

     ____   Custody   ____   Visitation and contact

     ____   Abuse/neglect allegations   ____   Other (specify): _____

3.   The parties or their counsel shall immediately contact the court-appointed psychologist/psychiatrist to assure scheduling for their clients and the minor child(ren).

4.   The original report shall be filed with the court, and a copy furnished to each pro se party or the attorney for each represented party.

5.   The court determines payment for such psychological evaluation as follows:

_____

_____

_____

_____

The cost for each evaluation should not exceed $_____.

DATED: _____   _____

                                                        JUDGE

Copies furnished to:

All counsel of record or pro se parties

Psychologist/psychiatrist

This page intentionally blank.

[CASE STYLE]

MOTION TO PROCEED IN FORMA PAUPERIS

The undersigned _____, hereby moves this Court to waive court filing fees and other costs associated with bringing this action, and allow the undersigned to proceed *in forma pauperis*. This motion is based upon the following facts and circumstances:

I am insolvent and unable to pay the charges, costs or fees otherwise payable by law to any clerk, or sheriff in this civil action because (choose one):

____   a.   I am currently receiving public assistance: $_____
                per _____ Case No._____.

____   b.   I am unable to pay those clerk's fees and costs because of indigence, based
                on the following facts:

         INCOME: _____

         _____
         Employer name and address

         _____
         Length of employment

         $_____ $_____
          Average gross pay   Average net pay

         per ___week ___month ___2 weeks

         ASSETS: [State value of car, home, bank deposits, bonds, stocks, etc.]

OBLIGATIONS: [Itemize monthly rent, installment payments, mortgage payments, child support, etc.]

_____

Signature

Name: _____

Address: _____

_____

Telephone: _____

Acknowledged before me on _____, by _____ _____, who is personally known to me or produced _____ as identification, and who did take an oath.

_____

NOTARY PUBLIC
My Commission Expires:

[CASE STYLE]

FINANCIAL AFFIDAVIT

STATE OF   )
COUNTY OF   )

BEFORE ME, this day personally appeared _____,
who being duly sworn, deposes and says that the following information is true and correct:

EMPLOYMENT AND INCOME

OCCUPATION: _____
EMPLOYED BY: _____
ADDRESS: _____
                   _____
                   _____
SOC. SEC. #:   _____
PAY PERIOD: _____
RATE OF PAY: _____

AVERAGE GROSS MONTHLY INCOME FROM EMPLOYMENT $_____

Bonuses, commissions, allowances, overtime, tips and similar payments   _____

Business Income from sources such as self-employment, partnership,
    close corporations, and/or independent contracts (gross receipts
    minus ordinary and necessary expenses required to produce income)   _____

Disability benefits   _____

Workers' Compensation   _____

Unemployment Compensation   _____

Pension, retirement, or annuity payments   _____

Social Security benefits   _____

Spousal support received from previous marriage   _____

Interest and dividends   _____

Rental income (gross receipts minus ordinary and necessary expenses
    required to produce income)   _____

Income from royalties, trusts, or estates   _____

Reimbursed expenses and in kind payments to the extent that they
    reduce personal living expenses   _____

Gains derived from dealing in property (not including nonrecurring gains)   _____

Itemize any other income of a recurring nature   _____

TOTAL MONTHLY INCOME $_____

LESS DEDUCTIONS:

Federal, state, and local income taxes (corrected for filing
     status and actual number of withholding allowances) $_____

FICA or self-employment tax (annualized)   _____

Mandatory union dues   _____

Mandatory retirement   _____

Health insurance payments   _____

Court ordered support payments for the children actually paid   _____

TOTAL DEDUCTIONS $_____

AVERAGE MONTHLY EXPENSES

HOUSEHOLD:

Mtg. or rent payments	_____
Property taxes & insurance	_____
Electricity	_____
Water, garbage, & sewer	_____
Telephone	_____
Fuel oil or natural gas	_____
Repairs and maintenance	_____
Lawn and pool care	_____
Pest control	_____
Misc. household	_____
Food and grocery items	_____
Meals outside home	_____
Other:	
_____	_____
_____	_____

AUTOMOBILE:

Gasoline and oil	_____
Repairs	_____
Auto tags and license	_____
Insurance	_____
Other:	
_____	_____
_____	_____

CHILDREN'S EXPENSES:

Nursery or babysitting	_____
School tuition	_____
School supplies	_____
Lunch money	_____
Allowance	_____
Clothing	_____
Medical, dental, prescriptions	_____
Vitamins	_____
Barber/beauty parlor	_____
Cosmetics/toiletries	_____
Gifts for special holidays	_____
Other expenses:	
_____	_____
_____	_____

INSURANCES:

Health	_____
Life	_____
Other Insurance:	
_____	_____
_____	_____

OTHER EXPENSES NOT LISTED ABOVE:

Dry cleaning and laundry	_____
Affiant's clothing	_____
Affiant's medical, dental, prescriptions	_____
Affiant's beauty salon/barber	_____
Affiant's gifts (special holidays)	_____
Pets:	
Grooming	_____
Veterinarian	_____
Membership Dues:	
Professional dues	_____
Social dues	_____
Entertainment	_____
Vacations	_____
Publications	_____
Religious organizations	_____
Charities	
_____	
Miscellaneous	_____

OTHER EXPENSES:

_____	_____
_____	_____
_____	_____
_____	_____
_____	_____
_____	_____
_____	_____
_____	_____

CHILDREN'S EXPENSES:

Subtotal $_____

TOTAL ABOVE EXPENSES $_____

PAYMENTS TO CREDITORS:

TO WHOM: BALANCE DUE: MONTHLY PAYMENTS:

_____   _____   _____
_____   _____   _____
_____   _____   _____
_____   _____   _____
_____   _____   _____
_____   _____   _____
_____   _____   _____
_____   _____   _____
_____   _____   _____
_____   _____   _____

TOTAL MONTHLY PAYMENTS TO CREDITORS: $_____

TOTAL MONTHLY EXPENSES: $_____

ASSETS (OWNERSHIP: IF JOINT, ALLOCATE EQUITY)

Description	Value	Husband	Wife
Cash (on hand or in banks)	_____	_____	_____
Stocks/bonds/notes	_____	_____	_____
Real estate:			
Home:	_____	_____	_____
_____	_____	_____	_____
_____	_____	_____	_____
_____	_____	_____	_____
Automobiles:			
_____	_____	_____	_____
_____	_____	_____	_____
_____	_____	_____	_____
Other personal property:			
Contents of home	_____	_____	_____
Jewelry	_____	_____	_____
Life Ins./cash surrender value	_____	_____	_____
Other Assets:			
_____	_____	_____	_____
_____	_____	_____	_____
_____	_____	_____	_____
TOTAL ASSETS:	$_____	$_____	$_____

LIABILITIES

Creditor	Security	Balance	Husband	Wife
_____	_____	_____	_____	_____
_____	_____	_____	_____	_____
_____	_____	_____	_____	_____
_____	_____	_____	_____	_____
_____	_____	_____	_____	_____
_____	_____	_____	_____	_____
_____	_____	_____	_____	_____
_____	_____	_____	_____	_____
TOTAL LIABILITIES:		$_____	$_____	$_____

_____

Affiant's Signature

Acknowledged before me on _____, by _____
_____, who is personally known to me or produced _____ as
identification, and who did take an oath.

_____

NOTARY PUBLIC
My Commission Expires:

CERTIFICATE OF SERVICE

I HEREBY CERTIFY that a true and correct copy of the above was delivered by mail this _____ day of
_____, _____, to: _____.

_____

Signature

Name: _____

Address: _____

_____

Telephone: _____

[CASE STYLE]

AGREEMENT REGARDING

_____

The undersigned parties stipulate and agree to the following terms and conditions as full settlement of this action, and further agree that this agreement shall be incorporated into a final order:

This court shall retain jurisdiction to enforce the terms of this agreement.

DATED:_____   DATED:_____

_____   _____
Signature   Signature
Name:_____   Name:_____

_____   _____
Signature   Signature
Name:_____   Name:_____
Address:_____   Address:_____

_____   _____
Telephone No._____   Telephone No._____

This page intentionally blank.

[CASE STYLE]

MOTION TO SET HEARING

The _____ hereby moves the Court to set a hearing on the

matter of _____.

DATED :_____   _____

                               Signature

                               Name: _____

                               Address: _____

                               _____

                               Telephone: _____

ORDER

A hearing before the Court is set for _____, _____, at

_____ _____. m., at the following location: _____

_____.

                               _____

                               Judge

This page intentionally blank.

[CASE STYLE]

CERTIFICATE OF LAST KNOWN ADDRESS

Pursuant to rule ____ of the _____, I certify that the last known mailing address of the _____, _____, is

_____.

DATED: _____

_____

Signature

Name: _____

Address: _____

_____

Telephone: _____

Index

A

absent parents, 40

abuse, 17, 37, 38, 39, 40, 44, 47, 48, 53, 73, 90, 91

access, 12, 16, 17, 43, 74, 84, 91, 95

addiction, 38

adoption, 14, 23

affidavits, 64

agreed orders, 71

Agreement, 71

Alabama, 4, 26

Alaska, 4, 43, 96

alternative dispute resolution, 23

American Jurisprudence, 5

appeals, 4, 86, 87, 93, 95

Appel v. Appel, 12

Arizona, 4, 13, 18

Arkansas, 4, 18, 81, 82

attorney ad litem, 73, 74

attorneys, 2, 5, 10, 17, 39, 55, 57, 58, 59, 60, 61, 66, 67, 68, 73, 74, 77, 86, 87, 95, 97

   selecting, 58

   working with, 60

B

Bass v. Bass, 96

best interest, 6, 10, 11, 12, 13, 15, 16-17, 29, 38, 40, 42, 43, 44, 45, 47, 52, 73, 74, 81, 82, 90, 91, 94, 96

born out of wedlock, 19, 27, 30

C

California, 4, 11, 12, 18, 74, 95
care and custody affidavit, 22
case citations, 5
case law, 6, 12, 13
case style, 24, 25, 26, 27, 28, 31, 33, 46, 50,
    51, 53, 54, 65, 66, 67, 69, 71, 72, 73, 74,
    75, 77, 83, 84, 86
Certificate of Last Known Address, 70
Certificate of Service, 32, 54, 66, 67, 70,
    72, 74
change in the circumstances, 35
child abuse, 17, 44, 47, 48, 73, 91
closing statement, 82
codes. *See statutes*
Colorado, 4, 12, 18, 22
Complaint for Grandparent Visitation, 29
Complaint/Petition for Grandparent
    Visitation, 24, 25
Complaint/Petition for Custody, 51
Connecticut, 4, 12, 17
conservatorship, 54, 86
constitutional, 11, 12, 13
contested cases, 70
Corpus Juris Secundum, 5
Court Appointed Special Advocate
    (CASA), 73
court procedures, 33, 55, 63
    filing your petition, 63
    notifying others, 64
court rules, 3
courtroom manners, 78
cover sheet, 64
custody, 1, 2, 6, 10, 13, 18, 19, 22, 27, 29,
    30, 31, 32, 34, 37, 38, 39, 40, 41, 42, 43,
    44, 45, 46, 47, 48, 49, 50, 51, 52, 53, 54,
    55, 57, 58, 61, 64, 65, 67, 68, 69, 71, 72,
    73, 74, 75, 81, 83, 84, 85, 86, 87, 89, 91,
    92, 95, 96, 97

evidence you will need, 91
filing for, 49
laws, 6
notifying the other parties, 55
obstacles to getting, 41
preparing your petition, 49
qualifying to file for, 37
reasons to consider filing for, 38
should you file for, 37
Custody Order, 84

D

death of a parent, 18, 19
Decree for Child Custody, 85
Decree Granting Grandparent Access, 84
default judgments, 68, 69
Delaware, 4, 17
depositions, 66, 75, 76, 78
digests, 5
discipline, 41
discovery, 75, 76
District of Columbia, 4, 6, 44
divorce, 1, 13, 18, 22, 23, 24, 30, 31, 34, 37,
    48, 50, 53, 54, 81, 82, 95, 96
docket number, 24, 29, 50
drug, 1, 37, 38, 40, 91

E

emotional development, 43
evidentiary rules, 79
expert witnesses, 78, 96

F

final order, 71, 82-83, 85
Financial Affidavit, 55
fit, 10, 13, 15, 16, 25, 28, 47, 93
Florida, 4, 11, 18, 22, 25, 28
form 1, 25
form 2, 169
form 3, 29
form 4, 30, 31
form 5, 31
form 6, 29, 45
form 7, 66, 67, 70, 72
form 8, 68, 69
form 9, 76
form 10, 67, 72
form 11, 23, 33
form 12, 65, 84
form 13, 70, 83
form 14, 70, 84, 85, 86
form 15, 51
form 16, 53, 54
form 17, 54
form 18, 70, 84
form 19, 70, 84, 85
form 20, 72, 91
form 21, 73
form 22, 73, 91
form 23, 74
form 24, 74, 91
form 25, 74, 75
form 26, 55
form 27, 71
form 28, 67
form 29, 70
foster a good relationship, 14
foster care, 74

G

Georgia, 4
good cause, 35
great-grandparents, 23
grounds, 42
guardian ad litem, 73, 74

H

Hawaii, 3, 4
hearsay, 79
home study, 71, 72, 92

I

Idaho, 4, 17
Illinois, 4, 18, 74
Indian Child Welfare Act, 19
Indiana, 4, 18, 52
instability, 40
interrogatories, 75
Iowa, 4, 11, 18, 25, 94

J

Jackson v. Tangreen, 13

K

Kansas, 4, 12
Kentucky, 4, 12, 17

L

law library, 2, 24, 50, 64, 67, 68
laws, 1, 2, 3, 5, 6, 7, 9, 13, 18, 19, 23, 32,
    35, 40, 43, 44, 47, 55, 90, 91, 97
    custody, 6
    visitation, 6
legal encyclopedia, 5
legal research, 2
Louisiana, 4, 12

M

Maine, 4, 11, 17, 22
managing conservator, 43
Mansukhami v. Pailing, 96
married parents, 17
Maryland, 4, 12, 18
Massachusetts, 4, 12, 18, 22, 23, 25, 29
mediation, 22, 23, 33
Michigan, 4, 22, 50, 89, 90
Minnesota, 4, 11, 18
Mississippi, 4, 18
Missouri, 4, 18, 22, 23, 33
Montana, 4, 17
Motion for Social Study (and Order), 72
Motion for Appointment of Guardian Ad
    Litem, 73
Motion for Default, 68, 69
Motion for Psychiatric/Psychological
    Examination, 74
Motion to Proceed In Forma Pauperis, 74
Motion to Set Hearing, 67
motions, 71

N

Nebraska, 4, 11
neglect, 38, 39, 44, 53, 90, 91
Nevada, 4
New Hampshire, 4
New Jersey, 4, 18
New Mexico, 4, 18
New York, 4, 17, 22, 94
noncustodial, 13, 14, 15, 17
North Carolina, 4
North Dakota, 4, 17, 96
Notice of Hearing, 67, 72

O

Ohio, 4
Oklahoma, 4, 17
opening statement, 80, 81
Order Appointing Guardian Ad Litem, 73
Order for Psychiatric/Psychological
    Examination, 74
Oregon, 4
Original Petition for Grandparent Access,
    30, 31
Original Petition in Suit Affecting the
    Parent-Child Relationship, 53

P

parental preference, 38, 42, 43, 97
Pennsylvania, 4, 18
Petition for Grandparent Visitation, 25,
    26, 30, 31, 65

Petition of Grandparents for Intervention in Suit Affecting the Parent-Child Relationship, 31, 54
Petition for Grandparent Visitation, 28
practice manuals, 3
psychological parents, 96
Punsley v. Ho, 95

R

relevancy, 80
reporters, 4, 93
Request for Mediation, 22, 33
requests for production of documents, 75
Rhode Island, 4, 11, 18

S

Santi v. Santi, 94
service by publication, 68
service of process, 64, 70
sexual abuse, 39, 47, 90
South Carolina, 4, 12, 18
South Dakota, 4
standing, 37, 42, 43
statutes, 3, 6, 10, 11, 12, 15, 17, 18, 22, 23, 26, 37, 43, 44, 52, 81, 82, 84, 97
Subpoena, 66, 76, 77, 91
subpoena duces tecum, 76, 77
Sullivan v. Sapp, 11
summons, 64, 65, 66
surviving parent, 43

T

Tennessee, 4, 17
Texas, 3, 4, 5, 18, 23, 25, 30, 31, 32, 43, 51, 53, 54, 83, 84, 85
trial procedures, 80
Troxel v. Granville, 6, 7, 9, 10, 11, 12, 13, 25, 90
    impact of, 11

U

unconstitutional, 7, 10, 11, 12, 87, 94, 95
uncontested cases, 70
unfit, 38, 39, 95
Uniform Child Custody Jurisdiction and Enforcement Act (UCCJEA), 6, 29, 44, 45
Uniform Child Custody Jurisdiction and Enforcement Act Affidavit, 45
unstable parents, 40
Utah, 4, 11

V

Vermont, 4, 12
Virginia, 4, 18
visitation
    after the court order, 34
    evidence you will need, 89
    failure to exercise, 15
    filing for, 21
    laws, 6
    modifying, 35
    notifying the other parties, 33
    preparing Your petition, 23
    reasons not to file, 16

reasons to file, 13
should you file for, 9
stability, 13, 15, 40, 41
Visitation Order, 83

W

Waiver, 65, 74, 84
Washington, 4, 9, 10, 11, 12, 24, 25
West Virginia, 4, 18
Wisconsin, 4, 12, 17
witnesses, 47, 61, 70, 75, 76, 77, 78, 79, 80, 81, 91, 96
writ of habeas corpus, 22
Wyoming, 4, 18, 19

ABOUT THE AUTHOR

Traci Truly received her law degree and undergraduate business degree from Baylor University. She has practiced family law in Dallas, Texas since 1985. In her general practice, she has handled various types of cases, representing many parents and grandparents in domestic relations matters. Ms. Truly has written or coauthored several legal guides, including *Teen Rights*, which was named to the New York Public Library's 2003 Books for Teen Age list. Her other works include *Child Custody, Support, and Visitation in Texas*, *Making Music Your Business*, and *How To Start a Business in Texas*. She has appeared on Fox Television (The Rob Nelson Show), on the Fox News Channel (Dayside with Linda Vestor), in *Seventeen Magazine*, and in the *AARP Bulletin*.

Sphinx® Publishing's National Titles
Valid in All 50 States

LEGAL SURVIVAL IN BUSINESS

The Complete Book of Corporate Forms (2E)	$29.95
The Complete Hiring and Firing Handbook	$19.95
The Complete Home-Based Business Kit	!4.95
The Complete Limited Liability Kit	$24.95
The Complete Partnership Book	$24.95
The Complete Patent Book	$26.95
The Complete Patent Kit	$39.95
The Entrepreneur's Internet Handbook	$21.95
The Entrepreneur's Legal Guide	$26.95
Financing Your Small Business	$17.95
Fired, Laid-Off or Forced Out	$14.95
How to Buy a Franchise	$19.95
How to Form a Nonprofit Corporation (3E)	$24.95
How to Form Your Own Corporation (4E)	$26.95
How to Register Your Own Copyright (5E)	$24.95
HR for Small Business	$14..95
Incorporate in Delaware from Any State	$26.95
Incorporate in Nevada from Any State	$24.95
The Law (In Plain English)® for Small Business	$19.95
The Law (In Plain English)® for Writers	$14.95
Making Music Your Business	$18.95
Minding Her Own Business (4E)	$14.95
Most Valuable Business Legal Forms You'll Ever Need (3E)	$21.95
Profit from Intellectual Property	$28.95
Protect Your Patent	$24.95
The Small Business Owner's Guide to Bankruptcy	$21.95
Start Your Own Law Practice	$16.95
Tax Power for the Self-Employed	$17.95
Tax Smarts for Small Business	$21.95
Your Rights at Work	$14.95

LEGAL SURVIVAL IN COURT

Attorney Responsibilities & Client Rights	$19.95
Crime Victim's Guide to Justice (2E)	$21.95
Legal Research Made Easy (4E)	$24.95
Winning Your Personal Injury Claim (3E)	$24.95

LEGAL SURVIVAL IN REAL ESTATE

The Complete Kit to Selling Your Own Home	$18.95
The Complete Book of Real Estate Contracts	$18.95
Essential Guide to Real Estate Leases	$18.95
Homeowner's Rights	$19.95
How to Buy a Condominium or Townhome (2E)	$19.95
How to Buy Your First Home (2E)	$14.95
How to Make Money on Foreclosures	$16.95
The Mortgage Answer Book	$14.95
Sell Your Own Home Without a Broker	$14.95
The Weekend Landlord	$16.95
Working with Your Homeowners Association	$19.95

LEGAL SURVIVAL IN SPANISH

Cómo Comprar su Primera Casa	$8.95
Cómo Conseguir Trabajo en los Estados Unidos	$8.95
Cómo Hacer su Propio Testamento	$16.95
Cómo Iniciar su Propio Negocio	$8.95
Cómo Negociar su Crédito	$8.95
Cómo Organizar un Presupuesto	$8.95
Cómo Solicitar su Propio Divorcio	$24.95
Guía de Inmigración a Estados Unidos (4E)	$24.95
Guía de Justicia para Víctimas del Crimen	$21.95

Guía Esencial para los Contratos de Arrendamiento de Bienes Raices	$22.95
Inmigración y Ciudadanía en los EE.UU. Preguntas y Respuestas	$16.95
Inmigración a los EE.UU. Paso a Paso (2E)	$24.95
Manual de Beneficios del Seguro Social	$18.95
El Seguro Social Preguntas y Respuestas	$16.95
¡Visas! ¡Visas! ¡Visas!	$9.95

LEGAL SURVIVAL IN PERSONAL AFFAIRS

101 Complaint Letters That Get Results	$18.95
The 529 College Savings Plan (2E)	$18.95
The 529 College Savings Plan Made Simple	$7.95
The Alternative Minimum Tax	$14.95
The Antique and Art Collector's Legal Guide	$24.95
The Childcare Answer Book	$12.95
Child Support	$18.95
The Complete Book of Insurance	$18.95
The Complete Book of Personal Legal Forms	$24.95
The Complete Credit Repair Kit	$19.95
The Complete Legal Guide to Senior Care	$21.95
Credit Smart	$18.95
The Easy Will and Living Will Kit	$16.95
Fathers' Rights	$19.95
File Your Own Divorce (6E)	$24.95
The Frequent Traveler's Guide	$14.95
Gay & Lesbian Rights	$26.95
Grandparents' Rights (4E)	$24.95
How to File Your Own Bankruptcy (6E)	$21.95
How to Make Your Own Simple Will (3E)	$18.95
How to Parent with Your Ex	$12.95
How to Write Your Own Living Will (4E)	$18.95
How to Write Your Own Premarital Agreement (3E)	$24.95
The Infertility Answer Book	$16.95
Law 101	$16.95
Law School 101	$16.95
The Living Trust Kit	$21.95
Living Trusts and Other Ways to Avoid Probate (3E)	$24.95
Mastering the MBE	$16.95
Nursing Homes and Assisted Living Facilities	$19.95
The Power of Attorney Handbook (5E)	$22.95
Quick Cash	$14.95
Seniors' Rights	$19.95
Sexual Harassment in the Workplace	$18.95
Sexual Harassment:Your Guide to Legal Action	$18.95
Sisters-in-Law	$16.95
The Social Security Benefits Handbook (4E)	$18.95
Social Security Q&A	$12.95
Starting Out or Starting Over	$14.95
Teen Rights (and Responsibilities) (2E)	$14.95
Unmarried Parents' Rights (and Responsibilities)(3E)	$16.95
U.S. Immigration and Citizenship Q&A	$18.95
U.S. Immigration Step by Step (2E)	$24.95
U.S.A. Immigration Guide (5E)	$26.95
What to Do—Before "I DO"	$14.95
What to Do When You Can't Get Pregnant	$16.95
The Wills, Estate Planning and Trusts Legal Kit	$26.95
Win Your Unemployment Compensation Claim (2E)	$21.95
Your Right to Child Custody, Visitation and Support (3E)	$24.95

SPHINX® PUBLISHING ORDER FORM

BILL TO:		SHIP TO:	
Phone #	Terms	F.O.B. Chicago, IL	Ship Date

Charge my: ☐ VISA ☐ MasterCard ☐ American Express

☐ **Money Order or Personal Check**

Credit Card Number ☐☐☐☐ ☐☐☐☐ ☐☐☐☐ ☐☐☐☐   Expiration Date ☐☐☐☐

Qty	ISBN	Title	Retail	Ext.
		SPHINX PUBLISHING NATIONAL TITLES		
____	1-57248-363-6	101 Complaint Letters That Get Results	$18.95	____
____	1-57248-361-X	The 529 College Savings Plan (2E)	$18.95	____
____	1-57248-483-7	The 529 College Savings Plan Made Simple	$7.95	____
____	1-57248-460-8	The Alternative Minimum Tax	$14.95	____
____	1-57248-349-0	The Antique and Art Collector's Legal Guide	$24.95	____
____	1-57248-347-4	Attorney Responsibilities & Client Rights	$19.95	____
____	1-57248-482-9	The Childcare Answer Book	$12.95	____
____	1-57248-382-2	Child Support	$18.95	____
____	1-57248-487-X	Cómo Comprar su Primera Casa	$8.95	____
____	1-57248-488-8	Cómo Conseguir Trabajo en los Estados Unidos	$8.95	____
____	1-57248-148-X	Cómo Hacer su Propio Testamento	$16.95	____
____	1-57248-532-9	Cómo Iniciar su Propio Negocio	$8.95	____
____	1-57248-462-4	Cómo Negociar su Crédito	$8.95	____
____	1-57248-463-2	Cómo Organizar un Presupuesto	$8.95	____
____	1-57248-147-1	Cómo Solicitar su Propio Divorcio	$24.95	____
____	1-57248-507-8	The Complete Book of Corporate Forms (2E)	$29.95	____
____	1-57248-383-0	The Complete Book of Insurance	$18.95	____
____	1-57248499-3	The Complete Book of Personal Legal Forms	$24.95	____
____	1-57248-528-0	The Complete Book of Real Estate Contracts	$18.95	____
____	1-57248-500-0	The Complete Credit Repair Kit	$19.95	____
____	1-57248-458-6	The Complete Hiring and Firing Handbook	$18.95	____
____	1-57248-484-5	The Complete Home-Based Business Kit	$16.95	____
____	1-57248-353-9	The Complete Kit to Selling Your Own Home	$18.95	____
____	1-57248-229-X	The Complete Legal Guide to Senior Care	$21.95	____
____	1-57248-498-5	The Complete Limited Liability Company Kit	$24.95	____
____	1-57248-391-1	The Complete Partnership Book	$24.95	____
____	1-57248-201-X	The Complete Patent Book	$26.95	____
____	1-57248-514-0	The Complete Patent Kit	$39.95	____
____	1-57248-480-2	The Mortgage Answer Book	$14.95	____
____	1-57248-369-5	Credit Smart	$18.95	____
____	1-57248-163-3	Crime Victim's Guide to Justice (2E)	$21.95	____
____	1-57248-481-0	The Easy Will and Living Will Kit	$16.95	____
____	1-57248-251-6	The Entrepreneur's Internet Handbook	$21.95	____
____	1-57248-235-4	The Entrepreneur's Legal Guide	$26.95	____
____	1-57248-160-9	Essential Guide to Real Estate Leases	$18.95	____
____	1-57248-375-X	Fathers' Rights	$19.95	____
____	1-57248-517-5	File Your Own Divorce (6E)	$24.95	____
____	1-57248-450-0	Financing Your Small Business	$17.95	____
____	1-57248-459-4	Fired, Laid Off or Forced Out	$14.95	____
____	1-57248-502-7	The Frequent Traveler's Guide	$14.95	____
____	1-57248-331-8	Gay & Lesbian Rights	$26.95	____
____	1-57248-526-4	Grandparents' Rights (4E)	$24.95	____
____	1-57248-475-6	Guía de Inmigración a Estados Unidos (4E)	$24.95	____
____	1-57248-187-0	Guía de Justicia para Víctimas del Crimen	$21.95	____
____	1-57248-253-2	Guía Esencial para los Contratos de Arrendamiento de Bienes Raices	$22.95	____
____	1-57248-334-2	Homeowner's Rights	$19.95	____
____	1-57248-164-1	How to Buy a Condominium or Townhome (2E)	$19.95	____
____	1-57248-197-7	How to Buy Your First Home (2E)	$14.95	____
____	1-57248-384-9	How to Buy a Franchise	$19.95	____
____	1-57248-472-1	How to File Your Own Bankruptcy (6E)	$21.95	____
____	1-57248-390-3	How to Form a Nonprofit Corporation (3E)	$24.95	____
____	1-57248-345-8	How to Form Your Own Corporation (4E)	$26.95	____
____	1-57248-520-5	How to Make Money on Foreclosures	$16.95	____
____	1-57248-232-X	How to Make Your Own Simple Will (3E)	$18.95	____
____	1-57248-479-9	How to Parent with Your Ex	$12.95	____
____	1-57248-379-2	How to Register Your Own Copyright (5E)	$24.95	____
____	1-57248-394-6	How to Write Your Own Living Will (4E)	$18.95	____
____	1-57248-156-0	How to Write Your Own Premarital Agreement (3E)	$24.95	____
____	1-57248-504-3	HR for Small Business	$14.95	____
____	1-57248-230-3	Incorporate in Delaware from Any State	$26.95	____
____	1-57248-158-7	Incorporate in Nevada from Any State	$24.95	____
____	1-57248-531-0	The Infertility Answer Book	$16.95	____
____	1-57248-474-8	Inmigración a los EE.UU. Paso a Paso (2E)	$24.95	____
____	1-57248-400-4	Inmigración y Ciudadanía en los EE.UU. Preguntas y Respuestas	$16.95	____
____	1-57248-453-5	Law 101	$16.95	____
____	1-57248-374-1	Law School 101	$16.95	____
____	1-57248-377-6	The Law (In Plain English)® for Small Business	$19.95	____
____	1-57248-476-4	The Law (In Plain English)® for Writers	$14.95	____
____	1-57248-509-4	Legal Research Made Easy (4E)	$24.95	____
____	1-57248-449-7	The Living Trust Kit	$21.95	____
____	1-57248-165-X	Living Trusts and Other Ways to Avoid Probate (3E)	$24.95	____
____	1-57248-486-1	Making Music Your Business	$18.95	____
____	1-57248-186-2	Manual de Beneficios para el Seguro Social	$18.95	____
____	1-57248-220-6	Mastering the MBE	$16.95	____
____	1-57248-455-1	Minding Her Own Business, 4E	$14.95	____
____	1-57248-480-2	The Mortgage Answer Book	$14.95	____
____	1-57248-167-6	Most Val. Business Legal Forms You'll Ever Need (3E)	$21.95	____
____	1-57248-388-1	The Power of Attorney Handbook (5E)	$22.95	____
____	1-57248-332-6	Profit from Intellectual Property	$28.95	____
____	1-57248-329-6	Protect Your Patent	$24.95	____
____	1-57248-376-8	Nursing Homes and Assisted Living Facilities	$19.95	____
____	1-57248-385-7	Quick Cash	$14.95	____
____	1-57248-350-4	El Seguro Social Preguntas y Respuestas	$16.95	____
____	1-57248-529-9	Sell Your Home Without a Broker	$14.95	____
____	1-57248386-5	Seniors' Rights	$19.95	____
____	1-57248-527-2	Sexual Harassment in the Workplace	$18.95	____
____	1-57248-217-6	Sexual Harassment: Your Guide to Legal Action	$18.95	____
____	1-57248-378-4	Sisters-in-Law	$16.95	____
____	1-57248-219-2	The Small Business Owner's Guide to Bankruptcy	$21.95	____
____	1-57248-395-4	The Social Security Benefits Handbook (4E)	$18.95	____
____	1-57248-216-8	Social Security Q&A	$12.95	____
____	1-57248-521-3	Start Your Own Law Practice	$16.95	____
____	1-57248-328-8	Starting Out or Starting Over	$14.95	____
____	1-57248-525-6	Teen Rights (and Responsibilities) (2E)	$14.95	____
____	1-57248-457-8	Tax Power for the Self-Employed	$17.95	____
____	1-57248-366-0	Tax Smarts for Small Business	$21.95	____
____	1-57248-530-2	Unmarried Parents' Rights (3E)	$16.95	____
____	1-57248-362-8	U.S. Immigration and Citizenship Q&A	$18.95	____
____	1-57248-387-3	U.S. Immigration Step by Step (2E)	$24.95	____
____	1-57248-392-X	U.S.A. Immigration Guide (5E)	$26.95	____
____	1-57248-178-0	¡Visas! ¡Visas! ¡Visas!	$9.95	____
____	1-57248-177-2	The Weekend Landlord	$16.95	____
____	1-57248-451-9	What to Do—Before "I DO"	$14.95	____

(Form Continued on Following Page)   Subtotal _____

To order, call Sourcebooks at 1-800-432-7444 or FAX (630) 961-2168 (Bookstores, libraries, wholesalers—please call for discount)
Prices are subject to change without notice.
Find more legal information at: **www.SphinxLegal.com**

SPHINX® PUBLISHING ORDER FORM

Qty	ISBN	Title	Retail	Ext.
___	1-57248-531-0	What to Do When You Can't Get Pregnant	$16.95	___
___	1-57248-225-7	Win Your Unemployment Compensation Claim (2E)	$21.95	___
___	1-57248-330-X	The Wills, Estate Planning and Trusts Legal Kit	$26.95	___
___	1-57248-473-X	Winning Your Personal Injury Claim (3E)	$24.95	___
___	1-57248-333-4	Working with Your Homeowners Association	$19.95	___
___	1-57248-380-6	Your Right to Child Custody, Visitation and Support (3E)	$24.95	___
___	1-57248-505-1	Your Rights at Work	$14.95	___

CALIFORNIA TITLES

Qty	ISBN	Title	Retail	Ext.
___	1-57248-489-6	How to File for Divorce in CA (5E)	$26.95	___
___	1-57248-464-0	How to Settle and Probate an Estate in CA (2E)	$28.95	___
___	1-57248-336-9	How to Start a Business in CA (2E)	$21.95	___
___	1-57248-194-3	How to Win in Small Claims Court in CA (2E)	$18.95	___
___	1-57248-246-X	Make Your Own CA Will	$18.95	___
___	1-57248-397-0	Landlords' Legal Guide in CA (2E)	$24.95	___
___	1-57248-241-9	Tenants' Rights in CA	$21.95	___

FLORIDA TITLES

Qty	ISBN	Title	Retail	Ext.
___	1-57248-396-2	How to File for Divorce in FL (8E)	$28.95	___
___	1-57248-356-3	How to Form a Corporation in FL (6E)	$24.95	___
___	1-57248-490-X	How to Form a Limited Liability Co. in FL (4E)	$24.95	___
___	1-57071-401-0	How to Form a Partnership in FL	$22.95	___
___	1-57248-456-X	How to Make a FL Will (7E)	$16.95	___
___	1-57248-354-7	How to Probate and Settle an Estate in FL (5E)	$26.95	___
___	1-57248-339-3	How to Start a Business in FL (7E)	$21.95	___
___	1-57248-204-4	How to Win in Small Claims Court in FL (7E)	$18.95	___
___	1-57248-381-4	Land Trusts in Florida (7E)	$29.95	___
___	1-57248-491-8	Landlords' Rights and Duties in FL (10E)	$22.95	___

GEORGIA TITLES

Qty	ISBN	Title	Retail	Ext.
___	1-57248-340-7	How to File for Divorce in GA (5E)	$21.95	___
___	1-57248-493-4	How to Start a Business in GA (4E)	$21.95	___

ILLINOIS TITLES

Qty	ISBN	Title	Retail	Ext.
___	1-57248-244-3	Child Custody, Visitation, and Support in IL	$24.95	___
___	1-57248-206-0	How to File for Divorce in IL (3E)	$24.95	___
___	1-57248-170-6	How to Make an IL Will (3E)	$16.95	___
___	1-57248-265-9	How to Start a Business in IL (4E)	$21.95	___
___	1-57248-252-4	Landlords' Legal Guide in IL	$24.95	___

MARYLAND, VIRGINIA AND THE DISTRICT OF COLUMBIA

Qty	ISBN	Title	Retail	Ext.
___	1-57248-240-0	How to File for Divorce in MD, VA, and DC	$28.95	___
___	1-57248-359-8	How to Start a Business in MD, VA, or DC	$21.95	___

MASSACHUSETTS TITLES

Qty	ISBN	Title	Retail	Ext.
___	1-57248-115-3	How to Form a Corporation in MA	$24.95	___
___	1-57248-466-7	How to Start a Business in MA (4E)	$21.95	___
___	1-57248-398-9	Landlords' Legal Guide in MA (2E)	$24.95	___

MICHIGAN TITLES

Qty	ISBN	Title	Retail	Ext.
___	1-57248-467-5	How to File for Divorce in MI (4E)	$24.95	___
___	1-57248-182-X	How to Make a MI Will (3E)	$16.95	___
___	1-57248-468-3	How to Start a Business in MI (4E)	$18.95	___

MINNESOTA TITLES

Qty	ISBN	Title	Retail	Ext.
___	1-57248-142-0	How to File for Divorce in MN	$21.95	___
___	1-57248-179-X	How to Form a Corporation in MN	$24.95	___
___	1-57248-178-1	How to Make a MN Will (2E)	$16.95	___

NEW JERSEY TITLES

Qty	ISBN	Title	Retail	Ext.
___	1-57248-512-4	File for Divorce in NJ (2E)	$24.95	___
___	1-57248-448-9	How to Start a Business in NJ	$21.95	___

NEW YORK TITLES

Qty	ISBN	Title	Retail	Ext.
___	1-57248-193-5	Child Custody, Visitation and Support in NY	$26.95	___
___	1-57248-351-2	File for Divorce in NY	$26.95	___
___	1-57248-249-4	How to Form a Corporation in NY (2E)	$24.95	___
___	1-57248-401-2	How to Make a NY Will (3E)	$16.95	___
___	1-57248-469-1	How to Start a Business in NY (3E)	$21.95	___
___	1-57248-198-6	How to Win in Small Claims Court in NY (2E)	$18.95	___
___	1-57248-122-6	Tenants' Rights in NY	$21.95	___

NORTH CAROLINA AND SOUTH CAROLINA TITLES

Qty	ISBN	Title	Retail	Ext.
___	1-57248-508-6	How to File for Divorce in NC (4E)	$24.95	___
___	1-57248-371-7	How to Start a Business in NC or SC	$24.95	___
___	1-57248-091-2	Landlords' Rights & Duties in NC	$21.95	___

OHIO TITLES

Qty	ISBN	Title	Retail	Ext.
___	1-57248-503-5	How to File for Divorce in OH (3E)	$24.95	___
___	1-57248-174-9	How to Form a Corporation in OH	$24.95	___
___	1-57248-173-0	How to Make an OH Will	$16.95	___

PENNSYLVANIA TITLES

Qty	ISBN	Title	Retail	Ext.
___	1-57248-242-7	Child Custody, Visitation and Support in PA	$26.95	___
___	1-57248-495-0	How to File for Divorce in PA (4E)	$24.95	___
___	1-57248-358-X	How to Form a Corporation in PA	$24.95	___
___	1-57248-094-7	How to Make a PA Will (2E)	$16.95	___
___	1-57248-357-1	How to Start a Business in PA (3E)	$21.95	___
___	1-57248-245-1	Landlords' Legal Guide in PA	$24.95	___

TEXAS TITLES

Qty	ISBN	Title	Retail	Ext.
___	1-57248-171-4	Child Custody, Visitation, and Support in TX	$22.95	___
___	1-57248-399-7	How to File for Divorce in TX (4E)	$24.95	___
___	1-57248-470-5	How to Form a Corporation in TX (3E)	$24.95	___
___	1-57248-496-9	How to Probate and Settle an Estate in TX (4E)	$26.95	___
___	1-57248-471-3	How to Start a Business in TX (4E)	$21.95	___
___	1-57248-111-0	How to Win in Small Claims Court in TX (2E)	$16.95	___
___	1-57248-355-5	Landlords' Legal Guide in TX	$24.95	___
___	1-57248-513-2	Write Your Own TX Will (4E)	$16.95	___

WASHINGTON TITLES

Qty	ISBN	Title	Retail	Ext.
___	1-57248-522-1	File for Divorce in WA	$24.95	___

SubTotal This page   _____

SubTotal previous page   _____

Shipping— $5.00 for 1st book, $1.00 each additional   _____

Illinois residents add 6.75% sales tax   _____

Connecticut residents add 6.00% sales tax   _____

Total   _____

To order, call Sourcebooks at 1-800-432-7444 or FAX (630) 961-2168 (Bookstores, libraries, wholesalers—please call for discount)

Prices are subject to change without notice.

Find more legal information at: **www.SphinxLegal.com**